Bringing Soprano Arias to Life

WITHDRAWN

by BORIS GOLDOVSKY
and ARTHUR SCHOEP

Drawings by LEO VAN WITSEN

G. SCHIRMER / New York • London

CONTENTS

Part One

Part Two

PART ONE

Introduction

Except for the music itself, which is readily available in published piano-vocal scores and anthologies, this book is intended to supply a soprano with nearly everything she may need to perform the particular operatic arias discussed here.* There are descriptions of stage settings, costume sketches, and specific instructions for enacting each of the scenes. While it is not the intention of the authors that these arias be acted out on the concert stage, much of the information in this volume — the dramatic analyses, discussions of vocal and musical aspects, and translations of the texts which are given for each scene — should be profitable no matter how or where the arias are performed.

The heart of each discussion is a detailed description of the actions of the aria, and the essential terms and abbreviations used in these stage directions are explained on pages 4 & 5. While the scenic design may change from one production to another, the suggestions given here in regard to dramatic motivations, character building, and stage movement can be readily adapted for use in any theatrical environment. This book makes no attempt, however, to teach operatic acting.†

Students of singing and stage direction will find many details of operatic lore in this volume that can only be garnered from a variety of other sources. In connection with vocal and musical aspects, matters of style and tradition are touched upon, and there is a general discussion of this problem on pages 6 to 20.

On many occasions the material contained here should also prove useful to the professional opera singer. It is no secret that stage directors tend to neglect the mise-en-scène of arias, either because they lack the time to work with singers individually or because they feel that leading singers prefer to be left alone, dramatically speaking, to do as much or as little as they wish. Under these circumstances, exciting scenes that feature arias often disintegrate into static and theatrically barren concerts merely sung in costume.

---

* All of the piano-vocal scores that contain the arias in this book are published by G. Schirmer, with the exception of *Don Pasquale* and *The Old Maid and the Thief* (both published by Ricordi). In addition, most of the arias may be found in the following G. Schirmer publications: *The Prima Donna's Album*, newly revised and edited by Kurt Adler, and *Operatic Anthology*, Volume I Soprano, compiled by Kurt Adler.

A few arias are published separately.

† For a detailed treatment of this topic, see Boris Goldovsky, *Bringing Opera to Life* (Appleton-Century Crofts, 1968).

The arias included in this volume are chosen from among those that are most popular and most widely studied and performed. Those in Part I are true solo scenes in which the singer is alone on stage. The arias in Part II are really ensemble scenes involving partners whose presence and supporting action are essential for the dramatic interpretation of the words and the music. Several well-known arias which demand a more extensive vocal contribution by stage partners have been excluded. This explains the omission of such pieces as the first-act arias from *Il Trovatore* and *Lucia di Lammermoor*. Other important soprano scenes which can be sung unaided in concert performances — Elsa's "Dream" from *Lohengrin* or Lucia's "Mad Scene," for example — require the dramatic participation of large choral groups and were excluded for this reason.

The "Caro nome" from *Rigoletto* is included in this collection in spite of the fact that near the end of the aria Gilda is observed by courtiers making audible remarks about her. Since these men stand in the deep shadows beyond the wall of Gilda's garden and do not in any way interfere with her behavior, their presence can be disregarded. As far as Gilda is concerned, she is alone on stage.

While most American productions outside of New York — except those involving foreign artists — are given in English, single arias are usually studied and sung in their original languages. For this reason the actions described in this book were devised to fit the original texts. As a general rule, the same actions will also be applicable when translations are used. Minor adjustments will be necessary when the versions in the vernacular differ substantially from the original wording. Special problems arising from spoken lines are discussed in connection with Pamina's aria from *Die Zauberflöte* (see p. 320).

A literal version and an idiomatic translation of each text are given for each aria. For despite the fact that conservatory and university workshop productions are usually presented in English, American singers almost invariably study operatic arias — at least at first — in their original tongue. Unfortunately, the student is rarely sufficiently familiar with the foreign language to be able to shape the phrases with the necessary verbal inflection and vocal color. Teachers and coaches, preoccupied with the mechanics of singing and musical accuracy, seldom have time to translate each individual word or to clarify the meaning of idiomatic expressions. Hoping to make the student sound as if she had a real understanding of the text, they tend to rely on such remarks as, "Put more accent on that syllable" or "Make a little crescendo here." How much simpler and more effective it would be if the student had a complete and exact knowledge of what she was singing. The translations of the arias are intended to help her accomplish this. Since word by word renderings often result in awkward and confusing sentence structure, our idiomatic line by line translations will help to clarify the meaning of the literal ones.

Vocal Aspects

In the presentation of each aria there is a brief discussion of its vocal aspects; this is in no way intended to be construed as a "voice lesson." On the basis of hearing many singers perform these arias, the authors have noted difficulties that they have with certain phrases. Since each singer is unique, with individual strengths and weaknesses, our general remarks are intended only as guidelines. Such matters as the trill and the use of *messa di voce* are discussed in the Vocal Aspects sections.

Because of the great abundance of operatic recordings, there has been an inevitable emulation of famous artists by admiring and aspiring singers, but a student should not rely too heavily on recorded performances for vocal hints. A recording of an opera can be an immensely useful tool — the singer can hear orchestral color and even orchestral melodies and cues that are not present in a piano reduction of the score, she can study interpretative nuances by famous singers and conductors, and she can benefit from hearing how accomplished artists use vocal color to great advantage. But it does not follow that an aria sung at breakneck speed by an unusually agile voice in a recording should be performed by all other sopranos in the same fashion, nor is it advisable to imitate the mannerisms of one's favorite singer. One need only compare the various recordings of well-known operas to learn how diverse interpretations can be.

Musical Aspects

The discussions of each aria's musical aspects contain formal analyses of the music and also deal with notational problems related to traditional and other deviations from the published texts. This includes variants in embellishments and appoggiaturas of operas composed before the middle of the nineteenth century. Whenever questions of basic tempo or tempo changes within the aria present problems, these are fully discussed. Details of harmony, rhythm, and orchestration, however, are touched upon only to the extent that they have a special bearing on the musical and dramatic interpretation of a given aria.

Singers rarely pay much attention to the structure of music and tend to think of formal analysis as an unnecessary pursuit of fussy details. Quite to the contrary, such study not only offers fascinating intellectual exercise but it also provides an invaluable practical aid in memorizing the words and music. One can try to string together the sequence of single vocal phrases in, let us say, "Ritorna vincitor," but it is much less time-consuming to visualize its basic structure, and to realize that it consists of an introduction and four independent episodes. And in terms of stage movement each of the episodes is associated with a separate placement, with the total action unrolling in the easily remembered sequences of right, left, up, and downstage.

The Drama

To bring a dramatic role to life it is essential to know what that particular person is thinking, feeling, and doing while on stage. But this is not sufficient, for an adult is not only a creature of the moment, he is also a composite of all his past experiences. And while we cannot begin to duplicate our own wealth of personal memories, a conscientious actor must try to discover, and, in a way, relive at least some of his stage character's past.

Under the heading Drama, sopranos will find those details of the story with which they must be familiar in order to enact their roles with a rounded characterization and a convincing individual flavor. Chief among these details are the time and place of action, the character's nationality, family status, and social position, as well as her long-range concerns and immediate emotional problems. Whenever possible, the discussion pinpoints, or at least touches upon, such items as the character's exact age, hair and eye color, and other distinctive physical attributes. Because of the demands of musical elaboration, operatic texts are usually greatly condensed, and the information given in the libretto has to be supplemented either by studying the novels and plays on which the opera is based, or — when these do not exist — by completing the character's life history out of one's own imagination. The singer is always given the source of this information: whether it is generally known, mentioned in the score, or culled from an important background text. Thus, Butterfly's black hair is a national Japanese trait, and Tosca's dark hair and eyes are sung about in the opera, while the computation of Countess Almaviva's and Susanna's ages is based on remarks that are found in the Beaumarchais play rather than in the opera itself. A listing of the most important background texts — in readily available English translations — is given on page 326. This should enable singers to check on the information given in the Drama section of each aria and to gather additional dramatic details useful for the enactment of their roles.

Terms and Abbreviations Used in the Aria Stagings

Stage directions in this volume are always given from the point of view of the singer as she faces the audience. Thus, left and right (abbreviated L and R) remain stable, even though the character may have her back to the audience. Upstage (abbreviated U) is away from the audience, and downstage (abbreviated D) is toward the audience. When a character moves UL, therefore, she moves in a diagonal direction toward her left and away from the audience. Other diagonal directions are abbreviated similarly. Thus, DR stands for downright, UR for upright, and DL for downleft. The line dividing the R side of the stage from its L side is abbreviated CC. The term "depth" refers to the distance from the footlights line.

When a character moves between another character or prop and the audience, she is said to move "below" it; when she moves so that the character or prop is between her and the audience, she is said to move "above" it. When she changes her position on the stage from one location to another, she "goes" or "moves" to the new location. When she moves backward, she "backs," and when she passes below another character or prop to a new location, we ask her to "cross" (abbreviated as X). When she passes above another character or prop to a new location, we use the term "cross above" (abbreviated as X above). The abbreviation "Xing" is used for "crossing."

Various types of turns are employed on the operatic stage.* We use the terms "clockwise" and "counterclockwise" (abbreviated Clw and Cclw) to identify turns made in place, without changing location on the stage. Turns that move the character forward or backward are described by letters that indicate the necessary movement of the shoulder:

RSF — right shoulder forward   RSB — right shoulder back
LSF — left shoulder forward   LSB — left shoulder back

Alphabetical List of Terms and Abbreviations

above — in the direction away from the audience
backs — walks backward
below — in the direction toward the audience
BU — backing up (in the direction away from the audience)
CC — the line separating the R side of the stage from its L side
Clw — clockwise turn
Cclw — counterclockwise turn
D — downstage (toward the audience)
DL — downstage left
DR — downstage right
depth — distance from the line of the footlights
goes — walks forward
L — left (from the point of view of the singer facing the audience)
LSB — left shoulder back turn moving slightly to UR
LSF — left shoulder forward turn moving slightly to DR
R — right (from the point of view of the singer facing the audience)
RSB — right shoulder back turn moving slightly to UL
RSF — right shoulder forward turn moving slightly to DL
U — upstage (away from the audience)
UL — upstage left
UR — upstage right
X — cross
X'ing — crossing

* The proper way to execute all these turns, together with the principles of walking, posture, use of head and eyes, and moving on the proscenium stage, is treated fully in *Bringing Opera to Life.*

It is taken for granted that readers are familiar with conventional musical terms. The expression *Messa di voce* (literally: emission of the voice) is perhaps less well known. It refers to a sustained tone sung with a gradual crescendo followed by a diminuendo:

Another unusual term employed is SPRAYING. It refers to an unhurried Clw or Cclw turn performed while singing, so as to give everyone in the audience the full benefit of a high sustained vocal tone.

Motivations

Acting is communicating the thoughts and emotions of the characters portrayed by the singer. Every move performed on stage must reflect either a thought or an emotion or sometimes both of these simultaneously. It is not possible within the confines of this volume to discuss the exact motivation — the specific thought or emotion — behind each and every move of the singer. It will help the performers, however, to learn to distinguish between "reasons" which are the result of thoughts, and "urges" which are the outcome of emotions.*

The actress may want to approach a partner *in order* to address him, or go to a bench *in order* to sit down on it. These would be *reasons*. On the other hand, the character the actress portrays may be too nervous, elated, or unhappy to stand still and may want to move away from her present location simply because she cannot bear to remain standing or sitting there. This type of movement would be the result of an *urge*.

A competent actress will know how to communicate clearly the thought behind the *reason,* as well as the type and strength of the emotion that governs the *urge* to move.

Traditions in Opera

In opera, the word "traditional" is applied loosely to all habitual and widely accepted additions and deviations from the music as it appears in the printed scores. Such knowledge is not written down but passed on — usually from teacher to pupil — by word of mouth. But the conscientious artist is often caught in the predicament of having to choose between the evidence of the printed text and that of the inherited, oral tradition. Unfortunately, this conflict between "tradition" and "notation" is not easy to resolve, for musical notation is an inexact science, and both the value of tradition and the true meaning of the printed text must be evaluated in the light of the style of the music in question.

As products of an age in which we are taught to regard musical notation as indicating the exact intentions of a composer, we find it difficult to realize that in an earlier age the composer's intentions were not — in fact, almost *could* not be — notated exactly. Today we tend to believe that we should perform music exactly as it appears on the printed page.

---

* For a detailed discussion of motivations, see *Bringing Opera to Life*.

Yet to do so, in music written before the second half of the nineteenth century, would completely violate the expectations of its composers. Composers of the seventeenth and eighteenth centuries often provided only a bare harmonic and melodic outline that was expected to be ornamented and embellished by the performer. Singers were regarded as the experts in the art of elaboration, and indeed their fame and fortune depended upon this talent. But eventually excesses crept into their improvisations, and the natural reaction of composers was to write out more exactly what they wanted to be performed. In the first half of the nineteenth century some composers adhered to the old traditions while others notated in greater detail what they desired. The performer thus had no way of telling which pieces were already sufficiently notated and which required additional ornamentation. Very often the performer would further embellish compositions already fully ornamented by the composer. Berlioz, Verdi, and Rimsky-Korsakov are among the composers who wrote strong statements exhorting the performer or conductor to perform their music exactly as it was notated.

In the field of vocal music habits of traditional ornamentation persisted until the end of the nineteenth century, when Gustav Mahler, a greatly respected authority on music in his day, established what is known as the "Werktreue" principles: fidelity to printed notation and respect, supposedly, for the intentions of the composer. Mahler forbade the alteration of notation in any way whatsoever. His intent was admirable; his error lay in failing to take into account the changes in notational procedures that had taken place over a hundred years or more, and in thinking that his edict was as applicable to *Figaro* as it was to *Falstaff*. Though there were those who rejected Mahler's principle, his word was law in Germany and Austria, and a whole body of coaches and conductors sprang up who insisted on rigid adherence to the printed notes, even in music which was intended to be inflected and ornamented.

It is important, therefore, to become acquainted with the development of notational forms and to be able to discriminate between good traditions and those that are doubtful, optional, or downright bad. Furthermore, notation and tradition are not necessarily antagonistic. Good traditions are more often than not implicit in the style of the work and conform to the intentions of the composer. They may be quite simply the *correct interpretation* of notational mannerisms commonly employed at the time the opera was written.

Questionable and bad traditions, on the other hand, are almost invariably of later vintage and, while it is not always possible to trace them to their point of origin, they are apt to reflect a desire either for "more effective" or for "less troublesome" execution.

Among the good traditions, which composers of the seventeenth, eighteenth, and early nineteenth centuries expected singers to observe, was a choice in the following details of execution:

1. Appoggiaturas (inflections added to phrase endings)

2. Embellishments to be added at appropriate points
3. The elongation of certain sustained tones
4. The special emphasis placed on certain words and syllables.

Appoggiaturas

The vocal ornament about which there seems to be the most confusion is the appoggiatura, the nonharmonic tone which occurs at a point of rhythmic stress. It is found most often in recitatives of the eighteenth and early nineteenth centuries, in arias, and — more rarely — in ensembles. The appoggiatura may approach the note of resolution from above or below at any interval. A graceful ornament, it not only creates a dissonance and then resolves it, but it provides a most effective opportunity to give a melodic line correct stress and emphasis based on textual considerations. Since it combines melodic, rhythmic, and harmonic functions, it surpasses all other ornaments in importance and frequency.*

Not only did notation for the appoggiatura vary from composer to composer but indications for it were often omitted from the vocal lines because at that time singers were experts in the art of ornamentation and were expected to embellish according to their taste, which sometimes varied from performance to performance. Since the principles for the use of the appoggiatura had been established by a solid verbal tradition, there was little danger of misunderstanding them. Furthermore, appoggiaturas were not notated exactly because of the strict harmonic rules of the time, which forbade the indication of dissonances produced by the appoggiatura. In addition, the accompanying keyboard player for secco recitatives had to be able to know at a glance what harmonies were to be provided, since he was furnished with only the vocal line and a figured bass (more often than not, the bass was not even figured). The presence of countless nonharmonic tones in the vocal line would certainly have disguised the harmony and would have led to countless errors. Thus, composers, bound by the conventions of their métier in their time, did not notate dissonances they expected to hear performed; singers, in like manner, adhering to the traditions of *their* métier in their time, introduced the desired dissonances which the composers did not notate!

There are still performers today who insist that composers of the eighteenth and early nineteenth centuries "meant what they wrote." These performers often point out that on many occasions Mozart did write out appoggiaturas and therefore when he did not do so he must have expected singers to execute all pitches as indicated in his scores. This, however, is a totally mistaken assumption. The use of added inflections and ornaments throughout the eighteenth century is supported by ample and irrefutable evidence. In Mozart's case it seems likely that he employed the

---

*The authors are grateful to Mr. Ross Reimueller for his comprehensive and scholarly examination of the problems of the vocal appoggiatura. The conclusions set forth here are based in part upon his work.

more precise notational methods only when dealing with relatively untrained singers, or when he had a decided preference regarding the type
of inflection he desired.

Cherubino's "Non so più cosa son" furnishes a case in point. The
singer for whom it was originally intended was making her first appearance on the operatic stage. Being uncertain whether the young woman
was familiar with normal performance practices, Mozart played it safe by
writing

Non so più co-sa son, co-sa fac-cio, or di fuo-co o-ra so- no di ghiac-cio,

instead of the more conventional

Non so più co-sa son, co-sa fac-cio, or di fuo-co o-ra so- no di ghiac-cio,

Incidentally, the more exact notation of the first example might have
offended a more seasoned prima donna. There is no doubt that in the
eighteenth century singers resented being treated as if they were novices.
The famous voice teacher, Pier Francesco Tosi, writing in 1732, used
some pretty strong language when referring to non-Italian composers
who tried to introduce the concept of written-out appoggiaturas. Tosi
asked:

Do not singers nowadays know where appoggiaturas are to be added unless
they are pointed at with a finger? In my time their own knowledge showed it to
them. Eternal shame to him who first introduced these foreign puerilities into
our nation, renowned for teaching others the greater part of the polite arts;
particularly that of singing! Oh, how great a weakness in those that follow
their example! Oh, injurious insult to you, modern singers, who submit to
instruction fit for children! Let us imitate foreigners in those things only,
wherein they excel.

When dealing with vocal music written before the 1850s, the problem
is not *whether* to inflect and embellish, but rather *where* and *how* this
should be done.

Although the process of modernization had been going on for a long
time, we speak of the 1850s as the dividing line between two practices
because it was in that decade that Verdi, among others, broke completely with the old system. In the last act of *Rigoletto,* when the composer
wanted the leading baritone to omit the traditional inflections, he was faced
with the virtual impossibility of indicating his intention by means of musical symbols alone. He was therefore forced to insert the famous instruction
that a recitative be sung "without the usual appoggiaturas" —

RIGOLETTO: *(This recitative must be sung without the usual appoggiaturas.)*

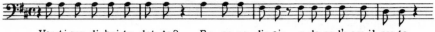

Ven-ti scu-di, hai tu det-to?   Ec - co-ne die ci;   e do-po l'o pra il res-to.

Again, in *La Traviata,* we find him writing out all vocal lines in full detail. Soon thereafter, in his letters and contractual arrangements, Verdi began a campaign against any alterations in his music, insisting that it be performed exactly as it was published.

At the time that Verdi was composing *Rigoletto* and *La Traviata,* the traditions governing vocal inflections and ornaments were still in full force; it is therefore useful to look at Verdi's written-out texts and compare them with the former method of notating the same music. The following excerpts from the last act of *Rigoletto* and from the recitative leading to "Ah, fors' e lui" are quite typical.

Allegro

È stra - no!   è stra - no!

Sa - ria per me sven - tu - ra   un se-rio a - mo - re?

Che ri - sol - vi,o tur-ba-ta a - ni - ma mi - a?   Nul

l'uo-mo an - co - ra t'ac - cen - de - va.

ch'io non co - nob - bi,   es - ser a - ma - ta a man - do!

These excerpts illustrate several characteristic varieties of appoggiaturas. Most common are the falling inflections approached from above.

Allegro

È stra-no!   è stra-no!

It would seem that when approached from a third above, the "filling out" was performed quite automatically. An uninflected execution of

È stra-no! È stra-no!

must have been regarded as unnatural or at least implausible.

Rising inflections are somewhat less common. Those approached by a skip from above are encountered occasionally in orchestrally accompanied numbers, as in Don Ottavio's aria from *Don Giovanni.*

dal-la sua pa - ce la mia di-pen - de, quel che a lei

pia - ce, vi - ta mi ren - de, _____

But these are not among inflections found in recitatives of either the Mozartian or the post-*Rigoletto* variety.

Rising appoggiaturas approached from below

con tal tem-po?

are used quite often and seem particularly apt in sentences involving questions.

When the syllables to be inflected were preceded by a note of lower pitch, the performer was allowed to choose between a rising appoggiatura

or a falling one prepared by a skip to a higher pitch.

This latter type of appoggiatura involves more of an effort than the rising inflections and is used when a sentence expresses the more energetic and violent emotions. It is interesting to note that this is the appoggiatura most often "written out" by Mozart, as can be seen in these examples taken from the vocal lines of Donna Anna in *Don Giovanni.*

Quel san-gue quel-la pia-ga quel vol-to

Other uses of the appoggiatura are discussed more completely in this volume in the Musical Aspects of the arias in which they occur.

Generally speaking, if a contemporary performer wishes to achieve a real and meaningful "Werktreue," he will want to perform works of the past in the style that was prevalent when it was composed; then the unwritten vocal appoggiatura will become a part of his vocabulary.

Vocal Ornaments

Many of the short ornaments are little more than special forms of the appoggiatura.

Ch'io   mor - - ra!

Extended ornaments are employed mainly to heighten the expressiveness of emotion-laden situations. They must *never* be used as mere vehicles for a display of vocal virtuosity. In this connection it is valuable to observe the difference in the embellishments on the words *gioja* and *gioir* as they appear in Violetta's first aria "Sempre Libera" in *La Traviata*. The *gioja* in the opening section

Oh gio - - ja ch'io non co-nob-bi

refers to the thrill, unknown to Violetta, of "esser amata amando," of "being not only loved, but responding to love!" On the other hand, the twice repeated *gioir* that precedes the Allegro section of the aria

Gio - ir! gio - - ir! _____

expatiates on the shallow joys of Violetta's present life. It is a comment on her gay but essentially loveless existence. The embellishment on *gioja* must therefore be imbued with sincere yearning, while those on *gioir* call for a more brilliant execution with a touch of bitterness and renunciation.

Italian composers of the first half of the nineteenth century — Rossini, Bellini, and Donizetti among them — continued to conform to the eighteenth-century traditions of relying on the singer to provide her own ornaments. Having the composer choose the ornamentation and include it in the published score was considered impractical because it might induce later performers to attempt passages unsuited to their particular vocal talents. This was a real danger, and the greater the prestige of the composer, the stronger the reluctance of performers to change his music and interfere with his expressed desires. Consider the problems this has created in Mozart's German operas where, unlike in his Italian operas, he wrote out the embellishments. Generations of sopranos have been con-

demned to perform the devilishly difficult *fioriture* in the arias of Kon-
stanze and the Queen of the Night, just because the notated embellishments were comfortable to Caterina Cavalieri* or Josefa Hofer, the
prima donnas for whom these roles were written.

Countless productions of *The Magic Flute* have been ruined for lack
of a soprano capable of doing even elementary justice to the stratospheric
fireworks of the Queen of the Night, while the written-out intricate ornament in the middle of Pamina's "Ach ich fühl's"

mei - nem_ Her - zen,_mei - nem_ Her -   - - - -

-    zen_mehr__   zu - rück.

must be held responsible for the habitual and most unfortunate slowing
down in the tempo of the entire aria.

Much as one may deplore the uninflected and unembellished style that
has long dominated performances of Mozart's Italian operas, it is in a
way preferable to the many disasters caused by the "notated" ornaments
of the *Abduction* and the *Flute*.

Rhythm and Tempo

Changes of tempo and irregularities of rhythm are much more prevalent
and frequent in opera than in purely instrumental music. They are caused
by the contradictory tendencies in the timing of the three basic elements
of opera: words, vocal lines, and instrumental accompaniments. There is,
on one hand, the habitual, fairly rapid speed of the spoken language, the
spacing of which depends on the import of the message and the construction of the sentence. At the other extreme is the natural expansiveness of
cantabile vocalization and the singer's instinctive desire to elongate sustained tones in the higher reaches of her voice. Both these inclinations are
kept in check by the orchestra, with its need for precise ensemble,
which more often than not depends on a stable tempo and on evenly
spaced divisions of time.

To put it briefly: words tend to move rapidly and not be shackled by
rigid rhythms, vocal tones incline toward slower speeds and elongation,
and the orchestra functions best at a steady pace. These considerations
affect most strongly the interpretations of recitatives (and of all recitative-
like passages) in opera.

As the name indicates, recitatives are devoted more to "reciting" than

---

* In a letter to his father, Mozart confessed that the "Martern aller Arten" aria
of the *Abduction* was "sacrificed to the fluent throat" of this singer.

to singing. The *secco* (dry) recitative is accompanied only by a keyboard instrument; the *stromentato* (instrumented recitative) is seconded by the orchestra. In the secco — where the orchestra is silent and where vocal demands are at a minimum — the speed of utterance is controlled entirely by the rules of the spoken language. One must not be misled by the fact that keyboard recitatives are organized in measures of 4/4 time having the appropriate number of quarter, eighth, and sixteenth notes. In the secco, all mathematics are entirely subordinated to verbal rhythms, and all note values are fictitious and maintained only for the sake of orderly visual presentation.

This does not apply to the *stromentati,* where the presence of the orchestra exercises a strong influence, and where rigidity and freedom often alternate from one measure to the next.

The following excerpt from the orchestral recitative that precedes Donna Anna's "Non mi dir" shows how verbal, instrumental, and vocal attitudes alternated and coexisted in the traditional notational forms of the eighteenth and early nineteenth centuries.

The first of these measures is counted in four quarter-note beats taken at approximately $\quarternote$ = 76. The second measure, however, has eight beats and lasts about twice as long as the first. The third measure again accelerates and returns to the tempo of the first.

In this sequence of fast-slow-fast, Mozart dispenses with all verbal tempo markings, trusting his performers to recognize instantly — from the very appearance of the page — the need for the doubling and subsequent undoubling of note values. And this is not all. The first two eighth notes of the vocal line — on which "Dio" is sung — are taken at the same speed as the "mondo" of the preceding fast measure. So that while the orchestra begins to play in the slower "instrumental" manner, the overlapping voice part continues at first to follow the fast, "verbal" style of the preceding measure. Finally, the high B♭ of the fifth measure can hardly be imagined without a slight elongation, and this again is not marked but rather taken for granted.

There are several ways in which these measures could be rewritten and made more explicit by modern notation. None of these versions, however, would have the simplicity and neatness of the traditional method used by Mozart. To state it in Tosi's colorful language, such detailed scoring might easily be interpreted as "an injurious insult submitting the singer to instruction fit for a child!"

Traditional Cuts and Changes

What is printed in a score is not always what a composer had in mind. In fact, composers have occasionally been known to change their minds regarding certain details of interpretation, and these changes — transmitted to us by the composers' friends or by artists who worked with them — are usually not indicated in the published scores. An instance of such a change is described in connection with the aria from Puccini's *Madama Butterfly* (see p. 249). It is not easy to evaluate information based merely on hearsay. And even when completely authentic, these word-of-mouth communications may be misleading, since a composer's acquiescence to the wishes of a performer is not necessarily based on artistic considerations.* Therefore, such changes should always be evaluated on their merits and accepted only if they clearly represent improvements over the printed directions.

An analysis of Violetta's first-act aria from *La Traviata* will introduce us to some very common types of optional and bad traditions. Considering the fact that this opera was composed after Verdi's injunction ("without the usual appoggiaturas"), which sounded the death knell of the old notational mannerisms, and in view of Verdi's later almost fanatical condemnation of any change from his notated instructions, we can safely conclude that in *La Traviata* he expected the singers to execute the actual notes exactly as he had written them down.

With all this in mind, let us look at the traditional changes in Violetta's first-act aria. They consist of:

1. The omission of the second verse in the Andantino section.

---

* When Leoncavallo conducted his *Pagliacci* on the West Coast, he permitted the famous baritone Battistini, who was performing the role of Silvio, to sing the Prologue, normally executed by Tonio. I have a copy of a letter in which the composer cautions Arturo Toscanini not to imitate this procedure, saying that he acceded to it only under duress. [B. G.]

2. The substitution of a different cadenza before "Follie! follie!"
3. The omission of two and a half measures of the vocal line, coupled
   with a sustained high E♭ near the end of the aria.

We will discuss the last of these changes first, since it will also serve
to clarify the distinction between an optional change and one that must
be unhesitatingly classified as bad. Here is what Verdi wrote down at this
point:

il ___ mio pen - sier, il ___ mio pen - sier, _____

_____ il_ mio__ pen - sier!

And this is what is normally heard after the initial *il mio pensieri*:

(sier.)   Il   mio,   Ah!_____

Verdi would probably have been opposed to the addition of the high
E♭ and to the elongation of the measure containing it. Yet this aspect
of the traditional change is not necessarily devoid of merit. Most lovers of
Italian opera find sustained high tones of this type very much to their
liking, and there is no doubt that when cleanly attacked and well sung
this note can be truly exciting. Singers who are asked to refrain from
executing this note feel robbed of a legitimate and sure-fire effect. They
claim that audiences and critics expect to hear this ending and that,
should they neglect to sing it, everyone will conclude that their vocal
range is insufficient for the role of Violetta. Given a tradition-oriented
audience and a soprano with a dead-certain high E♭, this deviation
from the printed text is defensible and belongs to the type of traditional
changes which we would call *optional*. However, a soprano who is not in
complete command of her highest notes should quite realistically weigh
the prospect of spoiling the effect of a well-sung aria by one badly produced tone.

While, the E♭ may be permissible, omitting the preceding vocal sentence
cannot be defended on any reasonable ground. Letting the orchestra alone
play

must unhesitatingly be denounced as a bad tradition. The sudden cessa-
tion of the vocal melody, leaving the instruments alone to scrub through
a conventional sequence of background harmonies, is a procedure of
lamentably poor taste. If a soprano cannot sustain this penultimate high
note without first "resting up" for it, she should not consider introducing
this traditional change.

The substitution of

for Verdi's cadenza

must also be labeled a bad tradition. The whole point of extended vocal
embellishments is to give the stage character a distinctive vocal personality. We need only compare the cadenzas Verdi wrote for his leading
sopranos in *Ernani, Luisa Miller, Rigoletto, La Traviata,* and *Un Ballo
in Maschera* to appreciate the care he took to give each one of them an
individual quality. Using the same final embellishments for Rosina's "Una
voce poco fa" and for Violetta's "Ah, fors' e lui" may have been, not too
long ago, in line with traditional habits, but it strikes us today as being
just as unimaginative and wrong as it would be to play both characters
in the same costume.

As we turn to the last of the three traditional changes in Violetta's
aria, we are faced with the general problem of operatic cuts.

Musical compositions are shortened basically because they are considered to be "too long." This expression, however, has two different
meanings depending on whether it is applied to a complete work or to a
reasonably short excerpt, such as a single scene or an aria. Most American
opera lovers will agree that works lasting more than four hours should
be shortened. When Wagner's *Die Meistersinger,* for instance, is presented
uncut — with two intermissions of normal length — it goes on for more
than five and a half hours. By making a number of judicious cuts, this
opera in most productions is reduced to less than five hours, which is certainly closer to the length of time that today's opera lover expects to
remain in the theater. For the same reasons *Così fan tutte, Tristan,* or
Der Rosenkavalier, to name a few others, are also rarely given without
extensive cuts.

When applied to arias, or other excerpts, however, "too long" refers to dullness rather than to duration. The danger of monotony is particularly serious when the excerpt features several stanzas with similar or even identical music. Unless the singer can vary the interpretation of these stanzas, the impression of repetitiousness and boredom is certain to occur. In Violetta's first-act aria this danger is aggravated by the fact that both its slow and its fast sections feature two verses. Making both stanzas of Violetta's Andantino interesting is by no means easy, and the traditional cut can therefore be recommended as an optional safeguard against monotony of execution.

Methods for achieving musical and dramatic variety are discussed in this book in connection with each individual aria. When additional interest cannot be created, it is certainly better to omit the repetition than to bore the audience.

Singing extended arias in their complete form without causing boredom is a challenge that should be welcomed by every ambitious singer. Verdi's own observations on this subject are very much to the point. When, after seeing *La Traviata* in Naples, his friend, De Sanctis, complained that the second-act duet between Violetta and Father Germont was too long, Verdi had this to say: "You are wrong in thinking it too long. I wish I could stage it for you with two competent artists. You would then discover that it is most effective, equal in ideas to any of my other duets, and superior in form and sentiment." In other words, "When well staged, sung, and acted, it is not too long!"

Acting Traditions

It is impossible to speak of established traditions in operatic acting. Eighteenth-century performers obeyed the rule of the *Standorte* (standing places — stage locations) according to which servants and slaves had to stand on the left side of the stage, while the right side was reserved for royalty and members of the nobility. This rule has long since lost its validity, as have nineteenth-century precepts advising operatic performers to face the audience and not walk about while singing.

Along with most present-day directors, the authors of this book subscribe to a more modern point of view. We feel that the behavior of singing actors should constantly reflect the thoughts and feelings of the characters they portray as well as express every nuance of the vocal line and the music played by the accompanying instruments. A detailed discussion of acting techniques and of the vocal and orchestral contribution to operatic behavior is not within the scope of this book.* But it is essential to know the more important musical aspects affecting the behavior of characters onstage. They are: the larger divisions of the musical form, and the energy, mood, and duration of individual musical phrases.

* For a thorough exposition of the principles of "musical acting" see *Bringing Opera to Life*.

Three general criteria are useful in evaluating the appropriateness of operatic actions:

1. Believability: the actions should be well suited to the dramatic situation and the music;
2. Clarity: the actions should be fully understandable to the listener and the beholder, and
3. Variety: the mise-en-scène should feature a sufficient number of changes of position and gesture to avoid the static quality and monotony of many operatic presentations.

The actions described in this book have been used in workshops with which the authors have been connected, as well as in complete productions directed by them.

Aida has added an Egyptian collar to her native Ethiopian dress. This is a gift of Amneris to her favorite slave. (Aida wears the same costume in the aria of Act III.)

"Ritorna Vincitor"
from *Aida,* Act I
by GIUSEPPE VERDI

The Drama

This aria concludes the opening scene of the first act of *Aida.* In the preceding episodes we learned of the Ethiopian invasion of Egypt and of Radames' hopes of becoming the leader of the Egyptian armies in the defense of his fatherland. Princess Amneris, who is attracted to the handsome Radames, wondered whether he may not be in love with some other woman and eventually guessed that the object of his desires was her lovely Ethiopian slave, Aida, who had been taken prisoner in an earlier war. Soon after her entrance, the weeping Aida revealed to us that her tears were caused not only by the horror of the impending war but also by the pangs of an ill-fated passion, the object of which, as we began to suspect, was the valiant Radames. When it was announced that the Ethiopian invaders were led by their king, Amonasro, Aida betrayed in an aside that he was her father. In the meantime, Radames was declared to be the supreme commander of the Egyptian armies, and the patriotic enthusiasm of the assembled populace rose to a climactic outburst in which everyone acclaimed the newly chosen general and wished him to "return victorious." Carried away by the enthusiasm of the crowd and by her love for Radames, Aida joined in this tumultuous shout. The Egyptians left the stage to accompany Radames to the consecration ceremonies in the temple of Vulcan. It is only now, when she remains alone, that Aida suddenly realizes that her enthusiastic response amounts to a betrayal of her country and to a wish for the defeat of her own people.

Although Aida's scene is primarily a succession of violent outbursts depicting the unhappy conflict of her emotions, it also helps to clarify a number of important dramatic points, not all of which were introduced earlier in the act. We are now given to understand that King Amonasro is attempting to rescue his daughter from bondage and to restore her to her noble position. We are no longer left in doubt of Aida's intense, burning passion for Radames, whose love comforted her in her servitude and "blessed her like a ray of sunshine." Finally, we are told that her exalted royal rank has remained hidden from the Egyptians, and, while it is not specifically stated by her at this point, we shall learn in the course of the opera that she has kept her identity secret even from her lover.

"Ritorna Vincitor" offers a particularly instructive example of the interrelation between words, music, and action. To illustrate how the harmonic progressions and formal structure of an aria can influence the placement and movements of the singer, we will analyze its musical and dramatic details in a combined discussion.

21

The Music and the Action

The aria's 117 measures are divided into five sections: a recitative-like introduction and four independent episodes.

> Introduction — measures 1–27
> First Episode in E minor — mm. 28–47
> Second Episode in F major — mm. 48–66
> Third Episode in A-flat minor — mm. 67–83
> Fourth Episode in A-flat major — mm. 84–117

Introduction: — Allegro agitato in 4/4 (mm. 1–27)
    Aida repeats Amneris' solo phrase

but in sudden recognition of its true meaning lowers the final note by a half step.

She realizes now that this triumphant A-major victory that Amneris was invoking is an "empia parola," a blasphemy concealing a disastrous A-minor side:

This new insight launches the music through C-sharp minor toward B minor, the traditional tonality of death; in this instance, the death of Aida's father.

    The opposing forces of the Ethiopians and the Egyptians which Aida

sees in her mind's eye can be presented in visual theatrical terms by
associating them with the two lateral sides of the stage: Aida's country-
men on the left, her lover's cohorts on stage right.*

It is most significant that each of the aria's four episodes is preceded by
an identical harmony based on the chord of the diminished seventh:

This ambiguous chord, which can be spelled with either sharps of flats

is ideally suited to symbolize Aida's tragic dilemma resulting from her
feelings toward her father and her lover. Since in the impending war these
two men, Amonasro and Radames, belong to opposing camps, any success
in battle that she might wish for one of them would necessarily imply
defeat and probable death for the other. Thus, at the end of the introduction, the horrifying vision of her defeated father evokes the crucial harmony:

and drives Aida away from the imagined sight on stage L, toward DR.

First Episode: Più mosso in ¢ (mm. 28-47)

In this section of the aria the implied B-minor cadence:

is sidetracked by a feverish più mosso in E minor.

* The Egyptians are now on their way to the temple of Vulcan which we place
in the far distance beyond the right wing of the stage.

After begging the gods to disregard her "insane words" invoking a victory
for Radames, Aida countermands them by a violent appeal to her own
people, urging destruction of the Egyptian oppressors. She soon realizes,
of course, that she is clamoring for the death of her lover, and this intoler-
able imagined event, occurring this time on stage R, drives Aida away from
the dreaded sight toward the DL portion of the stage. The critical moment
itself is highlighted by the second appearance of the chord of the diminished seventh:

As the sharps are converted into flats, the threatened B minor is again
averted and we are introduced to the theme that had accompanied Aida's
first entrance in the opera. This time, however, it is unmistakably identified as the music of Aida's love for Radames.

Second Episode: Andante in 4/4 (mm. 48–67)

We have seen how the versatile chord had led into the second, F-major
episode of the aria which is devoted entirely to the elaboration of Aida's
tender devotion for her lover. By the end of this section, she can no longer
conceal from herself the full extent of her tragic predicament. The
symbolic harmonic constellation is now entrusted to the orchestra:

and this permits Aida to turn her back on the audience and to proceed to the stone balustrade located further upstage.

Third Episode: Allegro giusto poco agitato (mm. 67–84)

This A-flat minor episode elaborates on the hopelessness of Aida's internal conflict. Torn between her loyalties and passions, she is unable to weep or to pray for either her father or her lover. She remains seated until the final appearance of the harmonic sequence based on the diminished seventh, which is now given additional significance by being sung twice in succession:

With the first of these sentences, Aida rises and with the second she moves D stage.

Fourth Episode: Cantabile (mm. 84–117)

In the beginning of this prayerful section, Aida kneels down to address the gods in heaven and to beg them to have pity on her. The mention of love gives her the energy to rise, and she remains standing until the final orchestral postlude. She then walks slowly toward the R, as if she also were drawn to the temple of Vulcan where the weapons of her lover are about to receive the benediction of the priests and the blessing of the gods of Egypt.

Note

To give Aida's opening sentence the necessary quality of sudden consternation, it is advisable to establish a sufficient contrast to the preceding triumphant A-major mood. This can best be accomplished by playing the entire orchestral postlude of the preceding scene, or at least its last four and a half measures. A single A-major chord — as it is printed in some anthology versions of the aria — is clearly insufficient for this purpose.

The Vocal Aspects

Although this aria is replete with emotional outbursts that demonstrate how Aida is torn between her love for her country and her father, and her love for Radames, care must be taken so that it is not sung entirely in a staccato and choppy manner. In other words, Aida's agitation must not lead to bumpy singing. More excitement can be created by singing the long phrases in a legato style.

Many sopranos, performing in acoustically imperfect auditoriums, fear that their lower range may be inaudible unless they resort to a full chest tone, with the result that it is very noticeable when they change registers. This aria has become the unfortunate victim of this practice, with less than pleasing results. Using a full chest tone in the lower register is certainly commendable when it is proper and called for, but the abuse of the chest register, by using it higher than it should be used and more frequently than absolutely necessary, has detracted from the artistry of more than one singer. In measure 23 of "Ritorna vincitor," for example, the octave skip downward from the high F♯ to the lower one does not require a change in registers; the orchestra is silent, and the singer will be heard without a chest tone being employed. The authors feel that a chest tone is not necessary for singing any of the opening twenty-seven measures.

The phrases in measures 28–32 and 33–36 should be performed unbroken, without a breath, and should be very legato. The high B♭ in measure 45 should be attacked without a glottal stroke — and quietly, not fortissimo — and should be swelled immediately to full volume. Since the orchestra is again silent, no chest tone is necessary for measures 47–48. However, in measures 61–63, the singer may choose to use a dark chest quality to provide the proper tone color to depict Aida's "cruel anguish" and "broken heart."

Since the section marked "Allegro giusto poco agitato" is also marked "triste e dolce," it seems proper that it should begin legato. Beginning at measure 69, however, and continuing for six measures, there are accent marks in several places, and the phrases are short. These short phrases can be interpreted as little gasps of excitement. However, as Aida soon regains control of herself, measures 75–83 need not be sung in a choppy manner, in spite of the marking "con più forza."

The character of the music dictates a smooth vocal line in the final section of the aria. A slight tenuto — not a fermata — is possible on the

Ab in measure 94. It is desirable that measures 100–105 be sung in one breath, with a slight portamento from "soffrir" to "ah!" This should be possible for most singers, especially if one observes the "poco stringendo" in measure 101.

There are a number of traditional changes at the end of the aria, involving the rearrangement of syllables sung on different notes from those indicated in the score. In measure 108, most singers extend the syllable "–ta" to the D♮, then sing "del" on the D♭ and the turn after it, with "mio" on the C and "sof–" on the last note in the measure.

- tà____ del____ mio   sof - frir,

This resetting of the text permits a breath after the D♮, and makes it possible for the fermata to be held comfortably. There is nothing unstylistic or incorrect about this minor change.

The next change is much more objectionable. Some singers sing "Numi" instead of the first "pietà" on the last quarter of measure 109, and the first quarter of measure 110. This change forces the singer to indulge in bad prosody, putting stress on the syllable "Nu–" on the last weak beat of the measure. It is better not to meddle with the text at this point and to sing "pietà" twice as written.

One final change is an anticipation before the very last note, so that "soffrir" is sung thus:

sof - frir!

The Text

Literal Translation

1. Return conqueror! And from-the my lip escaped the-impious word!
2. Conqueror of-the father my . . . of him who takes-up the-arms for me . . .
3. To give-back-to-me a fatherland, a royal-palace
4. and the name illustrious that here to-conceal to-me-is necessary!
5. Conqueror of-the my brothers . . . so-that-I him see, stained with-the-blood beloved,
6. triumph in-the cheers of-the Egyptian cohorts!
7. And behind the chariot, a king . . . my father . . . with chains bound!
8. The-insane word, O Gods, obliterate!
9. To-the bosom of-a father the daughter return;
10. destroy, destroy the troops of-the our oppressors!
11. Ah, unfortunate-one! What-have-I said? And the-love my?

12. Then to-forget can-I this ardent love that, oppressed and slave,
13. like ray of sun here me blessed?
14. Shall-I-invoke the death to Radames . . . to him whom-I-love, however, so-much!
15. Ah, not was on earth ever by more cruel anguishes a heart broken!
16. The sacred names of father . . . of-lover neither to-utter can-I,
17. nor remember . . . for the-one . . . for the-other . . . confused . . . trembling . . .
18. I to-weep would-like . . . I-would-like to-pray.
19. But the my prayer into blasphemy itself changes . . . crime is the weeping to me . . .
20. Sin the sigh . . . in night . . . deep the mind is lost . . .
21. And in-the anxiety cruel I-would-like to-die.
22. Gods, pity on-the my suffering!
23. Hope not there-has for-the my anguish . . .
24. Love fatal, terrible love, break-to-me the heart, make-me die!
25. Gods, pity on-the my suffering!

Idiomatic Translation

1. Return as conqueror! And from my lips escaped those impious words!
2. Conqueror of my father, of him who takes up arms for me,
3. in order to give me back my fatherland, a royal palace,
4. and the illustrious name that I am here forced to conceal!
5. Conqueror of my brothers, so that I will see him, stained with the blood of my beloved ones,
6. triumph in the cheers of the Egyptian forces!
7. And behind the chariot, a king . . . my father . . . with chains bound!
8. O Gods, obliterate the insane word that I uttered!
9. Return the daughter to the bosom of her father;
10. destroy the troops of our oppressors!
11. Ah, how unfortunate am I! What have I said? And my love?
12. Can I, oppressed and a slave, forget the ardent love
13. that has blessed me here, like a ray of the sun?
14. Shall I invoke death for Radames, for him whom I love so much?
15. Ah, never on earth was a heart broken by more cruel anguish!
16. The sacred names of father, of lover, I can neither utter
17. nor remember . . . I am so confused, I tremble so much, that for both of them
18. I would like to pray, I would like to weep.
19. But my prayer would turn into blasphemy; to weep is a crime . . .
20. To sigh is a sin . . . my mind is lost in deep night
21. And in cruel anxiety I would like to die.
22. Gods, have pity on my suffering!
23. There is no hope for my anguish . . .
24. Fatal, terrible love, break my heart into pieces, cause me to die!
25. Gods, have pity on my suffering!

The Scenic Picture

A square in the Egyptian city of Memphis surrounded by various monuments. One of the structures located near the center of the stage has a low stone balustrade suitable for sitting. The scene takes place in full daylight.

The Stage Actions Explained

Before she starts singing, Aida stands in the UR portion of the stage near CC and faces toward the R. Her arms are raised in a gesture of jubilation and acclaim. She is still completely caught up in the mood of enthusiasm that, a little while earlier, made her mingle her voice with the shouting Egyptians who were invoking victory for Radames.

Recitative

Measures

1. Suddenly realizing the import of what she had sung earlier, she drops her arms, and backs away in horror.
2. She turns Cclw to face D.
3. With "e dal mio labbro," she raises her hands closer to her mouth.
5. She goes slightly DR.
6. On "vincitor," she glances momentarily over her R shoulder.
7. With "padre," she turns LSB and backs to UR.
12. She illustrates the word "qui" (here) by gesturing toward the surrounding area of the stage.
13. Excited by her own words, she goes DL.
14. With "vincitor," she again looks over her R shoulder, imagining Radames in the role of the conqueror of her brothers.
15. With "fratelli," she turns LSB and faces toward DL. She now imagines the triumphal procession as it moves from L to R, led by Radames and followed by troops of Egyptian soldiers and by a chariot carrying her father bound in chains. As she describes her vision she points to the leader, to the soldiers, and to the chariot as if she were actually seeing them move toward her one by one.
27. With "avvinto," she buries her head in her hands and goes rapidly DR.

First Episode

28. She looks heavenward.
34. With "padre," she gestures toward the L.
35. With "figlia," she indicates herself.
37. With the first "struggete," she turns LSB and backs to UR.
39. With the second "struggete," she waves her L fist high in the air.
41. With the third "struggete," she goes a few steps L.
42. With "squadre," she turns Clw and points to the R, at the imagined Egyptians soldiers whom she wants to see destroyed by the Ethiopians.

45. Realizing that among the destroyed Egyptians will also be her be-loved Radames, she backs away in horror.
46. With "sventurata," she turns RSF and goes DL beyond CC.

Second Episode

49. She sings "e l'amor mio," looking heavenward over her R shoulder.
50. After "mio," she turns her head Cclw to look toward DL.
52. With "questo fervido," she turns RSB and backs slightly toward UL.
54. With "come raggio," she looks heavenward.
55. After "sol," she goes DR as if basking in the sunshine of Radames' love.
58. With "a lui," she looks over her R shoulder in the direction where she imagines Radames to be located now.
59. After "tanto," she looks heavenward and begins a slow LSB turn.
60. While singing the high Ab, she continues to turn LSB and backs slightly to UR.
62. With "angoscie," she goes DL, as far as CC.
63. After "affranto," she turns Cclw and goes U toward the stone balus-trade.
65. Having arrived below the balustrade, she turns Clw and sits down facing D.

Third Episode

68. With "padre," she glances toward the L.
69. With "amante," she turns Clw to look toward the R and then raises her eyes heavenward.
71. With "per l'un," she glances toward the R.
72. With "l'altro," she turns Cclw to look toward the L.
77. With "delitto," she turns Clw.
78. With "colpa," she rises.
79. With "in notte," she takes a step to the R.
81. With "e nell'ansia," she turns LSB.
83. She goes D along CC.

Fourth Episode

84. She kneels.
91. She rises and glances over her R shoulder.
94. With "tremendo," she turns LSB and backs to UR.
100. She goes DL.
103. She looks heavenward and raises her arms in an imploring gesture.
109. She kneels once more.
114. She raises and backs slightly; then turns Clw and exits into the R wing.

"Oh, Patria Mia"
from *Aida,* Act III
by GIUSEPPE VERDI

The Scenic Picture and The Drama

The third act of *Aida* is set by the shore of the Nile. There is a profusion of palm trees and granite rocks. At the summit of one of the rocks stands the temple of Isis, half hidden by the foliage of the trees. It is night time, with stars and a bright moon.

This is the scenic picture as described in the score. For the purpose of our staging, the Nile is flowing from DR to UL, while the back of the temple is visible in the UL part of the stage just below the imagined expanse of the river. In the DR area there is, in addition, a practicable rock on which Aida will sit while she sings part of her aria.

Princess Amneris, accompanied by the high priest Ramfis and several soldiers, arrived earlier by way of the river from the R. After the Princess's party ascended to the temple, and the barge on which she came was taken to its presumed anchoring place in the L wing, the stage remained deserted.

After a while Aida appears from DR, below the shoreline. According to the score, she does not enter until the seventh measure of her theme. The authors, however, can see no reason to delay her appearance. In line with our general principle of matching the action with the music, we prefer to see Aida as soon as her music is heard.

At the end of the preceding act, Aida witnessed her rival's triumph. The King announced publicly that his daughter, Princess Amneris, and Radames would be married and eventually would become the rulers of Egypt. Aida and her father, on the other hand, were ordered to remain captive in Egypt and to serve as hostages in case of another Ethiopian invasion.

These startling developments crushed Aida's hopes for a safe return to her native country and doomed all her hopes for happiness with Radames.

At the beginning of the second Stanza of this aria, Aida speaks of her fatherland as a quiet and blessed refuge that her lover promised she would one day see again, but now the dream of love has vanished and she will never again see her native country. This would seem to indicate that Radames had confided to his beloved the vow — expressed so eloquently in his "Celeste Aida" — that, should he become the leader of the Egyptian armies and win the war, he would take her back to her fatherland.

One can therefore guess quite accurately what passes through Aida's mind before she begins to sing: "Radames promised me that, should he return victorious, he would take me back to my country. Now, cruel man,

31

he seems only too willing to marry Princess Amneris! And yet he sent me a message to meet him here tonight."

This train of thought leads smoothly into the opening words of her Recitative: "It is here that Radames will come. What will he want to tell me? I tremble! If you come, cruel man, to bid me a final farewell . . . then the turbulent, dark waters of the Nile shall be my tomb; and there, perhaps, I shall find peace and oblivion."

The Music

This aria — which Verdi calls "Romanza" — begins with an eleven-measure orchestral introduction featuring the melody of Aida's love motive. It is played in unison by three flutes and is accompanied by gently murmuring violas and a softly sustained high G entrusted to a single stand of first violins. When it is performed with piano accompaniment, it is best to omit the eight-measure high G since it cannot be satisfactorily imitated on that instrument.

Although this aria is cast in the familiar two-stanza form framed by an introduction and a coda, Verdi enriched it by an additional episode employing an "oriental" oboe melody. This section — which, because of its obvious musical and dramatic content, we shall call the "Shepherd's pipe" — occurs three times and serves as the Prelude, Interlude, and Coda to the two stanzas.

> Orchestral Introduction and Recitative measures 1–27
> Shepherd's pipe — Prelude mm. 27–39
> First Stanza mm. 39–57
> Shepherd's pipe — Interlude mm. 57–63
> Second Stanza mm. 63–78
> Shepherd's pipe — Coda mm. 78–83
> Orchestral Coda mm. 83–85

To end the "Romanza," the authors recommend the following simple abridgment:

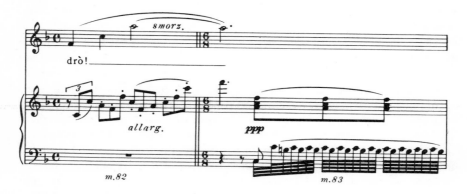

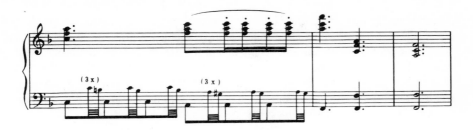

The Vocal Aspects

Very few sopranos will wish to refute the contention that — from the vocal point of view — this is one of the most difficult arias in the entire soprano repertoire. It requires a thorough command of the entire range, especially the upper middle and high voice. As is the case with "Ritorna vincitor," some singers are prone to use too much chest tone in the lower range because they are afraid of being inaudible. However, the opening recitative is *supposed* to sound fearful and excited, and even a breathy tone is more believable here than a dark, full chest quality. The singer need not fear being overwhelmed by the orchestra: either it plays a discreet tremolo, or is silent altogether. Most sopranos who attempt this aria should have a well-developed lower middle voice in order to sing all of the recitative, including measures 25–26, without a full chest tone. The marking "pianissimo," followed later by "morendo," in measures 24–26, should elicit the cooperation of the conductor.

Some degree of *messa di voce* should be possible on the long F in measure 31. Although it is not indicated by the composer, this device seems permissible and proper here. Measure 38 should be sung without an audible shift to chest voice. Care should be taken for the proper distribution of vowels on short notes in the 6/8 section. It is perfectly possible to distribute the three vowels *i, a,* and *u* in "dolci auri" in measure 40 so that none of them are slighted. The "–re" on the fourth eighth note of the same measure should be sung lightly to preserve proper prosody. In measure 42, care should be taken to make the *i* vowel in "mio" stressed, and longer, than the *o,* especially since it occurs on an octave skip and on a strong beat in the measure.

There are definite phrasing-breathing problems in the 6/8 sections of the aria. A good breath should be taken after "native" in measure 41. Then the "–lò" of measure 43 should be carried and connected to "o" with a slight portamento and without a breath, and the long phrase should end after "colli" in measure 44. A breath is possible but not obligatory after "rive" in measure 45.

The *i* vowel in "mia" on the high A in measure 55 is often uncomfortable for singers who dislike singing pure close vowels on high notes.

Kirsten Flagstad apparently preferred the sound of *ee* on high notes to all other vowels, but then she was an unusual singer in many respects! Most singing authorities condone — and teach — what is commonly known as "vowel modification." This is simply the process of changing the vowel sound of any close vowel to a more open sound. Thus the *ee* in this case would tend to become *ih,* as in the word "mitt," or even *eh,* as in the word "met." How much modification is necessary is up to the individual singer. The authors feel that a properly modified vowel, well sung, is preferable to a pure vowel badly sung. If the note is attacked softly, and not forte as marked, and then instantaneously increased in volume, a purer vowel can be attempted. It is generally good practice, incidentally, for *all* high notes to be attacked gently, regardless of dynamic marking, and then increased to proper volume as quickly as possible.

The low "mia" on C♮ in measure 56 need not be sung with a chest tone, for the orchestra is again silent. Neither should "mai più" in measure 59 be sung with a chest tone, since the orchestration is light and the phrase is marked "parlante." The same instructions hold for measures 61–62. Even though the composer has marked a slur from "–to" to "che‿in" in measure 65, the singer should probably take a breath there, first making a slight portamento between the two notes and then taking a catch breath, because the only alternative is to do the same thing two measures later. It is doubtful whether any singer will wish to attempt to sing measures 63–69 without a breath, and yet that is how the composer has marked the phrasing. The lesser of two evils would be the breath in measure 65, rather than the more exposed one (because of the larger interval) in measure 67. However, these are problems that can only be solved on an individual basis, and there is no pat solution.

Most singers will find it necessary to modify the *oo* vowel in the word "più" in measures 75–76 so that it becomes *aw* or even *ah,* on the high C. Though the authors recommend a little sobbing catch breath before the first "non ti vedrò," some singers may feel more comfortable vocally if they do not break the phrase at this point. Verdi did not write "a piacere" and "col canto" at measures 80–81, and adherence to the correct note values is preferred, especially on the "mai più" in measure 81, so that it is easy for the oboe to imitate the voice exactly. No chest voice should be necessary for measure 81. The final high A is marked "smorzando" (dying away) and thus no *messa di voce* is recommended here.

A final word is perhaps useful here about what may seem to be an ambiguous marking in many places in this aria. Verdi has marked many phrases . . . . in the two 6/8 sections of the aria. This should not be interpreted as a simple staccato. Rather the singer should sing as legato as possible and still give the notes marked with dots a distinct if discreet emphasis. No other interpretation of this marking seems possible: singing non-legato would spoil the musical phrase.

Also, Verdi uses a rather rare marking in two places in this aria. At measure 41 he indicates "sfumato il do♯" on the first beat, and again, at measure 65, he indicates "sfumate" on the first beat. Both terms literally mean "to vanish, evaporate, melt away," and we must assume that Verdi wanted a particular vocal effect obtained by making an extremely fine decrescendo on these two C♯'s to a light, spun-out head tone.

The Text

Literal Translation

Recitative

1. Here Radames will-come! What will-he-wish to-say-to-me? I tremble!
2. Ah, if you come to bring-me, O cruel-one, the-last farewell,
3. of-the Nile the dark whirlpools to-me will-give tomb . . . and peace perhaps . . .
4. and peace perhaps and oblivion.

Aria

5. O fatherland my, never more, never more you will-I-see-again!
6. O skies azure, O sweet breezes native, where serene the my morning shone . . .
7. O green hills . . . O perfumed shores . . . O fatherland my, never more you-will-I-see-again!
8. No . . . no . . . never more, never more!
9. O fresh valleys, O quiet refuge blessed that one day promised by-the-love to-me was . . .
10. Now that of-love the dream is disappeared . . .
11. O fatherland my, not you will-I-see ever again!

Idiomatic Translation

Recitative

1. Radames will come here! What will he want to say to me? I tremble!
2. Ah, if you are coming, cruel one, to say a last farewell to me,
3. the dark whirlpools of the Nile will provide a tomb for me . . . and give me peace perhaps,
4. yes, peace and oblivion, perhaps.

Aria

5. O my fatherland, never more will I see you again!
6. O azure skies, O sweet breezes of my native land, where the morning of my life shone serenely,
7. O green hills, O perfumed shores, O my fatherland, never more will I see you again!
8. No, no, never more, never more!
9. O fresh valleys, O blessed quiet refuge that one day was promised to me by love . . .
10. Now that the dream of love has disappeared,
11. O my fatherland, I will never see you again!

The Stage Actions Explained

Before indicating the various actions in a schematic, measure-by-measure listing, it may be useful to give a more leisurely analysis of the thoughts and motives that underlie the character's behavior on stage.

"Oh, Patria mia" belongs to the category of arias where so little seems to "happen" that singers tend to abandon any attempt at dramatic interpretation. They enter, make their way to the center-downstage area and, all too often, remain there to indulge in a static, concert-like performance, relieved only by occasional excursions to the right and the left.

It is admittedly not easy to bring Aida's third-act "Romanza" to full dramatic life. Let us begin by asking ourselves what Aida is singing about, and consider the possibilities of exteriorizing at least some of her thoughts and feelings. She begins by mentioning the place where she will meet her lover, then speaks of him, of herself, of the river Nile, and of her plan to commit suicide in its dark whirlpools. The first words she sings are: "Here Radames will come," and this thought suggests some acting possibilities for the orchestral interlude. "Is this the right spot? Yes! Here is the rear of the temple and the clump of palm trees to which he referred. Is Radames already here? Let me look on the other side. No! He is not here yet. Well, I must be patient. He mentioned that he might be delayed."* Acting out these ideas, she enters from DR and goes L to look at the temple of Isis, turns to observe the palm trees on stage R, and then turns in the other direction to give a searching look into the darkness of the L wing, wondering whether Radames may be waiting for her there. During the final three measures of the Introduction, she decides to sit down on the rock located R. She starts going in that direction, but as she walks, she recalls the events that occurred at Radames' triumphal reception and begins to wonder just why Radames asked her to wait for him here. Troubled by these thoughts, she forgets her earlier intention to sit down. Her first two sentences are sung toward DR in the direction from which she came and from which she also expects Radames to enter. At the end of her second short sentence, she turns to go UL and uses the second long pause to make her way to the U stage area where she will be able to look at the river while she sings of it, without turning her back to the audience. She then takes advantage of the repetition of "e pace forse," to change the focal point of her attention and to move toward the rocky seat. All at once she recalls to mind the shepherd of her native hills as he blows his

---

* The final sentence of our invented subtext may seem rather farfetched. But we must remember that Radames does in fact arrive at his rendezvous very much later than Aida. One wonders whether she would have remained here for such a long time if she had not become involved in the unexpected scene with her father. The idea that Radames feared a delay and asked Aida to be patient explains her willingness to wait for him and makes the actual sequence of later events more credible.

reed while guarding sheep. The sound appears to come from DL, from the far distant land of her people. She walks in that direction, listening to the melody she knows so well. She stops on the "Oh, patria mia" sentence and keeps standing there quietly listening to the repetition of the melancholy tune. With "mai più," she turns and retraces her steps to the seat where, with the second "mai più," she finally sits down.

Reminiscing on the beauty of her native land, Aida not only pictures it in her mind's eye but gives it an actual location DL, past the walls of the auditorium. As she gazes into the distance, she changes the focal points of her attention, imagining the "azure skies" and "sweet breezes" as being located higher in the air than the "green hills" and "perfumed shores." The painful realization that she will never again be in the physical presence of these dear sights gives her the energy to turn away toward DR and the urge to get up, so that with the first orchestral interlude (m. 47) she can take a step or two to the R. The "Oh, patria mia" sentence gives her a reason to make an LSB turn and back slightly to look again toward DR, in the direction of her beloved Ethiopia. She then goes in that direction, Xing above the rocky seat. At the climax of this phrase — with the third "mai più" in measure 51 — she slowly turns Clw and finishes this sentence, facing DR to strengthen the idea that "not seeing" her country lies in the direction opposite to "contemplating its beauty." The two "Oh, patria mia" phrases that follow are given different emphases: the first one continues to be directed toward DR, but on the high A of the second "mia" Aida turns Cclw to face DL so that the final "mai più ti rivedrò" she can go DL as far as the center of the stage.

Hearing the shepherd's pipe again, Aida starts sobbing, covers her face with her hands and turns Cclw remaining with her back to the audience for the almost inaudible *parlante* "mai più" in measure 59. During measure 60 she continues to turn Cclw so that by the end of this episode she is once more facing in the "never again" direction, DR.

At the beginning of the second Stanza, Aida makes another Cclw turn and walks slightly L in the direction of her imagined fatherland. The mention of "love" in measure 66 makes her think of Radames, and she rotates Clw for the "vanished dream of love," returning again to look in the "Ethiopian" direction on "patria" in measure 69. During the orchestral interlude (m. 71 and m. 72) she walks L to get still closer to her "patria." She remains there, facing DL, until measure 76, when she turns slowly Clw to give everyone in the audience the full benefit of the climactic high C. The first "non ti vedrò" could be preceded by a gentle, soblike breath, at which time she also moves a bit to the R. With the last appearance of the "Shepherd's pipe," Aida walks toward the rock. On "patria mia" she gives a last look at the fatherland and continues toward the rock so that when she has finished the high A in measure 83 she can collapse there and hide her face in her hands.

Recitative

Measures

1. Aida enters from DR, stops, and looks around.
3. She goes L, Xing CC, to look at the temple of Isis at UL.
5. She turns Clw and goes UR to observe the palm trees on the R.
7. She turns Cclw, goes slightly L, and gives a searching look into the L wing, wondering whether Radames may be waiting for her there.
9. She goes DR, intending to sit down on the rock, on the R.
12. She changes her mind and stops UL of the rock.
14. With "dirmi," she turns Cclw and goes UL. The *lungo silenzio* (long pause) permits her to take several steps before continuing to sing.
15. She sings "io tremo" over the R shoulder, and then continues to go UL.
16. With "Ah," she turns very slightly Clw to face DL.
20. With "del Nilo," she turns RSB and backs slightly to UL so that she can address the river toward DR.
25. With the repetition of "e pace forse," she looks heavenward and goes DR toward the rock.
27. She looks over her L shoulder toward DL.
29. She turns Cclw and goes L as far as CC.
34. She takes another step or two toward the L.
35. With "mai più," she turns Clw and goes R toward the rock.
38. With "mai più," she turns Cclw and sits down to face toward DL.

Stanza 1: Lo stesso movimento in 6/8

39. She looks heavenward.
44. She lowers her glance as she imagines the hills.
45. As she sings of the river, she lowers her glance still more.
46. With "mai più," she turns Clw.
47. After "rivedro," she rises and goes slightly DR.
48. With "Oh, patria," she turns LSB and backs slightly toward UR.
49. After "mia," she goes L, Xing above the rock to UL of it.
51. With "ma – – i," she turns Clw to face toward DR.
53. She sings the first "Oh patria," toward DR.
54. With the second "Oh patria," however, she turns Cclw to face DL.
56. With "mai più," she goes DL to CC.
58. She covers her face with her hands and turns Cclw to face UL.
59. She sings "mai più," in this position.
60. She continues to turn Cclw.
62. She faces toward DR.

Stanza 2

63. She turns Cclw and goes L to just beyond CC.
66. She turns Clw.

69. With "patria," she turns Cclw to face DL.
71. After "più," she takes several steps toward L.
76. She turns slowly RSB and back slightly to UL. The first "non ti vedro" is preceded by a gentle soblike breath at which time she also moves a little to R.
78. After "più," she walks DR toward the rock.
80. She stops UL of the rock and turns Cclw to face DL.
81. After "più," she turns Clw and goes DR to below the rock.
83. After she finishes the last note, she sits down and hides her face in her hands.

Rosina wears the "Goya" style dress of a young Spanish lady of the late 18th century.

"Una voce poco fa"
from *Il Barbiere di Seviglia*, Act I, Scene 2
by GIOACCHINO ROSSINI

The Drama

In the first scene of *The Barber of Seville* Count Almaviva serenaded Rosina under her window at dawn. She then wrote a note to the handsome, young admirer who first stared at her on the Prado in Madrid and who has now turned up in Seville. The note, asking the gentleman to state his name and his intentions, was dropped from the balcony of the house where she lives with her guardian, old Dr. Bartolo. Rosina is watched very closely by Dr. Bartolo and his servants, since he himself wishes to marry his young ward, who is not only pretty, but rich as well.

Rosina has had two snatches of conversation with her admirer: the first during the episode when she dropped the note; the second (after Dr. Bartolo had left the house) when the Count sang a reply to the note telling her that his name was Lindoro and that although he was not rich, he loved her very much. Caught near the balcony door talking to someone, Rosina was hustled inside by one of the servants and sent to her room.

At the beginning of the second scene, Rosina is anxious to find out whether her admirer is still beneath the balcony, and she needs a pretext to return to the living room so that she can peek out of the balcony window. Like many young ladies of refinement and position, Rosina often whiles away her time with embroidering, and in the living room is an embroidery frame with some unfinished work on it. She decides to pretend that she wants to match a skein of wool with that of the unfinished work on the frame. Disappointed that the admirer is nowhere in sight, and finding the living room empty, she has the sudden inspiration to write Lindoro another and more encouraging letter.

The Music

The aria is divided into two sections, the first an Andante of forty-two measures, and the second a Moderato of seventy-eight measures.* Each section has an orchestral introduction. The initial four notes of the Andante enunciate the central thought of the Cavatina: "La vincerò" (I'll win the day), and they appear again in measure 8 of the Moderato.

The introduction of the Andante consists of three phrases: the first (mm. 1–4) and the third (mm. 9–13) refer to Lindoro, with their dynamic contrasts and strong dotted rhythms; the second, with its whisper-

---

* The measures are numbered separately in each section.

41

ing sotto voce, is associated with Dr. Bartolo and the tactics needed to outwit him. The remainder of the Andante is an extension of these same ideas: measures 14–21 and 35–42 contain vocal and orchestral outbursts at the words, "Si, Lindoro mio sarà" (Yes, Lindoro will be mine), while measures 30–34 contain the same violin figures that are heard in measures 5–8, referring to Dr. Bartolo.

The first twelve measures of the Moderato have a few interesting features. The first eight measures of the introduction in E major are followed by a detour into f-sharp minor with a return to E major. These first eight measures are then repeated by the voice (mm. 13–20) but this time the little excursion into f-sharp minor is omitted, and new material consisting of four measures is introduced (mm. 21–24). Measures 10–11, with their excited, scrambling violin figures, may be interpreted as Rosina's writing of the letter.

Measures 25–40 are followed by six measures of excited passages in the violins which denote Rosina's finishing of the letter (mm. 41–46). Measures 49–64 are an exact repetition of measures 25–40, obviously intended to be embellished and ornamented by the singer when they appear a second time. The Coda, measures 65–78, is the last part of the aria. Mm. 72–78 are a repetition of Rosina's finishing of the letter in measures 41–47.

As in the Andante, there are notable contrasts in the Moderato. Rosina describes herself first as a docile, obedient girl, but when she is touched where it hurts, she becomes a viper, springing a hundred traps! The traps are set with insinuating vocal chromatics in f-sharp minor, but they are sprung with energetic sixteenths in a vocal line in E major.

The Vocal Aspects

All too often one hears this aria sung purely as a show piece, replete with vocal pyrotechnics that are meant to display the vocal flexibility, fluency, and range of the performer. Yet this does the aria but partial justice. A variety of tone color is also necessary, to accompany each of Rosina's rapid changes of thought: her love, her cleverness, her determination. When she thinks of Lindoro, her voice must reflect innocence and naivete; when she thinks of Bartolo, she must sound self-confident; when she comments on her docility and obedience, there should be a touch of irony in her voice. When she describes herself as a viper, her voice must sound angry; when she speaks of setting and springing traps, she must sound sly, then triumphant. All the musical skips, runs, and ornaments must express and emphasize her mood of the moment, and show Rosina's rapture, amusement, anger, laughter, or triumph.

This aria is often performed by high mezzo-sopranos in the original key and by sopranos in the slightly higher key of F major. Variants for certain passages are so numerous and so common that they scarcely need mention here. A number of them are found in the edition of Estelle

Liebling published separately by G. Schirmer. Many of these variations require the shifting of syllables in such profusion that any discussion of phrasing and breathing problems would become too involved.

Some of the variations are intended to accommodate higher voices and alleviate the necessity for singing notes below the staff. When the original is sung, care must be taken to avoid a glaring change of tone quality when shifting to a chest tone. When possible, it is preferable to sing measures 25–40 of the Moderato pretty much as written by the composer, and to introduce variations when this music is repeated in measures 49–64.

The Text

Literal Translation
1. A voice while ago here in-the heart to-me resounded.
2. The my heart wounded is already, and Lindoro it-was who it wounded.
3. Yes, Lindoro mine shall-be, it I-swore, it I-shall-win.
4. The guardian will-refuse, I the-cunning will-sharpen,
5. at-the end himself-he-will-quiet-down, and happy I shall-be.
6. I am docile, I-am respectful, I-am obedient, sweet, loving.
7. Myself I-allow to-be-ruled, myself I-make to-be-led.
8. But if me they-touch where-is the my weakness,
9. I-will-be a viper, I-will-be.
10. And hundred traps before to give-in I-shall-make to-play!

Idiomatic Translation
1. A voice, a little while ago, resounded here in my heart.
2. My heart is wounded already, and it was Lindoro who wounded it.
3. Yes, Lindoro shall be mine . . . I swore it . . . I shall win.
4. If my guardian refuses, I will sharpen my wits,
5. and finally he will quiet down, and then I shall be happy.
6. I can be docile, respectful, obedient, sweet, and loving.
7. I allow myself to be ruled and to be led.
8. But if someone dares to attack my weakness,
9. I will become a viper.
10. And I shall spring a hundred traps before I give in!

The Scenic Picture

The living room of Dr. Bartolo's house has two doors, one DR leading to Rosina's room, the other UL leading to the rest of the house. There is an archway DL which leads to Bartolo's room and French windows UC which lead to the balcony. Inside of these windows are shutters, in the fashion of many European houses. A small harpsichord stands along the R wall above the R door. A small square table, with inkwell and quill on it, is located on stage L. There are two chairs, one above the table, the other on stage R some distance to L of the harpsichord. An embroidery

frame stands by the U wall to R of the French windows. (For a drawing
of this setting, see *Bringing Opera to Life,* p. 188.)

The Stage Actions Explained

As the music begins, Rosina enters from her room, DR. She carries the
skein of wool in her L hand.

Section 1: (Andante)

Measures

1. *(the partial measure at the beginning is not counted)* Rosina looks
   around to make sure that she is alone.
2. She closes the door with her R hand.
3. She tiptoes UL toward the balcony window, hoping to catch a glimpse
   of Lindoro.
4. She glances toward the archway and decides it would be better to see
   whether Bartolo has returned. She puts the skein of wool on the harpsichord with her L hand and runs to the archway, Xing table, to look
   and listen.
7. Reassured that Bartolo has not returned, she starts UR toward the
   balcony window, above the table.
8. Nearing the main entrance, she imagines she hears a noise outside and
   makes a slight detour to it, opens the door, finds no one, and closes
   it again.
9. She continues UR to the balcony window.
10. She opens one of the shutters.
11. She opens the other shutter. She sees no one below.
12. *(on forte)* She closes the shutters and turns Clw to face DL.
22. She turns Clw and goes DR slightly.
26. She goes slightly more DR.
29. *(2nd quarter)* She turns Cclw and goes L to R of the table, looking at
    the archway.
31. When she refers to herself ("io") she turns slightly Clw.
32. When referring again to Bartolo ("Alla fin s'accheterà"), she turns
    Cclw and looks at the archway again.
33. Referring once more to herself ("e contenta io resterò"), she turns
    slightly Clw a second time.
35. She goes R to CC.
39. She goes further R to below the armchair.

Section 2: (Moderato)

Measures

1. With a sudden inspiration to write Lindoro another letter, she turns
   Cclw and runs UL to the L chair, sits down, and takes from its open
   drawer space *(to avoid the danger of sticking, it is safer to remove the*

drawer completely and keep the necessary props in the open compart-ment) the stack of six sheets of paper, the sander, and the saucer. She places the sander to her right and the saucer to her left.

8. *(on forte)* She looks up with determination and takes the quill from the ink bottle.
9. She writes briskly.
12. She replaces the quill in the ink bottle.
14. She picks up the sander with her R hand.
    (3rd quarter) She shakes the sander lightly over the paper to coincide with the flute scale in the accompaniment.
16. She puts the sander down again to her R.
18. She picks up the sheet of paper and moves it gently back and forth to make sure that the sand has blotted the ink.
    (3rd quarter) She shakes the paper over the saucer to empty the sand into it *(coinciding with the second flute scale)* and puts the paper down in front of her.
24. She gets up and steps slightly L to L of the table to face the archway.
27. She goes slightly L to the archway.
31. She turns Clw and goes R to below the table.
32. She sits on D edge of the table.
35. She turns Cclw to face the archway and shakes her finger in its direc-tion.
37. She leans back, reclining on the palms of her hands *(on the table),* in an almost provocatively relaxed pose.
39. She gets up and goes slightly R.
41. She turns Cclw, goes UL to the L chair, sits down, takes the quill, and finishes the letter.
47. She replaces the quill in the ink bottle and gets up to R of the chair.
48. *(3rd quarter)* She goes slightly R.
51. She turns Cclw and shakes her finger in the direction of the archway.
53. She turns Clw and goes slightly further R.
55. She turns Cclw to sing in the direction of Bartolo's room.
56. She goes further R and sits in the armchair.
63. She gets up and goes slightly R.
65. She turns Cclw and goes UL, Xing above the armchair, to CC.
72. She runs DL to the table, picks up the letter, folds it, returns to CC, dances in a complete circle, and kisses the letter.
78. She puts the letter in the bodice of her dress.

The rigid, heavily embroidered costume of Micaëla is typical of Spanish folk costumes.

"Je dis que rien ne m' épouvante"
from *Carmen,* Act III
by GEORGES BIZET

The Drama

Bizet's *Carmen* is based on Prosper Merimée's story of the same name, and depicts the gradual ruination of a decent, upright soldier by a fascinating, but totally conscienceless Spanish gypsy.

Although the librettists of the opera, Meilhac and Halévy, borrowed most of the incidents from Merimée, they felt impelled to make Carmen's conquest of José more difficult. Therefore they strengthened his ties with his native Navarra, elaborated his sentimental attachment to his mother, and provided an additional and contrasting love interest in the shape of the virtuous country girl, Micaëla.

José's mother, incidentally, is not a complete stranger to Merimée's novel. There is a fleeting mention of her near the end of the second chapter. The captive José, who is shortly to be executed, asks the narrator of the story if on his way to France he expects to pass through Navarra: "Should you go to Pamplona . . . I will give you this medal (he showed me a little silver medal that he wore around his neck); you will wrap it in paper . . . he stopped for a moment to control his emotion . . . and you will give it or send it to a good woman whose address I will give you. Let her know that I am dead, but don't tell her how I died."

On the other hand, Micaëla is a pure invention of the librettists and for everything regarding her person we must turn to the text of the opera, of which there exist two different versions. Most operagoers are familiar only with the later, grand opera version of *Carmen* which contains the orchestrally accompanied recitatives added to the opera by Ernest Guiraud several months after Bizet's death. The spoken lines of the original version are more extensive, however, and provide considerably more detail about the various characters and their relationship to each other. Since the Opéra Comique version has not been published in the United States,* we shall translate those portions that refer to Micaëla and to her relationship with José and his mother.

We first meet Micaëla in the opening number of the opera when, having just arrived in Seville, she comes to the square that faces the tobacco factory and asks the soldiers standing guard there† whether they can help

---

* The complete French text of this version is included in the edition published by Alkor (Kassel, Germany).

† During the nineteenth century tobacco was a governmental monopoly in Spain, and the factories where cigars and cigarettes were manufactured were guarded by soldiers.

47

her find Corporal José. She is told that José belongs to the relief guard which is expected to arrive shortly. Corporal Morales tries to persuade the pretty visitor to wait for José in the guardhouse, a suggestion that is enthusiastically seconded by his subordinates. Flirting with strange soldiers does not, however, appeal to our heroine and she manages to escape from her admirers telling them that she will return later.

During the change of guard, after José's arrival, we then hear the following conversation:

MORALES

A pretty girl was here asking for you. She said she would return.

JOSE

A pretty girl?

MORALES

Yes, and nicely dressed: blue skirt and braids falling on her shoulders.

JOSE

That is Micaëla! That can only be Micaëla!

MORALES

She did not give her name.

Up to this point the two versions of the opera are practically identical. It is in the next exchange between José and Lieutenant Zuniga that we can observe to what extent Guiraud has condensed Meilhac and Halévy's spoken lines. The beginning of this episode — where Zuniga questions José about the cigar factory — does not concern us here. It is only when Zuniga asks whether the girls working there are young and pretty that the conversation becomes of interest to us:

ZUNIGA

Are there young ones among them?

JOSE

Why, of course, sir!

ZUNIGA

And pretty ones?

JOSE *(laughing)*

I suppose so . . . But, to tell the truth, even though I have been on guard here several times, I don't really know, since I have never looked at them that much.

ZUNIGA

Go on!

JOSE

Believe me . . . these Andalusian girls frighten me. I am not used to their ways . . . always teasing, never a sensible word . . .

ZUNIGA

And then, of course, you have a weakness for blue skirts and for braids falling on shoulders . . .

JOSE *(laughing)*

Ah! The Lieutenant overheard what Morales was telling me?

ZUNIGA

Yes.

JOSE

I won't deny it . . . blue skirts and braids . . . that is the costume of Navarra . . . it reminds me of home* . . .

ZUNIGA

You are from Navarra?

JOSE

And of an old Christian family. Don José Lizarrabengoa . . . that is my name. I was destined for the church and was made to study for it. But I did not profit from the instruction. I was much too fond of playing *pelota*** . . . One day when I had won, a fellow from Alava picked a quarrel with me. I bested him again . . . but this forced me to leave Navarra. I turned to soldiering! My father was dead; my mother followed me and found a little place some twenty-five miles from here† . . . with little Micaëla . . . She is an orphan who did not want to be separated from my mother who brought her up.

ZUNIGA

How old is she, your little Micaëla?

JOSE

Seventeen.

ZUNIGA *(laughing)*

You should have said so right away! Now I understand why you could not tell me if the factory girls were pretty or ugly . . .

The spoken dialogue that precedes the duet between José and Micaëla is not much different from Guiraud's recitative, and the duet itself — in which Micaëla gives José his mother's gift of money, her letter, and the all-important kiss — is the same in both versions. It is worth noting, however, that having learned from the spoken lines that José's mother and Micaëla are now located only twenty-miles from Seville, we are no longer puzzled by the girl's statement that she will be home the very next day. Singers who are familiar only with the recitative version, and who quite naturally imagine that Micaëla's return trip must take her all the way to

---

* This is borrowed from Merimée's story where José, describing the scene that preceded his first meeting with Carmen, observes: "I was young then; all my thoughts were for Navarra, and I did not believe any girl could be pretty unless she wore a blue skirt and had braids falling on her shoulders."

** A form of tennis, also known as jai-alai: the national sport of the Basque country.

† Actually, *dix lieues:* ten leagues. The French league is equal to approximately two and a half miles.

Navarra, are usually amazed when they discover that Pamplona, the capital of Navarra — where according to Merimée's story, José's mother was living — is seven hundred miles from Seville.

In the spoken section which comes after the duet, we can again observe a considerable gain in informative detail.

JOSE

Now wait a little . . . while I read the letter.

MICAELA

I will wait, Mr. Corporal, I will wait.

JOSE

Ah! . . . *(kissing the letter before he reads it) (reading)* "Continue to behave well, my child! They promised to make you a sergeant: perhaps you will then be able to retire from service, to obtain some small administrative post, and to move closer to me. I am getting quite a bit older. You would live near me and get married. We won't have any trouble finding you a wife; as far as I am concerned I know only too well whom I would advise you to choose: surely the one who brings you my letter . . . I don't know anyone who is better behaved and nicer . . .

MICAELA

I think I better be going!

JOSE

But why?

MICAELA

I just remembered that your mother asked me to take care of some chores. I must do them at once.

JOSE

Wait until I am finished . . .

MICAELA

You'll finish after I am gone.

JOSE

But the answer?

MICAELA

I'll be back in time to take your answer to your mother. Good-bye!

JOSE

Micaëla!

MICAELA

No, no . . . I will return . . . I would much rather . . . I will return. *(She leaves.)*

JOSE *(continuing to read)*

"I don't know anyone who is better behaved and nicer . . . and if you are willing . . ." Yes, mother, Yes. I will do as you desire . . . I will marry Micaëla . . .

This is not what happens, of course. Carmen's torrid charms soon erase from José's mind the image of the "well-behaved" girl with her braids and her blue skirt. Micaëla is neither seen* nor heard of again until her third act aria with which, however — if she is a first-rate performer — she can steal the show from her glamorous rival. This is true mainly because not a single one of Carmen's three celebrated songs is a true solo number. Though it is hard to believe, Micaëla's third-act aria is the only vocal piece in the entire score where there is just a single person on stage.

The events of the third act take place in the secret mountain retreat which the gypsies use as a way station for storing contraband before smuggling them into Seville.

Some seven or eight months† have elapsed since Micaëla has last seen José. She comes to this den of thieves looking for José and hoping to persuade him to give up Carmen and to return to his former, orderly existence. His mother's declining health and her desire to see her son before it is too late are not the only reasons that bring Micaëla here. Although she speaks of having "once" loved him, it is fairly obvious that she still does and hopes against hope that he might return to her.

In spite of the relative brevity of her role, Micaëla's words and behavior, coupled with what José has to say about her, gives us quite a few clues to her character. Her opening scene with Morales and the soldiers shows us that she has a sense of humor and is eminently able to take care of herself. It is true that in her first-act scene with José she seems rather shy, but it is fairly certain that she has been worshipping him ever since she was a little girl in Pamplona. She has only recently blossomed into full-fledged womanhood and is of course well aware of her foster mother's match-making scheme. It is even highly probable that the old woman made Micaëla promise to kiss José on the lips and, since this is undoubtedly the first time that she has ever kissed a man, the anticipation of this tender caress causes her quite a bit of embarrassment. And the dangerous task she performs in the third act calls for great courage and determination.

This role is often unfairly denigrated because of its supposed sentimentality, but there is no reason to sing or act it in a sugary manner.

There was a time when all Micaëlas were made to wear blond wigs but this is completely unnecessary. There is no reason in the world why Micaëla cannot have dark hair. The contrast with the swarthy Carmen should be accented by the whiteness of Micaëla's skin and by the general wholesomeness of her personality. Where Carmen seems to exude an aura

---

* It is possible to bring Micaëla back on stage at the very end of the first act, so that she can witness Carmen's escape and José's inglorious arrest; but with all the commotion attending this episode, the "return" of our poor little messenger does not produce much of an impression either on her presumed fiancé or on the audience.

† It is rather curious that Guiraud keeps José in prison for two months while the original version speaks of only one month. Escamillo's words in his third-act scene with José establish the fact that an additional six months have elapsed since José threw in his lot with Carmen and the smugglers.

of reckless danger and the odor of musk, Micaëla must smell of new-mown hay and fresh milk.

Most opera lovers are so used to the instrumental recitative that introduces Micaëla's third-act aria that it comes as a shock to them to learn that it was composed not by Bizet but by Guiraud. Here again the spoken version is more informative, although the recitative version unquestionably has great musical charm.

The spoken lines of the original version help to explain how Micaëla is able to find her way to the hide-out of the gypsy smugglers. They also serve to inform the audience that Escamillo has been seen in the vicinity, so that his eventual arrival should not come as a complete surprise. To a modern opera lover the notion that Escamillo spends his time escorting a herd of wild bulls in the Andalusian mountains may seem rather preposterous. French playwrights of the 19th century, however, felt that it was their duty to "prepare" the entrances of important characters. Saint Saëns writes in his memoirs that one of the main reasons why the management of the Paris Grand Opera turned down his *Samson et Dalila* was that Delila's entrance in the first act was not properly "prepared!"

Even though it is unlikely that the spoken lines would be performed today without drastic cuts, the soprano entrusted with Micaela's aria should find the complete text of the original version instructive and helpful.

Complete Text

THE GUIDE
(enters surreptitiously, then signals to Micaela who is not visible, at first)
　　Here we are!

MICAELA *(entering)*

Is it here?

THE GUIDE
Yes . . . it is a deserted spot and not at all reassuring!

MICAELA
I do not see anyone.

THE GUIDE
They have just left, but they will soon return, for they have not yet taken all the merchandise. I know their habits . . . Be careful . . . One of them must be on guard nearby and should we be seen . . .

MICAELA
I want to be seen . . . since I came here expressly to speak to . . . to speak to one of the smugglers.

THE GUIDE
There's no doubt that you have a lot of courage! A while ago when we were caught in the middle of that herd of wild bulls that were led by the famous Escamillo, you did not tremble . . . And now, you come here to face these gypsies!

MICAELA

I do not get frightened easily.

THE GUIDE

You say that because I am here . . . if you were alone here . . .

MICAELA

I would not be frightened, I assure you.

THE GUIDE

Really?

MICAELA

Really!

THE GUIDE

Then please permit me to leave . . . I brought you here and you paid
me well. But now that you are here . . if you don't mind, I'll wait
for you at the place where you hired me . . . at the tavern near the
bottom of the mountain.

MICAELA

Very well. Wait for me there.

THE GUIDE

You are sure, you want to remain?

MICAELA

Yes, I am staying.

THE GUIDE (*as he leaves*)

May the Saints protect you . . . but it's a strange notion you have
there . . .

MICAELA (*looking around*)

My guide was right . . . this place is not very reassuring . . .

For those sopranos who want to omit Guiraud's recitative and preface
Bizet's aria with a few spoken lines, the authors recommend the following
greatly abridged acting version:

THE GUIDE

(*tiptoes in from the R and signals to Micaela who is not visible at first*)
Here we are!

MICAELA (*enters from the R*)

Is it here?

THE GUIDE

Yes . . . it is a deserted spot, and not at all reassuring.

(*Micaela goes L, Xing the guide, and looks around.*)

THE GUIDE

Are you sure that you want to remain here?

MICAELA

Yes, I am staying. (*She pays the guide.*)

THE GUIDE

May the Saints protect you. (*He leaves to R.*)

MICAELA

He was right . . . this place is not very reassuring . . .

Guiraud's Recitative

The Music

The recitative has nineteen measures. A ten-measure instrumental introduction is followed by a vocal section of nine measures. A strong accent (*sFp*) that for some reason has been omitted in most piano-vocal scores should be added on the down beat of the fifteenth measure.

Literal Translation
1. This is of the smugglers the retreat ordinary.
2. He is here, I him will see.
3. And the duty that me imposed his mother
4. Without trembling I it will accomplish.

Idiomatic Translation
1. This is the usual hide-out of the smugglers.
2. He is here, I will see him.
3. And the task that his mother imposed on me
4. I will undertake without trembling.

The Stage Actions Explained

Micaëla enters from DR in the second measure and stops with the third measure to inspect the surroundings. In the fourth measure she goes farther UL and notices the trunk and the bales of the merchandise that stand on stage L. She looks fearfully from L to R and then in the sixth measure turns Clw and starts going R as if ready to leave. She changes her mind, however, and returns to R of CC where she remains until the fifteenth measure. With the strong accent in the fifteenth measure she takes a few steps to DR.

Bizet's Aria

The Music

Song form with Introduction and Coda: 72 measures

A   Andantino Molto in 9/8 — 24 measures
Instrumental introduction — mm. 1–6*
First section — mm. 7–22
Instrumental transition — mm. 23–24

B   Allegro Molto Moderato in 4/4 — 20 measures
Second section — mm. 25–42
Transition — mm. 43–44

* Measure 1 is the incomplete measure with the upbeat G in the accompaniment.

A   Tempo I   (Andantino Molto) in 9/8 — 28 measures
        First section repeated — mm. 45–60
        Vocal postlude — mm. 61–68
        Instrumental postlude — mm. 69–72

The Vocal Aspects

It is puzzling that this aria is so often well performed when accompanied by a piano, and so often badly performed when accompanied by an orchestra. Perhaps the reason is Bizet's overzealous orchestration. Not only is the orchestral accompaniment thick and heavy but it is burdened with those relentless cello arpeggios which are almost always played badly. Conductors are prone to slow down the tempo, so that these arpeggios will sound more in tune and somewhat less sluggish, with the result that the singer must labor throughout the entire aria. If one listens to two recordings of this aria, one by Licia Albanese (Vic. LM 6102) made some years ago, with Fritz Reiner conducting, and the other by Janine Micheau (Angel 3613) with Sir Thomas Beecham conducting, one can hear some differences of interpretation — but each of them is burdened with a phlegmatic accompaniment. Sir Thomas is almost always somewhat behind the singer; Reiner manages to keep up.

It goes without saying that the aria should be sung legato; to do so is difficult for a lyric soprano in the middle range, when competing with a full orchestra. One must be careful to sing lightly the many final unstressed syllables in French, with the mute *e* vowel as in "–te" (mm. 8, 12, 46, and 50), in "–ge" (mm. 16, 20, 54, and 58), in "–me" (mm. 26 and 29), and in "–le" (mm. 33 and 39). It is common to hear a slight portamento from the high G to the lower one in measures 10 and 48.

It is common practice to hold the high B♮ in measure 39 for an extra two beats, cutting it off on the third beat of measure 40 with the orchestra. When this is done, then "Seigneur, vous me protège–" is sung unaccompanied. Though the high G in measure 43 is marked "forte," with diminuendo molto beginning immediately, many singers who can manage it prefer to attack the note piano, and make a *messa di voce* before the portamento to the lower octave. A rather full crescendo must be made on the high G in measure 56, so that the next measure can be forte. Many singers find the *messa di voce* on the D in measure 67 very difficult. If the note were somewhat higher in pitch, the *messa di voce* would be easier, but on D it is often quite difficult. It is no doubt for this reason that often one will hear an interpolated high B♭ between the D and the final E♭. It would seem preferable to hear the interpolated high note well sung rather than an out-of-tune D with a poorly modulated *messa di voce*. As a matter of general advice, singers should be cautioned to sing this aria on the light side, avoiding the pitfall of trying to compete with the rich and heavy sound of the orchestra.

The Text

Literal Translation

1. I say that nothing me frightens,
2. I say, alas, that I answer for myself;
3. But I have in vain to-make the brave-one,
4. At-the bottom of-the heart I am-dying of-fright!
5. Alone in this place wild, all alone I have fear, but I have wrong to have fear.
6. You will give me some courage, you me will protect, Lord!
7. I am-going to-see from close-by this woman,
8. whose the tricks cursed have ended by to-make an infamous-one
9. of him that I-loved once.
10. She is dangerous, she is beautiful! But I not wish to-have fear. No—
11. I will speak loud before her.
12. Ah, you me will-protect! Give me some courage!

Idiomatic Translation

1. I say that nothing frightens me,
2. I say, alas, that I can take care of myself;
3. But I'm only pretending to be brave,
4. Deep down in my heart, I am dying of fright!
5. Alone in this wild place, all alone I am afraid, but I'm wrong in being afraid;
6. You will give me courage, you will protect me, Lord!
7. I am going to see this woman face to face,
8. the one whose cursed tricks have succeeded in making a criminal
9. of him that I once loved.
10. She is dangerous, she is beautiful! But I do not want to be afraid. No—
11. I will speak boldly to her.
12. Ah, you will protect me, Lord. Give me courage!

The Scenic Picture

A secluded spot in the mountainous country not far from Seville. Micaëla's actions take place on the level ground, but farther in the background, a path starting at L leads uphill to the place where Don José (who is not visible during this scene) is presumed to be standing on guard. Bales with contraband goods are piled up in the DL section of the stage. A heavy trunk — low enough for sitting — is placed in the downstage area approximately six feet L of CC. There are several campfires, one of which is standing some distance UR of the trunk.

The third act of the opera begins at dawn, but by the time Micaëla arrives, it is the middle of the morning.

The Stage Actions Explained

Andantino Molto

Measures

1–4. Micaëla who, in the beginning of the aria, stands on stage R, looks around, making a Clw semicircle.

4–5. She sees the glowing campfire upstage, near CC, goes to it, X's it, and turns Cclw to crouch beside it, facing DR.

6. She warms, her hands at the fire.

9. After "hélas," she rises.

14. She turns Cclw to look at the overhanging rocks on L.

15. She turns Clw and goes R to CC.

16. After "sauvage," she turns Cclw and backs slightly to R.

18. She goes D to R of CC.

19. She looks to heaven, D.

22. After "Seigneur," she turns Cclw and goes L and in a Cclw semi-circle around the trunk, ending up above it, facing R.

Allegro Molto Moderato

27. She goes R to CC,

29. Turns slowly LSB, spraying the high B♭.*

30. She faces DL, looking into the distance.

32. She turns Clw to gaze DR.

33. She goes slightly DR,

34. Turns Cclw,

35. Goes a few steps L,

37. Goes slightly DL.

38. She looks to heaven, DL.

39. *(3rd quarter)* She turns RSB spraying the high B♮, and backs slightly to UL.

40. She looks to heaven, DR.

43. *(3rd quarter)* She turns Cclw and goes L, Xing above trunk to L corner of trunk.

44. *(4th quarter)* She sits down on L corner of trunk.

Tempo I *(Andantino Molto)*

52. After "effroi," she rises and looks L.

53. With "lieu," she turns to look UR, and then looks again to L.

56. She goes R, Xing trunk to CC.

57. She addresses heaven, DR.

58. She addresses heaven, D.

60. She kneels.

* For a definition of spraying, see p. 6.

66. She rises.
68. After she finishes singing, she turns Cclw and goes L below trunk.
69. With the eighth-note rest, she turns Cclw and looks at heaven, over L shoulder.
80. With the eighth-note rest, she continues to go L, then U to the platform elevation where she turns Cclw to face R and look at the rocky height UR.

To the simple burgher dress of the period Marguerite has added the jewelry she found in the casket.

"Song of the King of Thule" and "The Jewel Song"
from *Faust,* Act II
by CHARLES GOUNOD

The Drama

While Gounod's opera is ostensibly based on Goethe's *Faust,* it limits itself to just a few episodes culled from Part One of the original drama. The score informs us that the action takes place in Germany in the sixteenth century and tells the story of old Faust's pact with the devil and of the rejuvenated Faust's love affair with Marguerite. For additional information, however — particularly where our operatic heroine is concerned — we must turn to the play. Even though Gounod's Marguerite is more elegant and "ladylike" than Goethe's somewhat coarse Gretchen, several sections of the German work throw an important light on the details of her everyday existence. Here, for instance, is a relevant excerpt from Bayard Taylor's translation.

FAUST

No doubt you're much alone?

MARGARET

Yes, for our household small has grown,
Yet must be cared for, you will own.
We have no maid: I do the knitting, sewing, sweeping.
The cooking, early work and late, in fact;
And mother, in her notions of housekeeping, is so exact!
Not that she needs so much to keep expenses down:
We, more than others, might take comfort, rather;
A nice estate was left us by my father,
A house, a little garden near the town.
But now my days have less of noise and hurry;
My brother is a soldier,
My little sister's dead.

Goethe also tells us that Gretchen's father died before her sister was born and that her mother was ill for a long time thereafter. In the drama, Gretchen agrees to let Faust visit her at night, and gives her mother a sleeping potion, thus unwittingly causing her death. Gounod's librettists must have felt that such a display of immorality would not be tolerated by operatic audiences of their time. In the opera, Marguerite lives alone in her cottage, and while she tells Faust that she had "lost her mother," she does not offer any explanation of either the time or the circumstances of the death.

61

This is Marguerite's second appearance in the opera. She was first seen and heard as she was passing the town square in the middle of the preceding *Kermesse* scene, on her way home from church. The opera's text does not mention the church, but from Mephisto's words in the drama we learn that she had gone there for confession, even though — to the devil's chagrin — she had not a single thing to confess.

This earlier episode dealing with the meeting of Faust and Marguerite was quite short. Enchanted with the girl's appearance and charm, Faust offered to accompany her, but was told that she preferred to proceed home "unescorted." Under the circumstances, it is rather surprising that, even though she leaves the preceding scene well ahead of Siebel, Mephisto, and Faust, she arrives in her garden so much later than the three men. To account for this delay, it is possible to imagine that on her way home from church Marguerite changes her mind and decides to visit Marthe Schwerlein.* Finding that her neighbor is not in, Marguerite leaves her a note and continues on her way. As she enters her garden, her thoughts are filled with the handsome stranger who accosted her on her way from church. While walking in the garden, she stops to wonder whether the young man had perhaps followed her home. She returns to the gate to listen for his footsteps, but then, realizing that this is but a figment of her imagination, she decides that she might as well resume the domestic task which was interrupted when she went to church.

The libretto indicates that there is a spinning wheel standing in the garden. This is hardly what we would expect of a properly brought up girl, however. An innocent German maiden who goes to confession without having anything to confess, who gives a protective medal to her brother, who curtly rejects the arm of a handsome stranger; a girl whose room is so tidy that (again in Goethe's play) Faust is moved by its "Quiet orderliness and contentment" (even the devil admits that "not every girl is so neat"); this girl does not leave her spinning wheel outside when she goes to church! Domestic work may be taken to the garden, but it is kept inside the house.

Most Marguerites spin and keep the spinning wheel turning lustily while they sing the Song of the King of Thule. This surely is wrong. The rotation of spinning wheels happen to belong to ideas that lend themselves particularly well to orchestral illustration, as in fact they are so illustrated in *Faust* in the vision of the Prologue and the spinning aria of the third act. But this idea is not depicted musically in the Garden Scene and it is therefore essential that Marguerite should work in a manner *not* requiring the turning of wheels.

When staging this scene, we have found it necessary to explain the purpose of the act of spinning.

---

* Near the end of the seventh scene of Goethe's play, when Faust is anxious to inspect Gretchen's dwelling, Mephisto cautions him that this will have to wait until the girl goes out to visit her neighbor.

Spinning consists in converting short tangled fibers into yarn. A quantity of wool, cotton, or flax — that looks very much like a large snarled wig — is first separated into smaller pieces; each of these is then carded, that is, combed out with one or two small rectangular paddles closely set with bent wire teeth. The carded pieces are then arranged on the distaff — a short wooden staff — which stands on the left side of the spinning wheel. The worker twirls some of the fibers between the fingers and thumb of her right hand, draws them out in a strand by both hands, and attaches this strand to the spindle. This, a small rotating spool at the right side of the spinning wheel, is connected by a belt with a large wheel operated by a pedal kept in motion by the spinner's right foot. In the final act of spinning the yarn is collected on the rapidly turning spindle while the worker keeps the thread running through the fingers of both hands.

During the Song of the King of Thule, Marguerite goes through all the preliminary steps, but stops before pedaling the large wheel.

*   *   *

The flowers which Marguerite discovers during this scene were left for her by her young admirer, Siebel. Mephisto's casket, which is placed under the flowers, must contain earrings, a bracelet, a necklace, and a hand mirror. Besides the hand mirror, there is also a second mirror that lines the inside of the casket's lid.

It is interesting to note that in the opera these jewels are connected with the power of evil. It is probable that the French librettists felt that Marguerite's sudden giving-in to Faust would be less reprehensible if she were at first affected by the magic of the enchanted bracelet and then later by the emanations of the flowers over which Mephisto pronounces suitable incantations.

Marguerite's exact age is not given either in the play or the opera. Faust's remark that Gretchen is "over fourteen" can be interpreted as a hint that she is in the full flower of feminine development; one imagines her to be seventeen or eighteen years old. At one time, a blond wig was considered to be an indispensable attribute of a typical, blue-eyed German maiden, but such stereotypes are no longer taken seriously. It is true that Gretchen's long braids are mentioned by Goethe, but nowhere is there any indication of the color of either her hair or her eyes.

The Music

This is the longest piece in our collection. Its 306 measures consist basically of two separate arias connected by an independent Middle Link. The main features are:

Section I.   The Introduction and the two stanzas of the Song of the King of Thule — 77 measures

Section II.   The Middle Link (beginning with the words: "Les grands seigneurs ont seuls des airs si résolus") — 45 measures

Section III.   The Jewel Song, an A-B-A sequence with an Introduction and a Coda — 184 measures

Before embarking on a more detailed analysis of the music, we should like to discuss a few items of general interest. (Each section is numbered independently.)

The Tempo of the Various Sections

The metronome markings indicated in Gounod's *Faust* are, generally speaking, on the slow side. Even so, the modern tendency of greatly speeding up the music of eighteenth and nineteenth century works should not be exaggerated. We recommend the following speeds.

I Introduction (mm. 1–23)

Andantino   the opening eight measures as marked, ♩ = 66. Beginning with the 9th measure somewhat faster, ♩ = 80

The Song of the King of Thule (mm. 24–77)

Moderato maestoso as marked, ♩ = 72
Andante somewhat slower, ♩ = 66

II Middle Link (mm. 1–45)

Moderato ♩ = 88; Andante ♩ = 72; Andantino ♩. = 72 Recitative ♩ = 88; Allegro non troppo ♩ = 104; in the last five measures slow down to about ♩ = 84. The last measure should be sung in time, its eighth notes becoming equivalent to the first two quarter notes of the following Allegretto. Thus ♩ = 84 (or ♪ = 168) becomes ♩. = 56 (or ♩ = 168).

III The Jewel Song (mm. 1–184)

Allegretto ♩. = 56 The Coda can be taken somewhat faster: ♩. = 80

In the 27th and 125th measures it has become traditional to permit, and even to encourage, sopranos to elongate the F♯ half-note on the word "moi." There would be no harm in this if the instrumental accompaniment consisted of nothing more than the single sustained chord which is printed in most piano-vocal scores. This, however, is not so. For, in this measure, in addition to the chord, the flutes must execute a sequence of descending eighth notes:

Ré-ponds moi,   ré-ponds, ré-ponds, ré-ponds vi - te!

And this is just the type of passage that does not lend itself to a
rubato execution. The F♯ half note in the vocal line must therefore
be sung in time. Its unwarranted elongation shows how a bad tradition can have its origin in an over-simplified piano transcription.

The ritenuti notated in the 59th and 131st measures are usually
begun four measures earlier, permitting the soprano to sing the four
measures preceding the tempo with a heightened expression.

The Vocal Aspects

Several different styles of singing are called for in this scene — recitative,
simple folk-melody, and florid aria — and the conscientious soprano will
do well to remember to make clear distinctions between them.

Marguerite's opening recitative is contemplative and rather slow, as
she thinks aloud and recalls her meeting with Faust. When she sets about
doing the various chores prior to spinning, she sings a little "work song,"
a strophic folk-songlike melody which is interrupted by her thoughts of
Faust. Although her encounter with him has been very brief, he has obviously made a very deep impression on her. "The Song of the King of
Thule" must be sung in a quiet, simple manner — almost absentmindedly
— as if it were being sung by an untrained, vibrato-free voice in a most
ingenuous way. The interruptions, when her thoughts wander back to
Faust, call for a different tone color, and the manner of execution must
mirror the sentiments she expresses. When she has finished "The Song of
the King of Thule" and sings the recitative leading to the Jewel Song, the
rhythm can be rather free except for measures 12 to 14 where coordination with the orchestra is essential. Breathlessness, incredulity, excitement
must be present in the recitative after she discovers the jewel box, and
even more so after she has opened it. The aria which follows borders on
the ecstatic, because for the first time in her life Marguerite sees herself
not as a rather simple and devout young girl, but as the beautiful — perhaps seductive — daughter of a king, and she wishes that Faust could
see her now.

Most sopranos like to take a little extra time in measure 12* of the

* After the ninety-nine measures of "The Song of the King of Thule" and the
following recitative, the aria begins with measure 1, at the ¾ meter.

Jewel Song so that the scale can be executed cleanly and in tune; thus an
a tempo is necessary in measure 13. Another ritardando takes place in
measure 51, with further slowing down on the scale in the accompaniment
in measure 55, and molto ritardando in measure 59. Measure 60 returns
to the original tempo.

The end of the first A section is also marked with a ritardando
(measure 71), and the orchestral interlude in measure 73 returns once
more to the original tempo though it is possible for measures 73–90 to be
a trifle slower than the beginning tempo of the waltz. After the Poco più
lento in measure 91 and a gradual return to the original tempo, the second
A section begins in the voice like the first, with a slight slowing down in
measure 110 and an a tempo in measure 111.

The ritardandos in measures 127 and 129, and a molto ritardando in
measure 131, lead to a return to the original tempo in measure 132.
Though many sopranos like to hold the last beat of measure 156 an
inordinately long time, it seems to the authors that only a slight hesitation
on this note will do, since the longer, higher climax is just around the
corner. It has become customary for sopranos to sing only two measures
of the F♯ trill (beginning with m. 161) and to put the high B one measure
earlier (m. 163 instead of 164 as written).

The Text

Literal Translation
Recitative

1. I would-like much to-know who was this young man;
2. If he-is a great lord, and how he himself calls?

Song

3. He was a king of Thule, who, until the tomb faithful,
4. had, in memory of his beautiful-one, a cup in gold engraved.
5. [*dreaming*] (He had good grace, to that which it me-has seemed.)
6. No treasure had so-much of charm; in the great days he of-it made-use,
7. and each time that he there drank, his eyes themselves would fill with tears!
8. When he felt coming the death, stretched-out on his cold bed,
9. to it carry up to his mouth, his hand made a supreme effort!
10. [*dreaming*] (I not knew what to-say, and I-had reddened at-first.)
11. And then, in the-honor of his lady, he drank one last time.
12. The cup trembled in his fingers, and softly he rendered-up the soul!

Recitative

13. The great lords have only of-the airs so resolute, with this gentleness!
14. Let-us-go, not-of-it let-us-think longer! Dear Valentine!
15. If God me listens-to, I you will-see-again! Me there-is all alone!
16. A bouquet! It-is from Siebel, without doubt! Poor boy!
17. What see I there? From where this rich chest can-it come?

18. I hardly-dare it to-touch, and yet . . . Here-is the key, I believe!
19. If I it-would-open! My hand trembles! Why?
20. I not do, in it-opening, nothing of harm, I suppose!
21. O Lord! What of jewels! Is it a dream charming that me dazzles, or if I am-awake?
22. My eyes not-have ever seen of riches like-these!
23. If I-dared only myself to-adorn one moment with these pendants of ear!
24. Ah, here-is exactly, at-the bottom of the case, a mirror!
25. How not-to-be coquettish?

Aria

26. Ah! I laugh of myself to-see so beautiful in this mirror,
27. Is-it you, Marguerite, is-it you? Answer-me, answer quickly!
28. No! It not-is longer, no, it not-is longer your face; it-is the daughter of-a king,
29. Whom one salutes at-the passing! Ah, if-he were here! If he me would-see thus!
30. Like a young lady he me would-find beautiful; let-us-finish the meta-morphosis.
31. It me longs still to-try-on the bracelet and the necklace!
32. Lord! It-is like a hand, that on my arm itself places!

Idiomatic Translation

Recitative

1. I would like very much to know who that young man was;
2. Is he a great lord? What is his name?

Song

3. There was a king of Thule, who, faithful unto death,
4. had a cup engraved in gold, in memory of his loved one.
5. [*dreaming*] (He was very gracious, it seemed to me.)
6. No treasure had so much charm; he used it on important days,
7. and each time that he drank from it, his eyes would fill with tears!
8. When he felt death approaching, stretched out on his cold bed,
9. his hand made a supreme effort to carry the cup to his lips!
10. [*dreaming*] (I did not know what to say, and I blushed at first.)
11. And then, in honor of his lady, he drank one last time.
12. The cup trembled in his fingers, and peacefully he gave up his soul!

Recitative

13. Only great lords are so resolute and so gentle at the same time!
14. Come, let's think of it no more. Dear Valentine!
15. If God hears my prayers, I will see you again. I am all alone!
16. A bouquet! It's from Siebel, no doubt! Poor boy!
17. What do I see there? Where did this rich chest come from?
18. I hardly dare touch it, and yet . . . Here is the key, I believe!

19. If I would open it . . . My hand trembles! Why?
20. I won't do any harm if I open it, I'm sure!
21. O Lord! What jewels! Is it a dream that dazzles me, or am I awake?
22. My eyes have never seen riches like these!
23. If only I dared to adorn myself for a moment with these earrings!
24. Ah, here is exactly what I need — a mirror — at the bottom of the case!
25. How can I help but be coquettish?

Aria

26. Ah, I laugh when I see myself so beautiful in this mirror,
27. Is it you, Marguerite, is it you? Answer me quickly!
28. No! It is no longer you, no, it is no longer your face — it is the daughter of a king,
29. to whom one pays homage when she passes. Ah, if only he were here so he could see me like this!
30. Like a fine, noble lady he would think me beautiful; but let us finish my metamorphosis.
31. I long to try on the bracelet and the necklace!
32. Lord, the bracelet is like a hand, placed on my arm!

The Scenic Picture

The scene represents Marguerite's garden and a corner of her cottage. The visible six-foot section of the facade of the cottage — which runs parallel to the footlights from the DL corner of the stage — has a window in it. The R side of the cottage — with the entrance door in it — continues toward UR. The back wall and the inside of the cottage are visible only when the door or the window is open. Both are closed at first.

The garden wall runs for about twelve feet UL from the DR corner of the stage and continues toward the L until it disappears above the house. There is a gate in the middle of the R section of the wall. A flower bed is located in the center of the garden near its upper section. There are three benches — below the window, below the flowerbed, and near the DR corner. All of these stand parallel to the footlight line.

The casket with the jewels in it is on the ground near the corner made by the front and side walls of the house. It is placed under Siebel's bouquet, so that when the bouquet is raised the casket is revealed.

Inside the house are a chair and the spinning wheel, as well as a small table with a quantity of loose wool on it, two carding combs, and an apron.

The Stage Actions Explained

The following more detailed musical analysis, combined with a general description of Marguerite's actions, will help the performer to fix in her mind the overall structure of this lengthy scene.

Section 1. Introduction and the Song of the King of Thule

(a) Introduction (mm. 1–23)

Marguerite enters her garden. Wondering if she is being followed, she retraces her steps to look outside the gate. Realizing that she is mistaken, she proceeds to her cottage, opens the window, and begins to prepare for her daily chores. Tying on her apron and putting up her hair, she dreams about the handsome young stranger who addressed her earlier on the *Kermesse* square.

(b) First Stanza of the Song (mm. 24–50)

She picks up a quantity of wool and two carding combs and carries them into the garden. Sitting down on the nearest bench, she combs out several skeins of wool. She interrupts her work to reminisce about her recent encounter, and then combs out the remaining pieces.

(c) Second Stanza (mm. 50–76)

She returns to the cottage with the carding combs, leaves them there, and returns immediately, carrying a small spinning wheel. Sitting down behind the wheel, she attaches the combed pieces of wool to the distaff. She stops working again and recalls her embarrassment when addressed by the stranger. She finishes her work on the distaff, and then, pulling out a bit of wool, twirls it into a thread and attaches it to the spool in the spindle.

Coda (mm. 76–78)

She sits quietly, gazing into the distance.

Section II Middle Link

During measures 1 to 3 she rises and steps out from behind the spinning wheel.

Moderato Maestoso (mm. 3–7)

She goes once more to the garden gate and looks outside, hoping that perhaps Faust had followed her after all. Finding no one there, she decides not to think of him any more.

Andante (mm. 8–11)

As her thoughts turn to her brother Valentin, she returns to the spinning wheel.

Andantino (mm. 12–15)

She picks up the spinning wheel and starts carrying it toward the cottage.

Recitative (mm. 16–32)

As she approaches the cottage door, she notices the bouquet of flowers that Siebel left near the threshold. She places the spinning wheel near the cottage wall and stoops down to pick up the flowers. She discovers the jewel box that Mephisto put under the flowers and kneels down to inspect it. After some hesitation she unlocks the casket and rises in amazement, stunned by the sight of the jewels.

Allegro (mm. 33–45)

She looks around for the best place to put the casket and then runs to the bench in the R portion of the stage. Kneeling down above the bench, she takes out a pair of earrings and then, finding a hand mirror inside the casket, decides to try them on. As she attaches the second earring, she rises.

Section III   The Jewel Song

Introduction (mm. 1–8)

Thrilled by the chance to wear the earrings, Marguerite waltzes around in a circle and then, picking up the hand mirror, sits down on the upper side of the bench to the R of the casket.

Part A

First Episode (mm. 9–29)

Passing the mirror from hand to hand, she admires herself, finding it difficult to believe that she is seeing the reflection of her own face.

Second Episode (mm. 30–55)

She rises from the bench and, declaring that it is a King's daughter whom she sees in the mirror, she acts out the walk of a Princess who is being greeted by her subjects.

Third Episode (mm. 56–73)

Wishing that Faust could see her adorned by the earrings, she clasps the mirror to her breast and moves toward the L portion of the stage.

Part B

First Episode (mm. 73–91)

She returns to the R bench and sits down on its lower side. Turning the casket so that the mirror, set under the lid, is facing her, she replaces the hand mirror, and decides to try on a bracelet and a necklace.

Second Episode (Poco più lento) (mm. 91–106)

She puts the bracelet around her L wrist and then lifts the necklace over her head. As the necklace settles on her shoulders, she senses that a hand has touched her L arm, and grasps the bracelet with her R hand. She looks at her reflection in the casket's mirror, she feels lightheaded, indicating that the enchanted jewels are beginning to show their effect.

Return of Part A

First Episode (mm. 107–127)

She rises and steps back toward the R to admire herself in the casket's mirror. Then she looks at the bracelet and, lifting the necklace, admires it as well.

Second Episode (mm. 128–145)

Note that this episode corresponds to the third episode of the first A section. (The second episode of the first A section is omitted at this point and this accounts for the fact that the second A section is twenty-six measures shorter than the first.) Wishing that Faust could see her in all her bejeweled glory, she goes L to the center of the stage.

Coda

First Episode (mm. 145–165)

She runs to above the bench, kneels down, and turns the casket so that she can again admire herself in its mirror. Then she rises and returns to the center of the stage.

Second Episode (mm. 166 to the end)

She runs to the L of the bench, gives the casket a final quarter turn Clw, and then backs away from it toward the center of the stage. She makes a complete dancing turn, and with the last two chords of the aria, curtsies to her own reflection in the mirror of the casket.

Leonora wears the gray habit of a Franciscan monk. A scapula has been added to make it more flattering.

"Pace, Pace"
from *La Forza Del Destino, Act* IV, Scene 2
by GIUSEPPE VERDI

The Drama

A historical battle which happens to be part of the events of the third act of *La Forza del Destino* permits us to establish with fair precision a chronology for the rest of the opera. It was on August 11, 1744, in the village of Velletri, about twenty miles southeast of Rome, that the Spanish and Italian troops under the Neapolitan King Charles defeated the Austrians commanded by Lobkovitz.

Using this date as a point of departure, and aided by additional information given in the opera and in the play on which it is based, we arrive at the following sequence of events as they affect the role of Leonora.

Act I

It is summer of the year 1742. In this act the death of Leonora's father occurs and her flight from her family's country home near Seville. In the ensuing scuffle between her father's retainers and Alvaro's men, Leonora is separated from her lover; she eventually manages to find a safe harbor with an old aunt in the city of Cordova. Here she remains for a year. Then, at the advice of a distinguished cleric, Father Cleto, she decides to seek permanent refuge in the Franciscan monastery of Hornachuelos, a small town about thirty miles southeast of Cordoba.

Act II, Scene 1

It is the first of August, 1743, the eve of the annual "Jubilee of the Angels," a feast day on which a plenary indulgence is granted to the faithful who make a pilgrimage to a Franciscan monastery. Leonora, dressed in man's clothing, arrives at a tavern in the village of Hornachuelos and almost runs into her brother, Don Carlos, who holds her responsible for the death of their father. Afraid of her brother and appalled by his plans for vengeance, Leonora leaves the inn in the middle of the night and proceeds alone to the Franciscan monastery, which is located on a hillside overlooking Hornachuelos.

Act II, Scene 2

Next morning at dawn, outside the church of Our Lady of the Angels, Leonora, still in disguise, meets the head of the monastery, Father Guardiano. She persuades him to let her spend the rest of her life in solitary seclusion in a grotto on the grounds of the monastery, a hermitage that had once before harbored a repentant female sinner.

Act III

This act which features the battle of Velletri plays in Italy in August of 1744. Leonora does not, of course, appear in this act.

Act IV

Both scenes of this act occur on the same day. In the first scene we are told that five years have elapsed since Act III. It is therefore in late summer of 1749, and Leonora's seclusion has lasted six years.

The Music

Leonora's "Pace, pace" — Verdi calls it "Melodia" — opens the second Scene of the last Act.

The ninety-three measures of the Aria consist of two Stanzas and a Coda.

Stanza I (51 measures)
Section A
Allegro Agitato in 3/8 — (mm. 1–16)
Andante in 4/4 — (mm. 17–35)
Transition to G minor — (mm. 36–37)
Section B
Andante — (mm. 38–51)

Stanza II (42 measures)
Section A
Un poco stringendo — (mm. 52–60)
Andante — (mm. 61–68)
Section C
Andante — (mm. 69–75)
Coda
Allegro — (mm. 76–93)

The A sections of the two Stanzas are quite comparable in length. The ostensible difference in their measure length — 35 as compared with 17 — is more apparent than real. Each of these Stanzas is divided into two episodes: one excited, the other calm. But while the initial excited episode of Stanza I is marked "Allegro Agitato" and is notated in 16 measures of 3/8, its counterpart, the "un poco stringendo" of the Stanza II, is comprised of nine measures of 4/4, each measure thus being equivalent to four of those in 3/8. Were the "Allegro Agitato" notated in 4/4, like the "un poco stringendo," its 16 measures would be reduced to 4 measures and the total length of the first Stanza would number not 35, but 23 measures.

The Vocal Aspects

Roger Voisin, the eminent first trumpeter of the Boston Symphony Orchestra, used to say that one of the most difficult trumpet solos in the entire orchestral literature consisted of just one note — the opening A♮

of the overture to Wagner's *Rienzi*. It is a long solo note, and must be played with a perfect crescendo and decrescendo. "Pace, pace" presents the same problem. The opening note, F, which is difficult for some sopranos because it lies in the register change, is very long and must be executed with a perfect *messa di voce*.

Many singers make this note even more difficult by attacking it too softly and making the crescendo too long and the decrescendo too abrupt. We must admire the way it is performed by Leontyne Price (Vic. LSC-3828). But in listening to recordings one should remember that the artist has not had to perform the rest of the role before singing this treacherous aria. In recording sessions, no prescribed order is necessary, and the artist can record her role in short segments and when her voice is fresh. Nevertheless, Miss Price makes the most of this difficult moment.

Care must be taken to make the two *Pace's* in measures 19–21 different from those in measures 32–34. The first ones are both soft, with decrescendi; the second ones are, respectively, forte and piano with decrescendi. A ritardando (not indicated in some piano-vocal scores) is possible on the fourth beat of measure 31, to heighten "il mio soffrir." It is not difficult to sing "cotanto Iddio l'ornò, che l'amo ancor" (mm. 40–42) in one breath, and the crescendo-decrescendo in measure 41 sounds better without a breath after "l'ornò." It is worth noting that Miss Price does not resort to a chest tone for the low notes in measure 43.

Each "fatalità" (mm. 44–46) should be sung differently. The first one is forte. The second, an octave lower, can be almost breathy, while the third, although softest of the three, should have more tone and quality. The singer will do well to take "con passione" with a grain of salt at measure 48, and to sing this entire section of the aria, from measure 48 through measure 61, with considerable restraint.

The crescendo in measure 58 need not be overwhelming so that the decrescendo on the high G♭ in measure 59 will be easier to control. A ritartando at the end of measure 60, not indicated in most piano-vocal scores, is proper and stylistically acceptable. For many singers measures 62–68 are the most difficult passage in the entire aria. Here the vocal indiscretions committed earlier take their toll. A soprano without an impeccable vocal technique will find the high B♭ almost impossible to sing pianissimo; it would be prudent to sing it somewhat louder. A modest portamento from the high B♭ to the lower one is possible.

There is an admirable opportunity for using tone color for dramatic effect in measure 73. A breathy, almost suffocating, sound expresses very well Leonora's discontent and frustration with a life that seemingly is being prolonged without good reason. The tone quality should change abruptly in measure 76 when Leonora notices someone approaching. Whether to breathe after each "maledizione" (mm. 81–84) should be left to the singer; a rapid catch breath after each one seems unnecessary. The ending of the aria is sung by some sopranos (Miss Price, for instance) as follows:

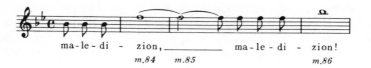

ma-le-di - zion,_____ ma-le-di - zion!
　　　　　m.84　　m.85　　　　　　　m.86

The authors prefer that it be sung as the composer wrote it, knowing full well that the high B♭ is doubly difficult without a break after holding the F for two measures! The last note, on the syllable "–ne," is much easier if sung with an *eh* (open *e*) vowel.

The Text

Literal Translation

1. Peace, my God! Cruel misfortune me-constrains, alas, to languish;
2. Like the day first since so-many years lasts profound the my suffering.
3. Peace, my God! Him-I-loved, it is true. But with good-looks and valor
4. to-such-an extent God him-endowed, that him-I-love still.
5. nor to-tear-to-me from-the heart the-image his will-I-know-how.
6. Fatality! A crime separated us-has here-below!
7. Alvaro, I you-love, and up in-the heaven it-is written:
8. not you will-I-see never again! O God, make that-I die;
9. that the calm can give-me death alone.
10. In-vain the peace here hoped this-soul,
11. in prey to so-much affliction, in midst of so-much grief.
12. Miserable bread . . . to prolong-to-me you-come the disconsolate life.
13. But who approaches? Who to-profane dares the sacred place? Curse!

Idiomatic Translation

1. Grant me peace, O Lord! Alas, cruel misfortune constrains me to languish;
2. My suffering has continued for these many years as deeply as on the first day.
3. Grant me peace, O Lord! I loved him, it is true. But with handsome looks and valor
4. God so endowed him that I love him still.
5. Nor will I ever be able to tear his image from my heart.
6. Oh, fatal destiny! A crime has forced us to separate here below!
7. I love you, Alvaro, and yet heaven has ordained
8. that I will never see you again! Let me die, O Lord!
9. For it is death alone that can give me peace.
10. My soul hoped for peace here in vain,
11. prey to so much affliction, in the midst of so much grief.
12. Lowly food! Why must you be brought here to prolong my disconsolate life?
13. But who is approaching? Who dares to profane this hallowed ground? A curse upon you!

The Scenic Picture

The description in the score speaks of "a valley, between inaccessible rocks, traversed by a brook. UR is a grotto with a practicable door. Over the door hangs a bell which can be rung from inside."

The brook can be imagined as running from the L to UR, where it disappears behind a straight wall of rocks. The food which Leonora handles in the course of the aria was brought in earlier by Father Guardiano and was deposited on a stone. The grove of trees — mentioned later in the act when Leonora rushes there to help her mortally wounded brother — stands in the DL direction. The monastery buildings must be imagined as being located some distance to the L of the stage, beyond the grove of trees. The stone with the provisions is located on stage L, UR of the trees and below the edge of the brook. There is also a fairly large flat rock C stage below the rocky wall. A crude stone structure in the form of a cross stands DR of the flat rock.

Leonora is living in the grotto in complete seclusion. The only person allowed near the hermitage is the prior of the convent, Father Guardiano, who comes once a week to supply Leonora with food and, occasionally, with other necessities such as the Franciscan monk's outfit which she is now wearing.

The Stage Actions Explained

In this aria, Leonora is tormented by two relentless emotions: her love for Alvaro and her nagging guilt for having been responsible for the death of her father. In the second act, when she came to the monastery to ask Father Guardiano's help, it had seemed to her that in this haven of Christian forgiveness she would eventually find comfort and peace. In the courtyard outside the church of Our Lady of the Angels, she assured Guardiano that her soul felt suddenly more at ease and that, kneeling by the cross, she was no longer pursued by visions of her father's bleeding ghost nor by the sound of his terrible voice cursing her. But after six years of solitude, this hope for tranquility has not been fulfilled. Her feelings of guilt and her craving for Alvaro have not abated.

As she tells us in her aria, the fatal forces of destiny which have manifested themselves in the crime that had so conclusively torn her from her lover are hounding her as relentlessly as on the first day of the tragedy. Her love for Alvaro is expressed in the B section of Stanza I, while awareness of her guilt is expressed by the emotional content of the agitated instrumental passage at the beginning of the aria and in the opening portion of Stanza II.

The dramatic interpretation of the opening Allegro Agitato presents a curious problem. At the end of the staging directions for this scene we read: "Leonora, pale and disheveled, comes out of the grotto in great agitation."

This, of course, fits the music perfectly. But it is disconcerting to find that sixteen measures later the score directs her to sing her opening "Pace" *dentro la grotta* — from inside the grotto — and to appear "on the threshold of the grotto" only two measures later, during the rest elongated by the fermata.

These directions are obviously contradictory. The only way in which Leonora could enter in great agitation with the orchestral introduction and still sing her opening "Pace" offstage would be for her to return to the grotto immediately after emerging from it. This quite ridiculous procedure is not, of course, what Verdi intended. We know that several years after its first performance in St. Petersburg this opera was quite thoroughly revised by the composer, and we are therefore dealing here with two different versions of the final scene.

We suspect that the idea of singing the opening "Pace" offstage originated with one of the early impersonators of the role of Leonora who feared that the energetic entrance and agitated behavior implied in the instrumental prelude might interfere with the breath control needed for a smooth execution of the *messa di voce* effect demanded by the opening vocal phrase. The fact that both of these contradictory stage directions continue to be reprinted in all piano-vocal and orchestral scores is an illustration of the carelessness that is unfortunately rather typical in the publication of Italian operas.

While we prefer the introductory Allegro Agitato to be interpreted in the manner indicated in the acting instructions given earlier, we admit that having Leonora sing her first "Pace" unseen by the audience may have a certain merit. The singer can choose either of these procedures, but must not, of course, try to combine both in the same performance.

The agitated musical portions of the two A Sections reflect Leonora's emotional conflict. Her desire to be reunited with Alvaro motivates her movements *toward* the grove; this would be the logical direction if she were to proceed to the monastery and from there to the outside world. She is immediately aware of the futility of such craving and this realization drives her *away* from the grove and pins her down against the rocky wall which, appropriately and symbolically, is located halfway between the grotto and the grove.

Her movements toward the cross and toward the stone on the L are self-explanatory.

The peculiar construction of the sentence in measures 62 to 68 requires special attention. An unfinished sentence: "In van la pace quest' alma . . ." (In vain for peace my soul . . .) is repeated three times and is then completed by the words: "in van sperò" (in vain had hoped). This unusual procedure must be justified dramatically by making it clear that Leonora's emotional condition makes it difficult for her to finish her thought. The kneeling, the shaking of her head, and the eventual rising from her knees must be given an appropriate "emotional tone." This acting-out of Leonora's difficulty will also enable the singer to catch the necessary breaths which can, if needed, be taken after each "alma" although a soprano with a "long breath" may prefer to stop only once, at the place marked by the sixteenth-note rest (m. 66).

The acting direction indicated for measure 19 has a special significance. When, after a rest elongated by a fermata, the voice and the orchestra have to attack the music simultaneously, it is advisable to arrange for some form of signal between the singer and the conductor. Since it is always better if the singer can concentrate fully on the focal point of her action, watching the baton is not the best method. But agreeing that the vocalist would attack her note at the moment she takes the third step solves the synchronization problem in the simplest possible manner. Leonora's first step serves as a warning for the conductor, or the accompanist, and her second step corresponds to the preparatory beat, or the conductor's upbeat gesture. Although in this instance the difficulty is lessened by the fact that only one instrument, the harp, accompanies the voice, the problem remains and this particular method of solving it is recommended.

Measures

1. Leonora opens the door of the grotto just before the music begins and takes a few steps L, stopping at measure 4.
6. She continues going L, Xing above the flat rock, and stops UL of it at measure 9,
10. backs UR to the rocky wall,
14. leans against the wall, still facing DL, and
17. turns slowly Clw (*while singing*) to face the cross.
19. During the fermata rest, she takes three slow steps, going DR toward the cross, and begins to sing on the third step.
23. (*3rd quarter*) she goes DR to the cross, kneels UL of it, and prays, bowing her head and covering her forehead with her folded hands.
26. (*3rd quarter*) She raises her head and turns it slightly Cclw to look DL and heavenward.
32. She rises and BU slightly to UL, turning her head Clw to look at the cross,
36. BU slightly and turns LSB.
37. She goes L to above the flat rock,
38. looks toward the grove, and
41. BU slightly again. She turns Clw to look into the distance,
44. turns LSB to look at the grove, and
46. (*3rd quarter*) looks into the distance D.
48. She looks toward the grove,
49. (*3rd quarter*) goes DL, Xing above the flat rock and looking toward heaven.
52. She turns Clw and goes excitedly UR, Xing above the flat rock, and looking (*slightly over L shoulder*) at the cross.
54. She (*3rd quarter*) turns LSB to lean against rocky wall.

61. She(*3rd quarter*) takes a few steps toward the cross, but stops (with the first "in van),"
64. (*3rd quarter*) kneels (on second "in van"),
66. shakes her head (on third "in van") and
67. rises (on last "in van").
68. She (*3rd quarter*) turns Cclw and goes UL, Xing above the flat rock to L stone,
71. picks up a burlap bag containing food, turns Clw, and carries the bag DR to above the rock.
73. She sits on the U side of the rock and puts the bag to her L.
76. (*2nd quarter*) She rises and backs slightly to UR, while at the same time pulling the bag to the ground above the rock.
79. She points to grotto with R hand — still looking toward the grove DL, and
81. (*3rd quarter*) goes DL toward the grove stopping at measure 83.
85. She BU toward UR, turns Clw (m. 88), and goes UR, Xing above the flat rock, to the threshold of the grotto (m. 91), turns Cclw (m. 92), gets hold of the door handle (m. 93) and backs into the grotto, closing the door.

A large, brightly colored shawl has been added to Gioconda's simple 17th-century Italian dress.

"Suicidio"

from *La Gioconda,* Act IV
by AMILCARE PONCHIELLI

The Drama

Sopranos who commit suicide are not rare in opera. Cio-Cio-San and Gioconda stab themselves; Tosca jumps to her death from the tower of the Castel San Angelo while other heroines choose less direct or more prolonged forms of self-destruction. Gilda, who goes to certain death to save her lover, and Aida who joins Radames in his subterranean tomb, are terminating their lives as surely as Cio-Cio-San, Gioconda, and Tosca. The precise manner in which Elisabeth dies in *Tannhäuser* is not revealed to us, and even though it is not a question of suicide in the conventional sense of the word, her intention — essentially not unlike Gilda's — is to "save" the man whom she loves.

It thus appears that six out of the twenty-one soprano heroines* represented in this volume die by their own will, even though not always by their own hand.

It obviously requires a very strong motivation to want to take one's life. The basic drive for all these young women is the same: life without the men they love is not worth living. Gioconda's suicide, however, presents a special case, and not only because her aria is entitled "Suicidio." The soprano who wants to perform this piece is faced with a difficult assignment not only because it is so very taxing vocally but also because its psychological motivation is so unusual.

To unravel the twisted strands of Gioconda's emotional state, it is useful to turn to *Angelo, Tyrant of Padua,* the Victor Hugo play on which the opera is based. We will discover that in this drama the logic of events and the motivations of the characters are presented much more clearly and precisely than in Boito's operatic text.

The plot of both the drama and the opera revolves around the unusually strong ties that bind Tisbe (Gioconda in the opera) to her mother. But while in the opera Gioconda's mother (called La Cieca — the Blind Woman) appears on stage and takes an important part in the music and the action, Tisbe's mother has been dead for many years. This daughter-mother relationship, which is the central element and main driving force of the drama, is explained by Tisbe in one of the longest and most eloquent tirades ever entrusted to a theatrical heroine. Even a short extract

* We do not count Pamina whose attempt to end it all by stabbing herself is caused by what is surely only a temporary mental aberration.

from *Angelo* will demonstrate why it was the glory of Mlles Mars and Rachel, two of France's most celebrated actresses.

TISBE

You know what I am — a nobody, a child of the common people, an actress. Well, humble as I am, I had a mother. Do you know what it is to be a child, a poor child, penniless, hungry, alone in the world, and to feel that you have beside you a woman — no, you do not know yet that it is a woman — an angel who teaches you to laugh, who teaches you to love! Who gives you her milk when you are small, her bread when you are big, her life all the time! Well, I once had a mother like that. She was a poor woman without a husband, who sang popular ballads in the public squares at Brescia. One day, it seems, in the song she sang not understanding a word of it, there was some allusion insulting to the State of Venice, some couplet that made the servants of an ambassador in the crowd laugh. A Senator passed. He looked and heard, and said to the officer who followed him: "To the gallows with that woman!" In the State of Venice that is quickly done. My mother was seized on the spot. She took her crucifix and allowed herself to be bound. I can still see that crucifix; it was of polished copper. My name, "Tisbe," was carved roughly at the bottom with the point of a dagger. I was sixteen then. Petrified, as if in a dream, I watched those men bind my mother. But with the Senator there was a young girl holding his hand, his daughter doubtless, who was suddenly touched with pity. The poor child threw herself at the Senator's feet and wept so bitterly that she obtained my mother's pardon. When my mother was unbound, she took her crucifix — my mother did — and gave it to the lovely child, saying: "Signorina, keep this crucifix, it will bring you good luck." Since then, mother — blessed woman! — has died. I have grown rich, and I long to see that child again, that angel who saved my mother. She is a woman now, and perhaps she needs me in her turn. In every city I visit, I send for the chief of police; I tell him the story and promise that I will give ten thousand gold sequins to whoever finds the woman I seek.

ANGELO

Ten thousand gold sequins! And what will you give the woman when you find her?

TISBE

My life if she will have it!

ANGELO

But by what token shall you recognize her?

TISBE

By my mother's crucifix.

We would like to recommend that all sopranos who intend to sing Gioconda's aria make a very careful study of *Angelo,* but this is easier said than done. Unfortunately the complete English edition of Hugo's plays has been out of print for many years and is very difficult to obtain. We have decided, therefore, to include a short synopsis of the plot of the drama, and to present, abbreviated in form, a few of its most important scenes.

Angelo (Alvise, in the opera) is a nobleman and the emissary of the Venetian state. He is the *podesta* (mayor) of Padua who rules the city with an iron hand, and who is very proud of his name and of his wife Catarina.

Tisbe (Gioconda), a famous, much-admired, and very wealthy actress, is madly in love with Rodolfo (Gioconda's Enzo). She is also very temperamental and almost insanely possessive. As she says to her lover in the first act: "I am jealous, terribly jealous! I cannot bear to see you speak to other women . . . it drives me mad. What right have they to words from you? A rival! Oh, never give me a rival! I would kill her!"

Rodolfo, though he seems quite content to be Tisbe's lover, does not reciprocate her passion. On the contrary, he is violently in love with Catarina (Laura, in the opera) who returns his love with equal fervor.

Homodei (Barnaba, in the opera), a spy in the service of the Venetian State, has his own reasons for wanting Catarina's undoing and introduces Rodolfo into her bedroom while at the same time making it possible for Tisbe to catch the lovers.

When Tisbe arrives, Rodolfo has been locked in the next room by Catarina for fear that he might come out to defend her against her husband. Tisbe accuses Catarina of harboring a lover and, finding a man's cloak, becomes certain that her suspicions are justified. She does not know whether the hidden man is in fact Rodolfo and in order to discover the truth, is about to rouse Catarina's husband who is sleeping in the adjacent apartment. This is what happens in this crucial scene:

CATARINA

Don't wake my husband. He will kill me! Have pity on me! Don't go to that door, I implore you!

TISBE

That's enough! I'll listen to nothing more! (*calling*) Monsignore!

CATARINA

Stop! At least give me a moment to pray! No, I will not leave this room. You see, I am going to kneel there . . . (*Pointing to the copper crucifix over the prie-dieu*) before that crucifix. Come, in mercy's name and pray by my side.

TISBE

(*rushing to the crucifix and tearing it from the wall*) Where did you get it? Who gave it to you?

CATARINA

It does no good to ask me questions about that crucifix.

TISBE

How does it happen to be in your hands? Tell me quickly! (*She walks to the candelabra and examines the crucifix.*)

CATARINA

Well, it was a woman who gave it to me. A poor woman whom
they were going to put to death. I asked for her pardon. As it was
my father, he granted it. It was at Brescia, I was very young.

Having thus unexpectedly found the woman who once saved her mother,
Tisbe now does everything in her power to help her. She hoodwinks the
Podesta by alarming him about an imaginary assassination plot and thus
makes it possible for Catarina's lover to escape unseen by anyone. Even
the discovery, in the next act, that Rodolfo is indeed Catarina's lover
does not weaken Tisbe's determination to protect her rival. When the
husband, finally convinced of Catarina's infidelity, decides to avenge his
honor by killing his wife, Tisbe again saves Rodolfo's beloved by substituting a powerful narcotic for the deadly poison.

In the final scene of the play the lovers are reunited, but not until
Tisbe, who now has nothing left to live for, provokes Rodolfo into stabbing her to death. It is most instructive to compare the last scene of the
play with the last scene of the opera. Gioconda, who has promised to
give herself to the hateful Barnaba, fulfills that promise by stabbing herself and offering him her dead body. In the play, Barnaba's counterpart,
Homodei is killed in the preceding act. He is not comparable to Barnaba,
in any case, since his carnal desires are aroused not by Tisbe but by
Catarina. The form of "suicide" that Tisbe chooses is therefore of necessity quite different from that of Gioconda's. Here, in greatly abbreviated
form, is what takes place in the play:

RODOLFO

(*addressing Tisbe and unaware that Catarina, still unconscious, is
lying behind the curtains in the recess*)

Allow me to secure those two doors. (*He bolts both doors.*) Where
have you been? What have you done today? No, do not tell me.
I know all! I know all, I tell you! There was Catarina's maid,
within two steps of you, separated only by a door. She heard
everything. The Podesta said: "I have no poison." You said: "I
have some! I have some!" Did you say so — yes or no? Come, lie
a little! Ah! You had poison? Well, I have a knife! (*He draws a
dagger from his bosom.*)

TISBE

Rodolfo!

RODOLFO

You have a quarter of an hour to prepare for death, Signora!

TISBE

You propose to kill me like this, with your own hands, without
waiting, without being more certain! You kill me for the love
of another! O Rodolfo, tell me with your own lips, is it really true
that you never loved me?

RODOLFO

Never!

TISBE

Then it is this word that kills me! Your dagger will simply finish the work! And one more word — tell me, did you love her very dearly?

RODOLFO

Did I love her? She was my life, my blood, my treasure, my consolation, my only thought, the light of my eyes — that is how I loved her!

TISBE

Then I have done well! But are you quite sure of what I have done?

RODOLFO

Am I sure of it? (*taking a handkerchief from his breast*) This handkerchief I found in Catarina's room — whose is it? Yours! (*pointing to the crucifix*) This crucifix that I find in your room — whose is it? Hers! What have you to say to justify yourself?

TISBE

Nothing. All that you have been told is true. You have come most opportunely, Rodolfo, for I wanted to die. I have no desire at all to live. You do not love me, so kill me! To live without my love — I cannot do it. Ah! You are not listening.

RODOLFO

Am I sure of it? The Podesta went to summon the four guards, and meanwhile you whispered terrible things to make her take the poison! Tell me! Where is she? Do you understand that she is the only woman I ever loved, The only one! The only one!

TISBE

The only one! The only one! Oh, it is cruel to stab me so many times! Have pity! (*She points to the dagger that he is holding.*) Give me one final stab with this! Well, yes. I hate that woman, do you hear? I took my revenge, I poisoned her, I killed her!

RODOLFO

Ah! You say it yourself! By Heaven! I believe that you are boasting of it, you wretch!

TISBE

Yes, and I would do it again! I killed her, I tell you! Strike!

RODOLFO

Wretch! (*He stabs her. She falls.*)

TISBE

Ah! You have struck me to the heart. It is well! Now that I am dying, be kind, say one word of pity. Will you not? (*A voice is heard behind the curtains of the recess.*)

CATARINA

Where am I? Rodolfo!

RODOLFO

Whose voice is that? (*He turns and sees Catarina who has drawn the curtains partly aside.*) You here? And living? (*turning to Tisbe*) Ah! What have I done?

TISBE

You have done well. I wanted to die. I urged your hand! I deceived
the Podesta. I gave a narcotic instead of poison. Be happy. She
is free. Dead to the Podesta. Living for you!

RODOLFO

Catarina! Tisbe! (*He falls on his knees, his eyes fastened on Tisbe.*)

TISBE (*in a voice that grows fainter*)

I am going to die. Think of me once in while and say: "She was
a good girl, was poor Tisbe." Go quickly now. Live. I bless you!

As Victor Hugo tells us in the Preface to *Angelo,* it was his intention
"To present . . . two serious and sorrowful figures, the woman in society,
and the woman outside society. To defend the one against despotism, the
other against contempt. To show in what flood of tears the guilt of the
one is washed away, and what tests the virtue of the other resists; and
how her sensual passion is vanquished by filial devotion."

By substituting Gioconda for Tisbe and Laura for Catarina, we can
see that Hugo's main ideas have remained intact in the opera. Laura is
still the "woman in society" who suffers from her husband's despotism
and who — except for Gioconda's unexpected intercession — would have
paid for her adultery with her life. And Gioconda is the "woman outside
society" whose generosity and gratitude triumph over her love for Enzo.
But here the resemblance between the opera and the play ends. What
Ponchielli's librettist, Arrigo Boito, has done is to make the story infinitely
more spectacular and "operatic." He did so by introducing many scenic
effects as well as numerous vocal ensembles and splendid choral scenes,
not to mention the justly famous "Dance of The Hours" ballet. Boito's
changes in the plot, on the other hand, turned Hugo's carefully constructed drama into what one can only describe as a "badly made play."

In the final scene of the opera Gioconda also tries to provoke Enzo
into killing her, but Hugo's logical denouement cannot take place because
the Mephistophelian spy and the Blind Woman are waiting in the wings
like two loose threads that somehow must be tucked away before the
final curtain falls. By resuscitating Tisbe's mother and by failing to kill
off Homodei, Boito burdened the last act with two superfluous characters,
thus making it quite impossible to arrive at a satisfactory conclusion. The
final sentence of the opera in which Barnaba shouts that he had strangled
Gioconda's blind mother because "she had offended" him, is a supreme
example of a *diabolus ex machina,* a devil from the machine, ending.

It is true that what concerns us here is not the logic of the opera or
even that of the last act, but the believability of the situation and words
of the "Suicidio" aria. But here again the continued existence of Gioconda's mother causes a grave problem.

We are quite ready to believe that Gioconda's love for her mother is
so strong that she is willing to take endless risks to show her gratitude
to the woman who saved her mother's life. But should this make her

willing to endanger the safety of her mother who, to make matters worse, is also blind?

At the very beginning of the last act, the *cantori,* who are presumably Gioconda's theatrical colleagues and close friends, carry in the still unconscious body of the drugged Laura. After thanking them and offering to pay them, Gioconda asks another favor: "Last night," she tells them, "my blind mother disappeared. I was in despair trying to find her, but it was of no avail. Please, search all streets and squares for a trace of my dear old lady. If you find her, bring her tomorrow to Camareggio for I will soon be leaving this island of Giudecca." "You can trust us," one of the *cantori* assures Gioconda. When she is alone she turns to the table on which is the dagger and the poison and begins to muse upon her plan for committing suicide. "I've lost my mother," she says in the aria, "I've lost my beloved. Now, having conquered my feverish jealousy I am ready to sink exhausted into the dark realm of death." These words would suit Tisbe, who has really lost both her mother and her beloved, but they do not seem plausible for Gioconda who certainly cannot abandon her mother simply because she has become temporarily separated from her.

We know that Gioconda is distracted and even perhaps not quite in her right mind, but if her filial devotion is comparable to Tisbe's — and the whole plot hinges on this assumption — she cannot possibly abandon her mother at this point. From a practical point of view there is of course nothing much that one can do about this. One certainly cannot rewrite the opera and trim its plot to make it closer to that of the play.

Opera lovers occasionally remark that most people do not notice all these subtle psychological discrepancies and therefore it really does not matter whether an operatic plot can stand up to rigorous logical analysis. This point of view may be valid for some members of the audience but never for performers.

Actors or actresses cannot be convincing impersonators unless they themselves are convinced that the thoughts and emotions of the characters they are portraying are completely logical and consistent with all the details of the plot. The artist who is entrusted with the role of Gioconda must try and imagine a mental and emotional state in which her words and actions make continuous and logical "sense."

An acceptable sequence of Gioconda's thoughts in the last act can perhaps be conceived along the following lines:

I have every intention of finding mother and being reunited with her. She has wandered away on other occasions, and has always been found safe and sound either by myself or by my friends.

I am so unhappy about Enzo's betrayal that I am contemplating suicide, although I do realize, deep down in my heart, that mother needs me, and that I cannot afford the luxury of finding peace in the grave.

Before I do anything else, I must finish the task at hand and see to it that Laura and Enzo find their way to safety. . . . . . .

Now the lovers have left, but what of Barnaba? I promised him that if he releases Enzo, I will give myself to him. Almighty God, don't let this horrible thing happen!

When Barnaba arrives to claim his reward, I will be so overwhelmed with all the agonizing disasters that have befallen me in the last twenty-four hours, that in a fit of despair, I will lose all sense of reality, forget everything, including my poor mother, and stab myself just to escape from his fiendish embraces.

The Music

The five measures preceding the Andante assai sostenuto in 9/8 serve quite adequately as an introduction to the "Suicidio" aria. One could of course include a larger segment of the preceding scene, but it is well to avoid involving the *cantori,* whose only dramatic function would be to show who is hidden behind the screen, and to inform the audience that Gioconda's friends are returning to the mainland to start a search for her mother. The words and actions of the aria deal predominantly with the contemplation of death by suicide. An expansion of side issues would only confuse the listeners.

The a tempo indication at the beginning of the introductory measures refers to the very beginning of the act — sixty-seven measures earlier — when the same music was heard. To give Gioconda time to perform her actions, this introductory Andante can be started very deliberately: at ♩ = 60 or even somewhat slower and with the fermata in the first measure.

This aria, including an introduction (mm. 1–5), consists of sixty-one measures.

The Andante assai sostenuto (mm. 6–53) consists of three sections, each of which has its own musical and dramatic content. And eight-measure coda (mm. 54–61) concludes the aria.

Section 1: in F-sharp minor (mm. 6–26).

This section deals with thoughts of self-inflicted death, either by stabbing or by poison, and with the emotional qualms induced by these thoughts. The descending arpeggio phrase which gives this section its aggressively "desperate" character

bears a strong resemblance to the theme of Gioconda's unhappiness which was heard near the end of the first act.

It is almost as if the phrase associated with the thoughts of death is an amplification of the earlier lament over lost happiness.

The vigorous vocal and orchestral exclamations in measures 8 and 10 must be reflected in the movements and actions of the singer.

Section 2: A major returning to F-sharp minor (mm. 27–44)

This section of the aria elaborates on the contrast between past happiness and present sorrow. It begins pianissimo but this mood lasts for only four measures. A very rapid escalation in dynamics and tempo follows, rising from *pp* to *ff* and enlivened by such markings as "più animato," "crescendo con passione," "stringendo," and "con disperazione." The breakdown in energy, the "exhausted sinking into the darkness," is even more rapid, but it is quickly superseded by the reappearance of the exclamatory descending arpeggio associated with death by suicide.

This section with its enormous contrasts requires great control and stamina on the part of the performer.

Section 3: in F-sharp and in 3/4 (mm. 45–53)

The change of meter is only a notational convenience. The basic beat remains the same: the former dotted quarters are equal in duration to the new quarter-note beats and the triple subdivision becomes duple. In this section Gioconda seeks consolation in the hoped-for "peace in the hereafter." The music changes to tranquillo and dolcissimo, but the tempestuous personality of the passionate street singer soon breaks out again, and the second phrase of this section soars to a ringing high B♮, the highest tone in the aria.

Coda: in F-sharp major (mm. 54–61)

It begins with the descending arpeggio phrase played *ff* by the strings and winds, but the rest of this section is subdued. The final mood is one of resignation.

The Vocal Aspects

A dramatic aria like this one may tempt many a singer to resort to questionable vocal practices. The neophyte may feel that in order to be audible almost everything that can conceivably be produced with a chest tone should be sung that way. Granted that a certain amount of vocal coloring is not only justifiable but necessary, the place where to draw the line is difficult to find, and one will thus hear this aria sung with a great change of quality on all the lower notes at the ends of phrases. Maria Callas, for instance, resorts to a rather noticeable, thick chest tone on the descending octave skips in measures 13, 15, and 22, and throughout most of measures 37–40 (Angel recording S. 35940). It is unfortunate that Miss Callas has set an example that her countless admirers will try to emulate. What is right for Miss Callas is not necessarily correct for everyone.

Many singers find the first word of the aria ("Suicidio") difficult to sing and thus modify its pronunciation. However, it should not be difficult to take the time to sing the two vowels *oo* and *ee* on the first syllable, even though they do occur on a sixteenth note. The skip upwards to another *ee* vowel should not present a problem either, for the pitch is not high enough to warrant much vowel modification. It would be wise not to try to sing the first word too powerfully, and to use a certain amount of restraint in the forte attacks in measures 13 and 15; the lower octave notes will become easier to sing, and a chest tone will not be needed for the singer to be heard. An adequate breath before measure 17 will permit almost anyone to sing measures 17–20 in one phrase, though Miss Callas does not choose to do so. A portamento on the word, "croce," in measure 22 is permissible. A chest tone should not be necessary on the word, "cammin" (mm. 23–24), even though the orchestral entrance, marked fortissimo, may overshadow the second syllable. A portamento on the octave skip upwards on "vola–" in measure 29 is permissible. The alternate notes on the syllable "–van" in measure 29 are possible but not necessarily preferable.

The three short phrases, each one measure in length, that build in intensity (mm. 32–34) are followed by a short stringendo to add further excitement in measures 35 and 36; "vinsi l'infausta gelosa febbre!" should be sung in one phrase without a break. The last beat of measure 36 returns to the original tempo, and although the vocal line is marked "piano" at that point the piano-vocal score does not indicate a piano in the accompaniment until measure 37. It goes without saying, however, that the accompaniment must already be soft at the end of measure 36. With a truly pianissimo accompaniment, a chest tone is not necessary for measures 37–40, though many singers will resort to it, justifying the practice by claiming that such vocal color is necessary because of the text, to show "heaviness and exhaustion, in the darkness."

Measures 45–46 should be sung legato but distinctly. Some singers distribute the syllables somewhat differently from the printed score in measure 50, singing "cie–" on the first two eighth notes, then "–lo" on the B♯ only, with a break in the phrase after the B♯. Then "al" is sung on the last three eighth-notes in the measure. This, of course, permits the difficult skip to the high B♮ to be sung with a portamento on the same *ah* vowel. A breath after "queta" in measure 52 should permit the singer to finish the phrase easily, without a chest tone.

The last phrase of the aria, marked "stentando" by the composer, slows down considerably, and thus several breaths will be necessary. A slight portamento on the second beat of measure 57, from A♯ to F♯ (on "–lo") is possible, even if a catch breath is taken before "di." The same principle applies to the second beat of measure 58: a slight portamento from F♯ to C♯ (on "–ta") is possible, with a small catch breath before "dentro."

A young and inexperienced singer, even though she possesses the vocal equipment and size of voice for this aria, will be tempted to sing it much too loud and too big. Rather than always starting at the beginning, while studying this aria, it is suggested that the young soprano first study the soft sections (mm. 37–40, 44–49, 55–59). When sung well, they will be all the more effective when contrasted to the bombastic phrases of the first section.

The Text

Literal Translation

1. Suicide! In these fierce moments you alone to-me remain,
2. and the heart to-me you-tempt . . . final voice of-the my destiny,
3. final cross of-the my road.
4. And one day charming flew the-hours;
5. I-have-lost the mother; I-have-lost the-love;
6. I-conquered the-unfortunate jealous fever!
7. Now I-fall exhausted among the shadows! I-touch to-the goal . . .
8. I-ask to-the heaven to sleep quietly within the-tomb.

Idiomatic Translation

1. Suicide, in these fierce moments you are all that is left to me,
2. and you tempt my heart . . . you are the final voice of my destiny,

3. the final cross along my road.
4. The hours used to fly charmingly in the past;
5. I have lost my mother, I have lost my love;
6. I conquered the unfortunate fever of jealousy!
7. Now I fall exhausted among the shadows; I reach my goal . . .
8. I ask heaven only that I may sleep quietly in the tomb.

The Scenic Picture

Each of the four acts of *La Gioconda* is given a separate name. "The Lion's Mouth," "The Rosary," "The Golden Palace" are the titles of the first three acts. The last act, which concerns us here, is called "Il Canal Orfano." Orfano, with the accent on the first syllable, is the name of the largest of the Venetian canals, facing the Cathedral and the square of St. Mark.

Immediately following this title, we read:

A vestibule of a dilapidated palace on the island of Giudecca. A screen, behind which there is a bed, stands in the right corner of the room. The lagoon and the festively illuminated square of St. Mark are visible through the large gate, upstage. An image of the Madonna and a cross are suspended on a wall. A lamp, a lighted lantern, a vial with poison, and a dagger are placed on a table. Theatrical paraphernalia belonging to Gioconda are scattered on a sofa. To the right of the palace there is a long and dark street.

In the course of the action, the score also mentions a door that leads from the vestibule to the street on the R. It is used by the men to carry Laura in, and for the entrances of Enzo and Barnaba. Laura and Enzo depart in a gondola that docks near the center upstage gate.

The lantern is held by Gioconda when she admits the men carrying Laura. The theatrical paraphernalia are used by Gioconda only after Barnaba's entrance near the end of the act. They can be disregarded when the aria is performed separately. The image of the Madonna and the cross are hung on the DL wall. The sofa is placed in the UL corner of the room.

The Stage Actions Explained

Orchestral introduction (Andante in 4/4)

Measures

1. Holding the lighted lantern in her R hand, Gioconda stands at the threshold of the door (DR), looking after the departing *cantori*. She closes the door, hangs the lantern on a hook near the door, turns Cclw and, after taking a few steps UL, becomes aware of the dagger and the vial of poison lying on the table.
2. A moment before the fortissimo chord she turns Clw, horrified by the thought of committing suicide.
3. She turns slowly Cclw, as if hypnotized by the deadly articles on the table,

4. goes UL to above the table, turns Clw, and stares at the dagger and the vial.
5. On the second quarter note, with the accented C♯ of the French horn, she lifts the dagger and gazes at it.

First Section 1 (Andante assai Sostenuto in 9/8)
7. She puts the dagger down, turns Cclw, and takes several steps L,
9. turns RSB and backs slightly toward UL while facing the table.
13. She goes DR to above the table,
15. lifts the dagger again,
17. puts down the dagger and gazes into the distance.
23. She looks at the vial with poison and picks it up.
24. She puts down the vial and backs to UL, horrified at the thought of death,
26. goes DR, Xing the table, to DR of it.

Section 2
27. She gazes into the distance DR, recollecting the happiness that was hers before Enzo and Laura found each other.

(Più animato)
31. Remembering suddenly the disappearance of her mother, she becomes nervous and turns Cclw.
33. With increasing nervousness, she turns RSB.
34. Still more agitated, she turns LSB. The backing segments of the last two turns have brought her quite a bit further U than she was in measure 7.
35. She backs still more, getting into a position where, by looking to R, she can see Laura lying on the bed above the screen.
36. The words "gelosa febbre," are directed toward Laura, the object of Gioconda's "feverish jealousy."
37. With "piombo esausta," she turns Cclw.
38. The first "fra le tenebre," is addressed to heaven.
39. During the second "fra le tenebre" she keeps on gazing heavenward and goes L with faltering steps to above the table.
40. She touches the vial containing the poison.

Section 3: (a tempo, Andante assai sostenuto)
41. She picks up the vial, turns RSB, and backs slightly to UL while looking at the vial in her R hand.
42. She passes the vial into her L hand; then while holding it in both hands, she turns Cclw to face the wall on which is placed the Madonna and the cross.
43. After "meta," she goes DL.
44. Letting her hands drop to her sides, she kneels before the image of the Madonna.

49. After "avel," she arises and addresses the cross.
53. She turns RSB to face R.

Coda

54. She goes rapidly to the DL corner of the table,
55. puts the vial on the table, sinks to her knees by the table,
57. and looks to "heaven."
60. When she finishes singing, she buries her head in her hands.

Manon wears the simple and flattering "robe volante" of the early 18th century (and, naturally, a little lace headdress).

"Adieu, notre petite table"
from *Manon*, Act II
by J. MASSENET*

The Drama

Among the twenty-four heroines presented in this volume, we find a pretty even proportion of "good" and "bad girls," and an almost equal number of near saints and outright sinners.

The only widow in the group, Norina, is temperamental and capricious, but morally without a blemish. Devoted and faithful wives who are treated shabbily by their husbands are represented by Countess Almaviva, and Cio-Cio-San. In the contingent of virginal maidens who can boast of a solid and unquestioned purity we pay our respects to Mozart's Anna, Pamina and Susanna, Rossini's Rosina, Verdi's tragically enamored Leonora, Bizet's Micaëla, Gounod's Juliette, and Wagner's sublime Elisabeth.

The authors — being men of only limited perception in such matters — are not absolutely certain whether Zerlina and Aida deserve to be included among those claiming the highest marks for virtue. Our feminine readers must use their intuition to decide this issue.

There is, regrettably, not much doubt about the status of the other ladies. As we descend to the circle of maidens who have definitely forsaken the straight and narrow, we meet Gilda, Marguerite, and Santuzza, that sad trio of incautious virgins seduced by unscrupulous men.

In the group of gay ladies who have no compunctions and seem only too willing to enjoy themselves without benefit of clergy, we find such charmers as Mimi, Gioconda, Tosca, Louise, and Laetitia.

Descending still lower, we pass the lone adulterous wife, Nedda, and at the blackest depth reach the abode of the two professional courtesans, Violetta and Manon.

It is undoubtedly the unrepentant Manon who wins the prize for depravity, not only because she totally lacks personal morality but also because — unlike Violetta — she is so ready to ruin and drag into the gutter the well-intentioned young man whom she professes to love.

The novel by Antoine Francois Prévost, from which the opera is derived, describes the gradual destruction of a fine and upright man by a tantalizingly lovely and thoroughly unscrupulous woman. To give this theme maximum impressiveness, the author endowed the victim with very strong initial defenses. Young Des Grieux comes from a good family. While

* Massenet's dislike of his own Christian name amounted to a phobia. He never permitted Jules to be spelled out in full on any announcements or programs. There is no reason why one should not continue to go along with his wishes in deference to a great composer's harmless mental quirk.

still a boy, he was enrolled in the order of the Knights of Malta and took the required vow of celibacy. He has been attending a religious seminary and has reached the age of seventeen without — as he himself puts it — having given much thought to the difference between the sexes. His behavior has been so exemplary, in fact, that he has been granted permission to call himself chevalier and to wear the cross of the Maltese order.

Manon, on the other hand, comes from a humble background. When, by the age of fifteen she began to display rather alarming tendencies, her family decided to send her to a convent at Amiens. It is there, after her arrival from Arras, while waiting for her cousin to escort her to the convent, that the young chevalier Des Grieux happens to catch a glimpse of the lovely girl. He is on his way to spend his summer vacation at his father's home in Picardy, but at the very first sight of Manon he is struck as if by lightning. "I feel," he says in the opera, "as if my life were about to end . . . or to start anew!"

Manon finds the young man extremely attractive. "I am not a bad girl," she confides to him, "but my folks accuse me of being much too fond of pleasure . . . and so they are sending me to a convent."

Young Des Grieux finds this prospect unendurable and so, on an impulse, the two teenagers take advantage of the availability of a carriage belonging to an old roué who had been flirting with Manon and leave for Paris.

By evening they reach St. Denis where, to quote Des Grieux's words in the novel — operas are less outspoken — the lovers "defraud the church of her rights and become man and wife without reflecting on the consequences."

In the second act of the opera we find them ensconced in a little Paris apartment in the rue Vivienne.

A careful reading of the book's third chapter enables us to set the time of these events with considerable precision. The flight from Amiens occurred on the 28th of June and the second act of the opera takes place exactly one month later. Neither Prévost nor Massenet specify in what year all this occurs. The novel was first published in 1731 and this gives us one acceptable date. On the other hand, since it is believed that Abbé Prévost's tale was inspired by a youthful adventure of his own, it might be even more appropriate to set the opera in 1714 when the author himself was seventeen years old.

During their honeymoon in Paris, the little money that Manon and her lover brought with them dwindles away, and Des Grieux now decides to appeal to his father, begging forgiveness for his disappearance from Amiens and asking permission to marry his youthful companion. The enamored chevalier is convinced that once his father has met Manon, he will instantly succumb to her charms. And these charms are glowingly described in a letter which the lovers read aloud and from which we learn incidentally that the second act of the opera takes place on the day after Manon's sixteenth birthday.

In spite of her youth, Manon is more realistic than Des Grieux. Unbeknown to him she has made the acquaintance of the enormously rich Brétigny who makes it clear to her that fidelity to her present lover would be certain to result in a life of poverty and deprivation. Also Brétigny has informed Des Grieux père of his son's whereabouts, and he assures Manon that this very evening her young lover will be forcibly removed from Paris. Manon's first reaction is to warn Des Grieux, but her fear of poverty is stronger than her passion for the young chevalier, and she decides to throw in her lot, at least temporarily, with Brétigny, whose millions will make her the "queen" of Paris.

No one has described Manon's essential character more justly and eloquently than Guy de Maupassant. In his admirable disquisition on women,* this great connoisseur of the feminine soul has this to say about our heroine:

In the past those adorable beings, who so move us even at this distance, were named Cleopatra, Aspasia, Phryne, Ninon de Lenclos, Marion Delorme, Madame Pompadour . . . and then there is Manon Lescaut. More truly feminine than all the others, she is frankly *rouée,* perfidious, loving, distracting, *spirituelle, formidable,* and charming. . . . As soon as Des Grieux met this irresistible girl, he became . . . by simple contagion, by the mere contact with the depraved nature of Manon, a cheat, a blackguard, the almost conscienceless partner of a charming, conscienceless wretch. . . . And yet this wretch is sincere; sincere in her deception and frank in her infamy. Des Grieux points this out himself in some lines that show us more of woman's nature than most of the great romances having pretensions to psychology: "Never had a girl less fondness for money but she could not rest a moment in the fear of wanting it." . . . Let us look at this Manon as if we had actually met her, and loved her. We perceive the clear cunning look which seems always smiling and promising; we know the lively false mouth; the small teeth within the tempting lips; the fine penciled brows, the vivacious and coaxing movement of the head; the charming motion of the figure and the fresh fragrance of the youthful body beneath the perfumed exterior. No woman has ever been so clearly evoked . . . no woman has ever been so womanly — nor ever contained the quintessence of her sex as this celebrated girl so sweet . . . and so perfidious.

The Music

The aria, marked "Andante (sans lenteur)", begins with the words: "Adieu, notre petite table." It is preceded by a declamatory introduction of twenty-six measures which, in its varied and changing moods, is not unlike an instrumentally accompanied recitative.†

* An English translation of this essay is included in the Modern Library volume *Three Famous French Romances* which contains Daudet's *Sapho,* Prevost's *Manon Lescaut,* and Merimée's *Carmen.* (New York: Random House).

† Printed versions of this aria begin with the upbeat to measure 19. For those who do not happen to have a vocal score we are reprinting the complete musical text of the introduction. (see p. 102).

This declamatory introduction consists of four sections:

> Allegro agitato — mm. 1–11
> Andante espressivo — mm. 12–18
> Allegro — mm. 19–22
> Très retenu — mm. 23–26

The twenty-four measures of the aria consist of two stanzas (mm. 1–12 and mm. 13–24) of eleven measures each, framed by a one-measure-long introduction and a postlude of equal length.

The Vocal Aspects

Although the entire role of Manon abounds in stirring climaxes and high notes, Massenet wisely chose to set this aria in the middle voice, with the highest pitch only an F. The reason is obvious — Manon's mood of sadness and nostalgia would be improperly expressed in any other way. Because of the relentless middle tessitura, many sopranos are not fond of this aria: they find it hard to sing and difficult to make expressive.

The first eleven measures of the introduction need not be sung in strict time, since they are accompanied only by tremolo strings. Though the piano-vocal score indicates alternate notes in the opening measures, the lower notes are preferable. The entrance of the voice with "Non, non!" in measure 10 may be delayed until after the first beat in the measure.

Though measures 12–17 must be sung in tempo for proper coordination with the orchestra, the following measures (18–22) are free. Measures 23–26 are very slow; it is not necessary, however, to observe all the breath marks in measures 25 and 26.

Because of its tessitura, slow tempo, and lack of real climax, one may hear this aria sung with rather a thin tone and somewhat out of tune. Even the recording by an artist such as Janine Micheau can be criticized for these shortcomings (London LLPA–7). Most singers would be wise not to attempt too slow a tempo, in spite of the Andante $\quad = 63$ metronome marking. Because of its delicacy and pathos, the gradations of dynamics must be definite without being overdone. Only "Ah! pauvre ami" in measure 19 should be sung forte with a crescendo; "comme il m'aimait!" immediately afterwards is suddenly pianissimo. In no instance is it possible for the singer to attempt a chest tone for the sake of audibility on the lower pitches. The last "Adieu!" is preceded by an audible sob, and it should be attacked forte, with a carefully controlled diminuendo to pianissimo.

This aria, although it seems to be a prime example of a seemingly easy piece with no apparent vocal difficulties, is nevertheless difficult to sing. A well-developed, full middle register is an indispensable attribute for the soprano who attempts it.

The Text

Literal Translation

Recitative

1. Let us go! It is necessary! For him himself . . . My poor Chevalier . . .
2. Oh, yes, it is he whom I-love. And yet, I-hesitate today. No, no!
3. I not am longer worthy of him. I hear this voice that me-leads against my will:
4. "Manon, you will-be queen by the beauty." I not am but weakness and but fragility!
5. Ah, in-spite-of myself, I feel flow my tears before these dreams obliterated!
6. The-future will-have-it the charms of these beautiful days already past?

Aria

7. Farewell, our little table, that us reunited so often!
8. Farewell, farewell, our little table, so large for us, however!
9. One occupies, it-is hard-to-believe, so little of space in oneselves embracing!
10. Farewell, our little table! The same glass was it ours,
11. Each of us when he drank there searched the lips of the-other —
12. Ah, poor friend, how he me-loved! Farewell, our little table! Farewell!

Idiomatic Translation

Recitative

1. Courage! It must be! For his own sake . . . my poor Chevalier . . .
2. Oh, yes, it is he whom I love. And yet, I hestitate today. No, no!
3. I am no longer worthy of him. I hear this voice that leads me on against my will:
4. "Manon, you will be a queen by right of your beauty." I am nothing but weakness and frailty.
5. Ah, in spite of myself, I feel my tears flow when I think of those lost dreams!
6. Will the future have the charm of those happy days already past?

Aria

7. Farewell, our little table, that reunited us so often!
8. Farewell, our little table, that was so large for us, however!
9. It is hard to believe that one occupies so little space while embracing!
10. Farewell, our little table! The same glass was shared by us,
11. And each of us, when drinking, searched for the imprint of the lips of the other —
12. Ah, poor friend, how he loved me! Farewell, our little table, farewell!

The Scenic Picture

A desk and a chair are located in the alcove near the DR corner of the stage. It is here, in the beginning of this act, that Des Grieux wrote the letter to his father and later read it with so much tenderness to Manon. A vase with a bouquet of red roses presented to Manon by Brétigny stands on a table farther UL beyond the open window. When questioned about them Manon lied to Des Grieux, pretending that they were tossed through the window by some unknown person. There are two other chairs on stage L; one above the little table, and the other to L of it.

The area below the table on stage L is associated in Manon's mind with Brétigny's promise that, if she leaves Des Grieux, she will be "queen by right of her beauty!"

Night is approaching. The lamp standing on the DL cupboard was brought in earlier by the maid who also put on the table a supper setting for two, but with only one glass.

As the scene begins, Manon is standing near the center door through which Des Grieux has just left to post the letter to his father.

The Stage Actions Explained

Declamatory Section

Measures

1. Manon leans against C door facing DL.

4. She turns Clw to look at the window on "Mon" and runs to window on "chevalier."
7. *(first quarter)* She turns Cclw and goes L to CC.
8. *(fourth quarter)* She turns RSB and starts towards the window, but stops at the sight of the roses.
10. She backs to L away from the roses.
12. She turns Cclw and goes DL beyond CC, landing UR of the table, gazing into the distance DL.
16. She BU slightly on repetition of the word "Reine."
17. She turns Clw and goes slightly R towards the desk.
18. On the fermata she goes to the chair next to the desk on stage **R.**
19. She leans on the back of the chair, and
21. *(first quarter)* sits on the chair.
25. She sings "De ces beaux jours" looking toward heaven DR.
26. Getting up on "déjà passés," she then turns Cclw and goes UL.

Aria

1. She turns slightly Clw, sees the table and begins a slow DL walk, reaching CC by the first beat of measure 2.
5. She goes further DL to UR of the table, and
9. leans on UR corner of the table.
12. She goes L along the upper edge of the table and sits down in the chair above the table.
15. *(third quarter)* She touches the glass and fondles it.
19. She rises to L of the chair, and RSB's to look at the window.
20. On "Adieu," she looks at the table again.
22. On "Adieu," she collapses in the L chair
24. and buries her head on the table.

Over a panniered petticoat, the Countess wears a lace negligee. The inevitable lace cap completes the costume.

"Porgi, amor"
from *Le Nozze di Figaro*, Act II
by WOLFGANG AMADEUS MOZART

The Drama

Sopranos are often misled into thinking that Countess Almaviva is a middle-aged woman who has been married for fifteen or twenty years. Such an assumption may unfortunately have come about from having seen the role interpreted by singers of middle age who portrayed the Countess in this fashion. Yet, Count Almaviva himself says in the fifth act of the Beaumarchais play on which the opera is based, "Three years make a marriage so respectable." Since we know that in *The Barber of Seville* Rosina could not wed Count Almaviva without her guardian's consent because she was under age, it is evident that the Countess is still a very young woman, at the most in her early twenties.

This is the Countess's first appearance in the opera. She is alone, and she feels deserted and unhappy. This aria, a *lamento,* is a touching prayer to the god of love. We know from Act I that the reason for the Countess's unhappiness is her husband's habits of infidelity. She fears that he no longer loves her, for not only has he been pursuing the gardener's little daughter, Barbarina, but he has been making more persistent advances to his wife's maid, Susanna, promising her a dowry if she will submit to his desires. Susanna, the epitome of virtue and proper behavior, does not intend to gratify the Count. This is the day of her wedding to Figaro and she hopes that somehow she can circumvent the Count without making him so angry that he will not permit the marriage to take place. The opening sentence of the conversation between the Countess and Susanna that immediately follows this aria makes it clear that the Countess has been informed of the situation before the curtain opens on the second act.

The Music

The long instrumental introduction, seventeen measures in length, can be divided into five episodes:

1. A short preliminary section to accompany the opening of the curtain. (mm. 1–2)
2. A principal theme played by strings introducing the Countess. (mm. 3–6)
3. A sudden interruption of the pensive mood by an exclamatory motive in the woodwinds; a strong conflict of emotions portrayed through the alternation of the forte and piano sections. (mm. 7–10)

4. A hesitation and uncertainty (syncopated rhythm in the strings), followed by a feeling of dejection (deceptive cadence). (m. 12 and first half of m. 13)
   A sudden energetic decision to act. (Second half of mm. 13 and 14)
5. A dissipation of energy. The soft arpeggio in the French horns leads to a mood of resignation and despair. (mm. 15–17)

The sung portion of the aria is broken by two interludes, the first of two and one half measures (mm. 25–27), the second of one and one half measures (mm. 30–31). Although there are but four lines of text in Da Ponte's libretto for this aria, Mozart's characteristic use of repetition expands them into eleven musical phrases, with "O mi rendi il mio tesoro" (Either restore to me my treasure) appearing three times, and "o mi lascia almen morir" (or at least let me die) appearing four times. The second appearance of the latter phrase is heightened by the scale passage to the high Ab, with added wind instruments, and the fermata on the high note (m. 36). The plaintive quality of the bassoon dissonance on the minor ninth Gb (first beat of m. 38) lends added poignancy to the word "sospir" (sigh). The brief postlude, which is a repetition of the last phrase of the orchestral introduction (mm. 16–17), concludes the aria and makes it seem as if it consists of two verses — one "sung" by the orchestra, the other by the soprano.

The Vocal Aspects

Very few operatic characters make their first appearance with the singing of a major, well-known aria. Most often the singer will have a recitative or some phrases with limited vocal demands, before being required to launch into an aria. But Countess Almaviva must begin singing "Porgi amor" without the benefit of "warming up." It is perhaps for this reason that so many sopranos are a little afraid of this aria. Yet its vocal demands are not great, and it is short.

The extended pantomime that precedes the aria is most useful to the singer, for it takes the place of vocal "warming up." All too often, the curtain is opened only two or three measures before the singing begins, and as soon as the curtain is completely open, the Countess must begin to sing. Having the curtain open as soon as the introduction to the aria begins, however, gives the singer time to settle down, to execute the business of the pantomime, and to get into the character before having to sing.

This aria is an exercise in the art of singing legato. All of the sixteenth notes must be sung with the greatest smoothness, especially in meaures 36 and 37, where there is a syllable for every note; this also applies to the scale in measure 41. The long dotted quarters (mm. 18, 28, and 32) can be sung with tiny crescendi after being attacked softly. The long slow scale (mm. 34–35) to the Ab climax has both a crescendo and a ritardando. Many singers have some breathing difficulties in the phrase that begins with the last two sixteenths of measure 40; care should be taken to take a very deep breath during the eighth rest in this measure. The syncopations in measure 42 should not be hurried. In addition to the appoggiatura indicated by the composer on the first beat of measure 43, the authors also prefer several others:

1. One from below on the first beat of measure 30 (A instead of B♭ on the first eighth note).
2. One from above on the first beat of measure 40 (A instead of G on the first eighth note).
3. One from above on the first beat of measure 47 (F instead of E♭ on the first eighth note).

The addition of these appoggiaturas does much to give the aria a plaintive quality: the extra dissonances enhance the sadness and melancholy mood of the Countess. One final word about tempo is perhaps useful. Though the aria is universally conducted with four beats to the measure, it must not be sung too slowly, lest it seem tedious and labored.

The Text

Literal Translation
1. Bestow, love, some consolation to-the my sorrow, to-the my sighs!
2. Either to-me restore the my treasure, or me allow at-least to die.

Idiomatic Translation
1. Grant me, love, some consolation for my sorrows and my sighs!
2. Either restore my treasured love to me, or let me die.

The Scenic Picture

The setting is the sitting room of Countess Almaviva's apartments. The main entrance to the room is on stage L. The door to the rest of the Countess's quarters, including the room of her maid, Susanna, is on stage R. There is a small dressing table with a chair above it on stage L and a sofa on Stage R. An embroidery frame stands to R of the sofa. We know from *The Barber of Seville* that Rosina was fond of embroidering — one of the more genteel activities in which young ladies of breeding indulged in in the eighteenth century. It is logical to assume that though she is now Countess Almaviva, Rosina would occasionally return to this pastime, especially when her husband left her to her own devices. The use of this embroidery frame at the beginning of Act II serves well to provide the Countess with a quiet and suitable occupation for the pantomime that precedes the singing of the aria.

The Stage Actions Explained

The music begins simultaneously with the opening of the curtain. The Countess is sitting near the R corner of the couch, embroidering flowers on the material on the embroidery frame standing to her R. For this activity, it is best to pretend that she has needle and thread than to use the actual properties (see Laetitia's aria in *The Old Man and the Thief*). Though it is early afternoon, she has not yet dressed and is still wearing a negligee. Although outwardly calm, she is very upset by what Susanna has told her about the Count's attempts to seduce her. She knows that the Count planned to go hunting, and she half hopes, half expects, that he will come to kiss her goodbye before he departs. But the Count does not arrive.

Measures

1. The Countess embroiders, pretending to be her usual calm self. The pantomime for this activity must not be overdone, and the singer would do well to practice with a real needle and thread. At times the Countess betrays her inner conflict and anxiety with a small sigh and a momentary hesitation before continuing her embroidering.

7. Unable to pretend any longer, she turns Cclw *(still seated)* toward the main entrance, perhaps thinking that she may have heard the Count outside her door. The action should be timed to precede the forte on the first beat of measure 7 ever so slightly, and the turn toward the door must not be too vigorous.

8. She disappointedly resumes her embroidering.

9. She turns Cclw and looks over her L shoulder toward the window, thinking that the Count has really gone away without coming to say goodbye.

10. She turns Clw to face downstage, thinking: "What shall I do? I just can't sit here, pretending that nothing is wrong."

11. She gets up, fighting to keep back her tears.

12. She picks up the frame, intending to carry it to the R corner of the room where it is usually kept, turns Clw, and goes R slightly. After a step or two she stops: the thought strikes her that she would rather die than lose the love of her husband.

13. She puts the frame down and shakes her head sadly.

13. *(2nd half)* Shaking off her despondency and determined to find the Count and present him with an ultimatum, she turns Cclw and goes L toward the main entrance, Xing above the couch.

15. As she nears the door, the weakness of her position becomes apparent to her, for she realizes that the Count would deny her accusations. She falters slightly.

15. *(2nd half)* She turns Clw, looks at the window, and goes R toward it, hoping to catch a glimpse of her husband riding away, but he is nowhere to be seen.

17. She turns Cclw away from the window and faces downstage.

18. Looking heavenward, the Countess begins her lament to the god of love, facing DL. She imagines the deity to be high in the sky far beyond the walls of the auditorium.

25. *(2nd half)* Thinking again of her husband, she turns Cclw and starts

toward the main entrance door, Xing above dressing table and chair to UL of them. She thinks: "If he could only see me now, I am sure I could persuade him I am still his own lovely Rosina!"

27. Happening to notice the hand mirror lying on her dressing table, her thoughts abruptly change: "Has my beauty faded in these last three years? Is that why he is attracted to younger and prettier girls?" She turns Clw and goes DR to L side of the dressing table.

28. She picks up the hand mirror with R hand and turns her head to address the god of love over her L shoulder.

29. She passes the mirror into her L hand while singing, not looking at it.

30. She extends her L arm so that she can look at the reflection of herself in the mirror.

31. At the sight of her pale, suffering face, she feels sorry for herself, and replaces the mirror on the table, passing it from her L hand to her R hand, and then BU slightly to UL of chair.

32. She faces DR, and looks heavenward at the first mention of death.

34. She goes R to UR of table, Xing above chair.

36. (after fermata) Though still facing DR, she turns her head slightly Cclw, addressing the god of love over her L shoulder.

37. Feeling tears welling up, she takes a small handkerchief from her L sleeve with her R hand and lifts it to her L cheek, but is careful not to hide her face with her R arm as she does so.

38. With her R hand, she lightly wipes away the hot tear that falls on her L cheek.

39. She lowers her R arm while continuing to address the god of love over her L shoulder.

41. She turns her head Clw and goes DR to L corner of the couch, looking heavenward.

43. (2nd half) She wipes the tears from her R cheek and puts the handkerchief back in her L sleeve.

45. (2nd half) She turns Cclw to face DL and BU a step or two, once more addressing the god of love.

47. (2nd half) She turns her head slightly Clw; her final sentence is sung over her R shoulder while looking heavenward.

49. (2nd half) Deciding that her husband's love will be returned to her, no matter what the cost, she goes L to the dressing table, and sits down in the chair above it to repair the damage done to her face by her sorrow and her tears.

"Dove Sono"
from *Le Nozze di Figaro,* Act III
by WOLFGANG AMADEUS MOZART

The Drama

Since the plan — of dressing up Cherubino and having him meet the Count in the garden instead of Susanna — has backfired (see p. 255) the Countess decides to take things into her own hands. Susanna must promise the Count that she will submit to his desires, but now it is the Countess herself who will pretend she is the maid and take Susanna's place. All this was made clear in the earlier recitative that opened the third act:

COUNTESS

Come, have courage! Tell him that he should wait for you in the garden.

SUSANNA

O heaven! And Figaro?

COUNTESS

Tell him nothing! Instead of you, I myself shall go there.

SUSANNA

O God! I do not dare . . .

COUNTESS

Remember that my peace of mind is in your hands!

Susanna executes the Countess's orders, but instead of reporting at once to her mistress, she follows her fiancé to the courtroom so as to be present at the hearing of Marcellina's complaint against Figaro.

Waiting for Susanna's return, the Countess becomes impatient and goes in search of her. Uncertain of how her husband has reacted to Susanna's proposal, she now begins to doubt the wisdom of the whole enterprise.

The Music

The Recitative (25 measures)

The rapid succession of the countess's moods is clearly indicated in the words and the music of the recitative. The opening measure expresses her impatience. Her growing concern is reflected in the string interludes of the opening nine measures: the first one (m. 4) is transposed to a higher register (m. 6) and is elaborated in a faster and more discordant passage (mm. 8 and 9).

In the next four measures (10–13) the Countess restrains her fears and tries a calmer approach: "What is the harm?" she asks herself. All that is planned, after all, is a simple exchange of clothing with Susanna.

The final twelve measures (14–25) of the recitative mark a return of her nervousness, which now is expressed in an eloquent appeal to heaven. The Countess pours out her indignation in what is probably the longest sentence in all opera: "O . . . to what a degrading and shameful state I am reduced by a cruel husband who — after serving me with a shocking mixture of infidelity, jealousy, and anger . . . and after having first loved, then offended, and finally betrayed me — now forces me to seek the help of my own servant girl!"

Throughout this recitative, the orchestral strings provide an emphatic and detailed commentary. While the instruments cannot tell us exactly what gestures, turns, and steps the Countess should be making, they leave no doubt as to the level of energy or the timing of such actions. Notice particularly the sudden relaxation of tension after "But what is the harm?" in the tenth measure and a similar relaxation at the reference to her husband's erstwhile love, in the twenty-first measure.

In the orchestral score the first chord of the recitative is notated as the conclusion of the preceding keyboard section, and the strings begin only after the Countess's opening sentence. When this aria is performed separately with orchestral accompaniment,

should be added to the string parts and notated on the first beat of the measure.

The Aria (110 measures)

The Andantino in 2/4 is conducted in four beats to the measure. The tempo must be fluent enough to permit the singer to take each of the recapitulation phrases (mm. 37–40, 41–44, and 45–48) in one breath, and yet slow enough to enable the oboe to execute the thirty-seconds in measures 8 and 44 without undue hurry. ♪ = 66 can be recommended as a sensible speed.

The form of the Aria is not complicated. It is divided into two sections, an Andantino and an Allegro. The Andantino in 2/4 has fifty-one measures and is set in a simple A-B-A song form with no Introduction or Postlude. The fifty-nine measures of the Allegro in 4/4 are divided into two stanzas connected by a bridge passage that anticipates the music of the final Coda.

The text consists of three quatrains,* the first two of which are allocated to the Andantino and the third to the Allegro section.

---

* This English version by Ruth and Thomas Martin, is from the G. Schirmer piano-vocal score.

Are they over, those cherished moments,
Hours together so sweetly shared?
Are they broken, those fervent pledges,
His deceitful lips declared?

If a bitter fate inclined me
Such unhappiness to know,
Why do memories remind me
Of those joys of long ago?

If at last my heart's devotion
Could achieve but one reward,
And revive the dead emotion
Of my false and heartless lord!

As usual, Mozart elaborates on this basic structure by repeating many lines of the text and by adding instrumental interludes. Quite apart from the formal restatement of the first quatrain in the recapitulation of the Andantino, and the expected recurrence of the third quatrain in the second stanza of the Allegro, there are eleven repetitions of complete lines and two repetitions of a half line. There are, in addition, nine purely instrumental portions of various lengths (Introduction, seven Interludes and Coda).

Since most of these elaborations reflect the increasing emotional tone of the situation and serve as stimulants for the larger actions executed by the character, they deserve the most careful attention on the part of the performer.

The Vocal Aspects

Recitative

The recitative is one of those masterly examples of Mozart's genius that highlight a monologue in which a character's thoughts and emotions change rapidly from anxiety to rationalization to self-pity. Not only must the singer know the exact meaning of each word, but she must have at her command a variety of vocal colors to express the changing moods and thoughts.

Although the recitative is accompanied by the orchestra, it need not be sung in strict tempo except in certain key places where coordination with the orchestra is essential. The first seven measures are rather deliberate, if not measured. Measure 8 must be sung in strict tempo to permit the orchestral entrance, and the subsequent Allegretto later in the measure, to function properly. Although the Andante does not appear until measure 10, the preceding phrase, "Ma che mal c'è?," is slower than the Allegretto of the orchestra. So that the *fp* entrances of the orchestra in measures 14 and 15 can be decisive and coordinated exactly with the voice, these two measures must be sung in strict tempo. The first half of measure 16 must also be in strict tempo, since the viola resolution from B♭ to A on the syllable "–dot" will otherwise be very difficult. Measures 17 and 18 are rather free, but measure 19 to the end should be sung in a relatively strict tempo, although the high A on the down beat of measure 24 can be elongated slightly.

    The following appoggiaturas are recommended. Although we recognize that other alternatives or omissions may be preferred, we feel that this recitative lends itself particularly well to the use of many inflections.

Recitative

qual u-mil sta - to fa-ta-le   io son ri-dot - ta   da un con sor- te cru-

del!   Che do-po a - ver-mi con un mi-sto in - au - di - to d'in-fe-del-

tà,   di ge-lo-si - a,   di sde - gno,   pri - ma a-

ma-ta,   in-di of - fe - sa,   e al-fin tra-di-ta,

fam - mi or   cer-car   da u - - na mia ser-va a - i - ta!

Andantino (51 measures)

To enhance the feeling of melancholy and sorrowful contemplation, the Andantino section of the aria must be sung as smoothly as possible. Even though there is an eighth rest at the end of measure 2, the singer should pause, but not necessarily breathe, so that the first four measures become one uninterruped phrase. Measures 9–12 should be treated in the same fashion. A catch breath after "–gner" in measure 15 is permissible.

An appoggiatura on the first eighth-note of measure 22 (C instead of B♭) is useful to highlight the word "pene." A breath after "bene" in measure 29 is possible if the singer is not able to sing measures 28–31 in one breath. An effort should be made to sing measures 32–36 in one breath. Measures 37–40 must be sung in one breath; the singer should be careful to note that Mozart has notated this phrase slightly differently the second time. A slight crescendo with a portamento from C to F is stylistically appropriate in measure 51.

Allegro (59 measures)

Singers with sufficient breath control should sing "mi portasse una speranza di cangiar l'ingrato cor" (mm. 5–9) in one breath. Most singers will wish to breathe after "costanza" in measure 22. The breath in measure 25 sometimes presents problems. It is safest to make a slight ritardando on the last beat of measure 24 so that the first two beats of measure 25 are somewhat slower. The dotted quarter- and eighth-notes should be sung accurately in the slower tempo; then after a good breath, the singer should continue on the third beat of the measure a tempo and sing the remainder of the phrase without a breath (through "cor" in m. 29). Those sopranos who find it difficult to execute a trill on the D in measure 47 should omit it.

The Text

Literal Translation

Recitative

1. And Susanna not comes? I-am anxious to know how the Count received the proposal.

2. Rather daring the project to-me seems . . . to a husband so full-of-spirit and jealous . . .
3. But what harm there-is? Changing the my clothes with those of Susanna,
4. and the hers with mine to-the protection of-the night . . .
5. Oh, heaven! To what lowly condition unfortunate
6. I am reduced by a consort cruel . . . who after having-me with a mixture unheard-of
7. of-faithlessness, of jealousy, of disdain . . .
8. first loved, then offended, and finally betrayed . . .
9. makes-me now seek from a my servant help!*

Aria

10. Where are the beautiful moments of sweetness and of pleasure?
11. Where have-gone the promises of that lip lying?
12. Why ever, if in tears and in griefs for me everything itself has-changed,
13. the memory of that goodness from-the my breast not disappeared?
14. Ah, if only the my constancy in-the languishing loving always
15. to-me might-bring a hope of changing the-ungrateful heart!

Idiomatic Translation
Recitative:

1. And Susanna still hasn't come? I am anxious to know how the Count received the proposal.
2. Our plan seems rather daring to me . . . my husband is so violent and so jealous ? . .
3. But what harm is there in it? I'll change clothes with Susanna
4. while she wears mine, under cover of night . . .
5. Oh, heavens! To what humiliation
6. I am reduced by a cruel husband . . . who, with an incredible mixture
7. of faithlessness, jealousy, and disdain,
8. having first loved, then offended, and finally betrayed me,
9. now drives me to seek help from my own maid!

Aria

10. Where have they gone, those beautiful moments of sweetness and pleasure?

---

   * At the end of the recitative's third sentence, all piano-vocal and orchestral scores print an exclamation point: "Alquanto ardito il progetto mi par, e ad uno sposo si vivace e geloso!" This translates as "Somewhat bold the project seems to me, and to a husband who is so violent and jealous!" It sounds, in both languages, like an unfinished sentence which, in fact, is just what the librettist had intended. In Da Ponte's original libretto this place is marked quite clearly with an ellipsis: "and to a husband who is so violent and jealous . . ." The unspoken continuation should no doubt be: "(and to a husband who is so violent and jealous . . .) this masquerade would quite certainly look foolish and undignified!" The string passage marked "Allegretto" expresses these unspoken words to perfection.

11. What has become of the promises made by those lying lips?
12. Why, if everything for me has changed into tears and grief,
13. does the memory of past sweetness not disappear from my breast?
14. Ah, if only my constancy, while I am languishing but still loving,
15. might bring some hope of changing his ungrateful heart!

The Scenic Picture

A stone terrace outside the palace of the Almavivas near Seville. The park is visible in the background. The façade of the building with the entrance door is at R. A table and a chair are placed in the DL portion of the terrace. An armchair is to the R of center.

The Stage Actions Explained

Recitative (25 measures)

Throughout the Recitative, the Countess displays various shades of impatience, nervousness, and unhappiness.

Measures
1. She enters from stage R, and stops at the R of the armchair. She is looking for Susanna. After the opening sentence, she goes UL, Xing above the armchair, to glance in the direction of the center entrance.
2. She turns Clw to face DR.
4. With "proposta," she goes DR to L of the armchair.
6. After "mi par," she continues to go DR more nervously, but stops below the armchair.
8. With "vivace," she turns Cclw and with "geloso," goes UL to UR of the table.
9. With "che mal c'è," she calms down somewhat, and turns very slightly to face DL.
12. After "cò miei" she goes D and then L, Xing the table to DL of it.
14. With "oh, cielo!" she turns RSB energetically.
15. With "stato fatale," she backs slightly to UL.
17. With "crudel," she goes R, Xing above the table, to CC.
19. & 20. The vigorous orchestral interjections in these two measures express the Countess's agitation. They must be acted out by nervous gestures and slight turns to L and R. With "prima amata," she calms down.
21. Recollecting the early days of her marriage, she goes slightly DR.
22. With "offesa," she again becomes excited and turns LSB.
23. After "tradita," she goes L to the UR corner of the table.
25. She goes toward the chair standing above the table, so that with "aita," she is ready to sit down.

Andantino (51 measures)
1. During measures 1–8 the Countess sits behind the table and faces toward DL.

8. After "piacer," she leans forward and puts her hands on the table.
12. After "giuramenti," she turns her head Clw, as if visualizing her husband's "broken pledges" in the distance toward DR.
18. This painful thought affects her strongly and induces her to rise.
19. She goes slightly to the R,*
20. takes a handkerchief from her L sleeve and
22. holding it in her R hand, she wipes a tear from her L cheek.
25. She goes DR slightly.
27. Just before "la memoria," she turns Cclw to face DL.
   (Notice that while the Countess's sorrows are associated mostly with the DR portion of the stage, the recollections of her past happiness are imagined in the opposite direction, toward DL.)
31. She looks at the wedding ring on her L hand. This symbol of her lost joys affects her so strongly that she repeats the preceding sentence, with a special emphasis on the word "ben."
34. With "ben," she passes her L hand to her R side, and
35. goes R to the armchair.
36. During the fermata, she continues to look at the ring, turns slightly Cclw and sits down.
37. Sitting in the armchair, she sings toward DL.
44. After "piacer," she turns Clw to face toward DR.
49. She rises and takes a few steps toward the R.

Allegro (59 measures)
1. During the fermata, the Countess turns LSB to face DL.
3. With "nel languire," she turns her head Clw and sings the sad C–minor phrase over her R shoulder.
5. With "mi portasse," she gazes heavenward, and turns her head slowly Cclw, so that with "speranza," she faces completely DL.
7. With "cangiare," the Countess makes a begging gesture with her L hand.† Two measures later, this word is stressed by an even more emphatic gesture and a slight backing toward UR.
12. She turns Cclw and goes UL, Xing above the armchair, but stops short of CC. (UL is the direction from which earlier, in the opening Recitative of this act, the Countess saw her husband enter the stage.) The musical phrase below occurs in measures 12–14, 17–19 and 52–54 and is always associated with the Count, and with the Countess's desire to look for and find him.
15. She turns her head slightly Clw, and sings the entire sentence looking over her R shoulder toward DL.

---

* The space between the table and the armchair should be apportioned into three approximately even segments which the Countess traverses during her walks in measures 19, 25, and 35.

† Since the entire Allegro section is dominated by the Countess's hope that by remaining faithful and loving she can induce her husband to change and to abandon his philandering, the word "cangiare" (change) should always be reinforced by a gesture or other bodily movement.

17. She continues to go toward UL.
18. She stops, turns Clw and goes D to UR of the table.
20. She begins this sentence facing toward DL.
22. With "nel languire," she turns Clw and goes DR to L of the armchair. (This C-minor phrase is an elaboration of what she sang in the fourth and fifth measures of the Allegro. It is again directed toward the "sorrowful" DR side of the stage, and should be sung and acted with great expression. Even though a change of tempo is not marked here, the mood of languor and the sixteenth notes in the vocal line point to a considerable relaxation in energy. We recommend a slowing down that begins in the twenty-third measure and continues until the middle of the twenty-fifth measure).
25. The conductor (or pianist) should permit the singer to take a comfortable breath after "ognor," and resume the fast tempo only with "mi portasse." This is also the place where — by analogy with the fifth measure of the Allegro — the Countess begins to turn LSB.
27. With "cangiar," she backs slightly to UR.
30. The Countess begins to go DL. She walks in a continuous movement that takes her first to DR of the table and then L, Xing the table, to DL of it. She reaches her destination not later than the middle of the thirty-third measure. Both high A's are "sprayed"* from DL to DR.
34. During the first A, she moves her head Clw so as to sing
35. over her R shoulder.
36. With "l'ingrato cor," she turns her head Cclw so as to face DL.
38. During the second high A, she makes an RSB turn and extends it with a slight backing toward UL.
41. With "cangiar," she goes R, Xing above the table, to CC.
44. With "cangiar," she turns Cclw and goes slightly D.
48. She remains there, addressing heaven toward D.
52. During the postlude, she turns Clw and goes U to the center entrance looking from one side to the other for the Count.
56. She sees him approaching with the gardener, Antonio. Not wishing to confront the Count at a time when he is involved with servants, she turns Cclw and leaves the stage via the DR door.

* For the definition of "spraying," see page 6.

Laetitia is the prototype of a maid. Here she wears the Hollywood idea of a maid's uniform.

"Steal me, sweet thief"
from *The Old Maid and the Thief,* Scene VI
by GIAN CARLO MENOTTI

The Drama

The Old Maid And The Thief was originally written for radio performance, which accounts for its many short, fast-moving scenes. The
opera has been performed on the stage for almost thirty years, however,
and is very easily adaptable for stage presentation through the use of
a multiple setting that encompasses Miss Todd's living room, kitchen,
and upstairs guest bedroom.

Miss Todd, who is in her late fifties or early sixties, lives in a small
town somewhere in rural America. The time is the present. We know
from the first scene that she is a reluctant spinster, who was deserted by
her lover many years ago. Laetitia, her maid, is still young and attractive,
but at the beginning of the opera she may be somewhat carelessly dressed
and dowdy looking. Both ladies are much attracted to a young drifter
who happens to knock on Miss Todd's door looking for a handout. The
dress and grooming of both Miss Todd and Laetitia change during the
course of the opera to indicate that they become more interested in their
appearance when a young and attractive man is on the scene.

Miss Todd invites Bob to spend the night. The next day the ladies learn
of the escape of a thief from a nearby town jail and assume that Bob is he.
They are caught in a dilemma: is it better to harbor the attractive criminal
and risk being robbed or attacked, or is it prudent to call the police and
lose the company of their charming guest? Laetitia persuades Miss Todd
to pretend that she is well-to-do, to give Bob money which she (Miss
Todd) will "borrow" from her church and her club, and to keep Bob with
them for the time being.

A week passes; with a smile Bob accepts Miss Todd's stolen money and
stays on. Laetitia has received but little encouragement from Bob, who
professes to hate all women. In this scene she is mending and pressing
Bob's trousers. Miss Todd is momentarily absent from the house (she is
probably out stealing money from the purse of a friend on whom she
goes to call) and Bob is asleep upstairs in the guest room.

The Music

Menotti has imitated the classic recitative and aria of the eighteenth
century but gives it a twentieth century twist. The first twenty-three
measures are more arioso than recitative, and they must be sung with
strict attention to proper note values. The aria itself, beginning with

measure 24, has many changes of meter. However, the quarter note remains the basic beat. Care should be taken to make the 7/8 measures (mm. 24 and 35) the correct length without letting them slip into ordinary 4/4 measures. Even though the aria itself is but thirty-six measures long, its form can be described as follows:

> A section — mm. 24–34
> A1 section abbreviated — mm. 35–40
> B section — mm. 41–59

The Vocal Aspects

Except for two high B♭'s, this aria presents few vocal difficulties for a competent singer. Measure 3 can be sung freely, but from then on the proper note values must be sung in a consistent tempo. Though measure 23 of the recitative is marked rallentando molto, the aria itself, beginning with measure 24, should not be sung too slowly, so that it is possible to sing longer phrases without needing a breath. The singer should breathe after "thief" (m. 25), "youth" (m. 27), "time" (m. 29), and "strife" (m. 32), but then should sing "And then with furtive step death comes and steals time and life!" in one breath. To indicate Laetitia's increasing emotion, little catch breaths are possible after "lips," "heart," and "cheeks," in measures 49 and 50, but "steal, oh steal my breath" should be one phrase, as should "and make me die before death will steal her prey." All of the composer's markings for change of tempo in measures 49–53 should be carefully observed.

Those singers who find an *ee* vowel difficult on high notes will wish to modify the word "steal" on the B♭ in measure 55 to more than an *eh* vowel sound. The last phrase should be sung unbroken, with careful attention to the numerous tempo changes. The last note should be held until curtain or blackout.

The Scenic Picture

Miss Todd's kitchen and living room occupy the main area of the stage. At center, on a platform reached by a flight of stairs, is the guest room. Only the kitchen and a portion of the living room are the playing areas for this aria. The kitchen occupies about a third of the stage, on stage R; the living room occupies the rest of the stage to the L of the kitchen. To separate the living room from the kitchen, there is a low cabinet that indicates a dividing wall. To move between the kitchen and the living room, one X's *above* this cabinet. To the L of the cabinet, in the living room, stands a small table with two chairs to its R and L. In the center of the kitchen area stands an ironing board. On it, sitting on its edge, is an iron which is heating as the aria begins.

The Stage Actions Explained

Laetitia is seated in the chair to the R of the table in the living room sewing a button on the back pocket of Bob's trousers, which are in her lap. With such tiny properties as a needle and thread, it is often preferable to pantomime their use since actual ones would constitute somewhat of a hazard and since they are almost always invisible to the audience. There is a sewing basket on the table to Laetitia's L.

Measures

1. Laetitia vigorously stabs the needle through the material of the trousers.
2. She then sticks the needle through the material from the other direction.
3. She stops sewing for a moment and sings to herself.
6. She resumes sewing.
8. (*second beat*) She finishes sewing.
    (*fourth beat*) She vigorously breaks the thread (*pantomime*) and drops the needle into the sewing basket.
9. She gets up, holding the trousers.
10. (*4th beat*) She turns Cclw, puts the trousers down on the table beside the sewing basket.
11. (*2nd*) She picks up the sewing basket, turns Clw and goes UR to above U corner of the cabinet, sets the sewing basket down on the cabinet, and continues R to above the ironing board.
13. (*2nd beat*) She picks up the iron with R hand.
    (*3rd beat*) She wets the index finger of her L hand with her lips.
    (*4th beat*) She touches this finger to the bottom of the iron. The iron is hot enough to iron the trousers.
14. She sets the iron down on its edge on the ironing board.
16. She shrugs her shoulders.
17. She goes L to above the cabinet, picks up the sewing basket, and continues L slightly to just UL of the cabinet.
19. (*2nd beat*) She turns Clw and kneels, facing the cabinet, opens its door, puts the sewing basket inside it, and closes the door again.
    (*4th beat*) She rises, turns Cclw and goes L to above the table, Xing above R chair.
20. (*4th beat*) She picks up the trousers vigorously.
22. She turns Clw and goes R to above the ironing board, Xing above R chair and cabinet.
23. She arranges the trousers on the ironing board so that she can press them and picks up the iron with R hand.
24. She presses the trousers, timing the speed of her ironing motions to coincide with the indicated changes of tempo, now faster, now slower.
38. She sets the iron down on its edge, to R of the trousers.
40. She turns the trousers over to press the other side and picks up the iron.

41. She presses the trousers again.
48. (*3rd beat*) She sets the iron down on its edge.
49. She looks heavenward, completely wrapped in her thoughts.
55. She impulsively grabs the trousers and clutches them to her breast.
56. Realizing what she has done, she looks at the trousers and finds that she has wrinkled them.
57. She lays them down on the ironing board to iron out the wrinkles, smoothing them with her hands.
58. She picks up the iron and slowly presses the trousers. The ironing continues until curtain or blackout.

Since Nedda refers to her gypsy background, she combines the style of the 1860's with a gypsy costume.

Ballatella

from *Pagliacci*

by RUGGIERO LEONCAVALLO

The Drama

It was described in the Introduction (see p. 4, The Dramatic Aspects) how one should proceed to bring an operatic character to life. In order to build a character the singer must study the complete text of the opera and note every remark — made by the character himself, or by others about him — which throws a light on his present and past activities.

To demonstrate amply how to collect this information and to go about filling out the character when the opera is not based on a literary text, we have chosen the role of Nedda.

The numbers in parentheses refer to the pages in the G. Schirmer piano-vocal score where such information can be found.

Information Culled from the Vocal Score and Other Sources

Nedda's mother was a fortune teller (p. 70).

After her mother died, the orphaned girl would have died of hunger (p. 192) if Canio, the head of a traveling theatrical troupe, had not picked her up "somewhere on the road" (p. 191).

The girl was very pretty and Canio eventually fell in love with her and married her (pp. 191–192).

Nedda became an actress and a regular member of the traveling company, playing roles of attractive young girls, such as Colombina (p. 164).

At the time the action takes place, Canio's company is giving open-air performances in small villages in the south of Italy.

In the introductory pages of the score it says: "The Scene is laid in Calabria, near Montalto, on the feast of the Assumption. Period, between 1865 and 1870."

In a letter dated Sept. 3, 1894,* addressed to his publisher Sonzogno, Leoncavallo is even more specific: "I left the setting of the opera as I saw it then, and as it can be seen now in Montalto, Calabria, at the Festival of the Madonna della Serra which takes place on August 15."

The villagers are on terms of such easy familiarity with Canio and his troupe (pp. 38, 46, 47, 48) that we can guess that this is not the first time the company has come to Montalto.

Nedda does not love her husband, and probably never did (p. 98).

Unbeknown to Canio, she is now involved in a passionate affair with Silvio, who, judging by his intimate knowledge of the village (pp. 93, 122), is a native of Montalto.

Since Nedda chides Silvio for his imprudence in coming to see her

* The complete text of this letter is quoted in H. E. Krehbiel's *A Second Book of Operas,* pp. 110–111. (Garden City Publishing Co., N. Y.)

during the day (p. 92), we must assume that they usually meet at night when they can be protected by the darkness.

Silvio is upset that the players will be departing from the village the next day (pp. 96, 109), and wants Nedda to leave her husband and run away with him (p. 99).

Nedda is afraid to do so (pp. 99–100), but eventually decides that she cannot fight her destiny (p. 103), and promises to meet Silvio later that night and throw in her lot with his (pp. 118, 153–154).

Alerted by Tonio, a fellow actor whose amorous advances Nedda has spurned earlier (p. 90), Canio catches his wife making love to Silvio (p. 118).

Silvio manages to escape without being identified by either Tonio or the jealous husband (pp. 119, 127, 128).

Enraged, Canio wants to find his wife's lover and avenge his honor. He threatens to kill Nedda if she does not tell him the name of the man (pp. 124, 203).

Nedda will not expose Silvio to her husband's murderous fury and refuses to reveal his name, even though she should die for it (pp. 200, 201).

If we add to this the sarcastic laughter with which Nedda rejected the advances of the obnoxious Tonio, and the physical courage it took to restrain and horsewhip him, it is apparent that we are dealing with a passionate woman of great determination and stamina.

Filling out the character

To gain a better understanding of Nedda's personality and emotional make-up, we should try and learn more about her relations with both her husband and her lover. In the absence of an authentic text, such details can be supplied only by one's own imagination. Taking advantage of all the data and hints derived from the text of the opera, we should like to offer — as only one of many possible extrapolations — the following *freely invented* additional details.

When her gypsy† mother died, Nedda was barely fifteen years old and was left entirely to her own devices. Canio, who met her when she was roaming the streets, took her in partly out of pity, because she looked so famished, and partly because he needed an actress to replace his regular ingénue who was getting old and quarrelsome. Canio started training the girl and, being a hard taskmaster, at first treated her rather brutally (p. 72). It turned out that she had a definite flair for the stage. As her beauty began

---

† Toward the end of her aria, Nedda refers to the flock of birds as "boëmi del ciel," gypsies of the sky. Since, in this song, Nedda obviously compares her own unhappy "chained" lot with the unfettered freedom of these birds, one wonders whether perhaps at this point she is remembering her carefree wanderings with her "fortunetelling" gypsy mother. Canio's vituperations in the last scene could perhaps, then, also be caused — at least in part — by his bitter regret of having married a fickle and untrustworthy gypsy girl.

to blossom, the much older Canio fell head over heels in love with her and, when she turned seventeen, proposed marriage.

Nedda felt no particular tenderness for Canio — she was in fact rather terrified of him — but the idea of becoming the boss's wife appealed to her and, at first, her husband treated her with great affection.

Canio, while not the most attractive of men, is not basically an unpleasant person. In the words of Peppe: "é violento, ma buon!" (he is violent, but kind) (pp. 126–127). And, as he himself tells the villagers, he truly "adores" his wife.

For the first two years their marriage remained fairly stable, but when Silvio came into the picture, things began to deteriorate.

In trying to imagine the origin and progress of Nedda's extramarital love life, one is at first struck by the apparent lack of opportunities available to a woman who is constantly traveling from one village to another accompanied by a suspicious, violent-tempered, older husband. But here again, the composer's letter from which we quoted earlier comes to our aid. "The players," Leoncavallo wrote, "arrive a week or ten days before the festival to put up their tents and booths in the open space which reaches from the church toward the fields." In a week or so during which her husband is busy in the "open space," his wife has ample time to spend in the village and to meet a number of young men. One imagines that Nedda and Silvio became acquainted during the troupe's earlier visit to Montalto in the preceding year. In the evening, when the husband and the other members of the company went to the tavern for a glass of wine and a game of cards, it was not too difficult to pursue a flirtation that had started during the day. One has the feeling that, in the first year, this flirtation resulted in only one, and fairly hasty, act of adultery. On this next visit, however, the spark that was ignited the year before turned into the *"febrile amor"* (p. 107), the feverishly passionate conflagration, the tragic outcome of which is portrayed in the opera.

* * *

Before we can proceed with the discussion of Nedda's actions during her aria, it is necessary to say a few words about her appearance and behavior in the preceding scenes. It is quite clear that, just before the curtain went up, three of the traveling comedians — Canio, Peppe, and Nedda — were drumming up trade for the evening's performance by making a tour of the village in a cart drawn by a donkey. After Canio's speech urging the villagers to attend the show "a venti tre ore," at seven o'clock,‡ we

‡ "Twenty-three o'clock" actually means two hours before dark. Since in those days, one o'clock designated darkness, twenty-four o'clock meant one hour before, and twenty-three o'clock, two hours before dark. Sunset in August occurs roughly around eight thirty, and darkness sets in thirty minutes later; so that if one o'clock equals approximately nine, twenty-three comes close to seven. It is worth noting that the combination of afternoon heat and lack of artificial stage illumination made "twenty-three o'clock" about the only possible curtain time for summer shows given in the south of Italy in the open air.

come to the important episode that establishes Canio's possessive attitude toward his wife. When Tonio attempts to help Nedda out of the cart, Canio boxes his ears and lifts her down himself. Tonio resents this treatment and, while Canio and Peppe express their willingness to join the villagers for a drink at the tavern, Tonio makes the excuse that he must take care of the donkey. It is at this point that one of the villagers decides to tease Canio by remarking that Tonio is staying behind in order to make love to Nedda. The husband does not take kindly to this joke, and makes it clear that anyone who thinks of making advances to Nedda will live to regret it. This warning is given with such a "fiery look" (p. 68) that Nedda shudders and remarks in an aside that her husband's words make her feel jittery (p. 52). Now the bagpipe players make their entrance and church bells are heard calling the faithful to Vesper services.

Canio and Peppe ask the villagers to wait for them (p. 47), but what of Nedda? To have her remain onstage during the choral number — as is often done nowadays — is quite wrong in our opinion. It is regrettable that there are no printed stage directions at this point, but it is certainly logical to assume that, during their tour in the cart, all three comedians were dressed in their traditional commedia dell'arte costumes: Canio as a clown, Peppe as Arlecchino, and Nedda as Colombina.

According to the score it is now three in the afternoon (p. 16), and since the show will not start until seven, the performers will naturally want to shed their stage outfits. This is what Canio and Peppe will be doing while the villagers wait for them. Nedda should also proceed to her dressing room, which is obviously attached in some way to the platform stage where the evening's performance will take place. When she emerges, shortly before the Recitative of her Aria, she has changed into a comfortable peasant outfit.

The Music

Nedda's solo scene consists of a Recitative, followed by a Vivace in 3/8 which is entitled "Ballatella," or little ballad.*

Recitative (36 measures)

The thirty-six measures of the Recitative are divided into three equal parts of twelve measures each. Near the beginning and ending of the first part, the cellos intone the sinister theme of Canio's jealousy, while in the middle of this section we hear Silvio's motive played con amore by the first violins. These orchestral phrases spell out Nedda's two dominant emotions: fear of her husband and passionate tenderness for her lover.

_____

* The G. Schirmer piano-vocal score has the title "Ballatella" printed three measures ahead of the Vivace section, but this is obviously a typesetting error. In the orchestral score published by Broude Brothers, the title is placed correctly.

The second part (mm. 13–24), where Nedda yields to the caresses of the afternoon sunshine and dreams of her "secret desires," serves to underline the young woman's voluptuous sensuality.

The third part (mm. 25–36) in which the orchestra illustrates the fluttering wings and twitter of birds, ends with the vocal flourishes by means of which Nedda — hoping to imitate her mother's occult art — tries to converse with her feathered friends.

Ballatella (142 measures)

The music of the Ballatella follows the structure of the poem and consists of four independent sections of approximately equal length. Counting the ten measures of the orchestral introduction, there are in all one hundred and forty-two measures.

The first quatrain (mm. 11–42), in which the music does not depart from the tonic of F-sharp major, describes in a gay and almost impersonal fashion the joyous abandon of the birds' flight.

With the second quatrain (mm. 43–74), the mood becomes more lyrical and almost sad. The flying feathered arrows "thirsting for the splendor of the blue sky" make Nedda think of her own thirst for freedom, while their pursuit of "the dream" and "the illusion" is closely akin to her own hopeless dream of happiness with Silvio. This escape into the dreamland of happiness and splendor is symbolized by a departure from F-sharp major, moving first to the "amorous" A major, and then to the "splendid" D major.

The third quatrain (mm. 75–101), filled with passionate agitation, provides the main contrast of the poem and of the music. Nedda envies the courage of the birds who, unlike her, are not afraid to challenge fate. How she wishes she could also brave the storms and the lightning of destiny, for only this courage and daring† could lead her "over the abysses" of her unhappy lot. The music throbs through a succession of ever-ascending chords of the diminished seventh, until it reaches the safe haven of the dominant of F-sharp major.

The final quatrain (mm. 102–142), (again in the home key of the piece) describes Nedda's enthusiastic greeting of the "strange country" to which those "gypsies of the sky" are driven by the "hidden power" of their indomitable desire.

The Vivace section of Nedda's aria has had its share of detractors. According to Ernest Newman, for instance,

. . . being young and romantic, (Nedda) dismisses her gloomy thoughts and gives herself up, in a lilting ballatella, to the joy of contemplating the birds in their carefree flight through the sunlit air. The situation seems to have been created only to give the prima donna a chance to show what she can do,

---

† In the final scene, she finally "dares" to tell her husband that if he finds her "vile and unworthy," he should get rid of her and allow her to leave him. And, of course, she does brave death in trying to save her lover's life.

and the music, with its slender intellectual content, to have been written with the same object.

This is not necessarily true. The "prima donna" who is a genuine artist will "show what she can do" less by displaying "joy in contemplating the birds," than by enacting her envious admiration for their courage in defying the winds and the lightning of the stormy skies, and by communicating a feeling of kinship for their vain pursuit of the land of dreams and illusions. Nedda may be "young and romantic," but she is also a prisoner who watches the outside world from behind the bars of a jail.

The Vocal Aspects

Most of the accompanied recitative should be sung with careful attention to correct note values. Only in measures 8–12 and 15–16, where the orchestra plays long notes, is one allowed the freedom of typical recitative singing. The fermata in measure 12 must not be held too long; a delicate portamento down to the A is possible after the fermata.

The high A in measure 15 is marked "dolce" and should be attacked softly, as if in surprise, almost as if Nedda notices the beautiful summer day for the first time. To give the feeling of "sweet languor," since the composer has indicated "con dolce languore" in measure 18, the six measures (18–23) must be sung extremely legato. This serves as a strong contrast to the more excited last section of the recitative, where Nedda notices the birds and recalls how her mother used to sing as if she were talking to them. There is no need to use a chest tone in measures 22–23. Measures 26–34 must be sung especially carefully in rhythm so that no problem of coordination with the accompaniment can arise.

Though the G. Schirmer piano-vocal score indicates that the trills in measures 35–36 are optional, it does not seem possible that they can be omitted. A singer who cannot sing the trills should not attempt the aria. Most singers prefer to sing the higher notes on the second trill. Although some prefer to sing "Ah" on these trills, there is no reason why they cannot be sung *oo-ee* with the *ee* on the upper note after the trill, though some modification of these close vowels may be necessary for the upper trill. *Oo* and *ee* are vowels that resemble the singing of birds more closely than does "ah."

The instrumental introduction lasting ten measures is obviously Leoncavallo's tone painting of birds in flight, with the beating of wings indicated by the relentless arpeggios in the accompaniment. Though the first two phrases that are sung are the standard four measures in length, making up an eight-measure period, one of the characteristics of Leoncavallo's style in this opera is his use of the irregular-length phrase. He often uses a seven-measure or a nine-measure period instead of one made up of two four-measure phrases. Measures 19–25, for instance, are a seven-measure period, and measures 34–42 are a nine-measure period. Singers, accustomed to four-measure phrases so prevalent in most of the standard operatic literature, sometimes find it difficult to feel the rhythm of a seven-measure or nine-measure period, and wish to add or omit a measure. It is necessary to study the irregular-length phrases in this aria carefully to prevent musical inaccuracies.

Though the marking, "a tempo giusto senza mai affrettare," is given when the voice begins, the admonition for a precise tempo without hurrying does not mean that there cannot be a change of tempo during the aria. At measure 34, con slancio permits some acceleration; a gradual slowing down begins in measure 43 until the original tempo is reestablished in measure 48. The animando in measure 75 again permits acceleration. Note that the composer has set the word, "lampi," (lightning) to two short notes; be sure to stress the first syllable sufficiently.

The indication "con anima e passione allargando la frase e ben cantato" at measure 102 may seem to be contradictory, but it simply means a slight slowing down, but with excitement and passion. At measure 123, the ritardando should be slight. Then the final few measures of the aria leap forward with excitement, beginning with "incalzando e crescendo" at measure 129. The presto at measure 136 cannot be too fast — there are too many notes in the accompaniment. Though the accompaniment is marked "col canto" at measure 140, it is better to maintain the strict tempo of the final presto and for the voice to cut off sharply (tronco) and exactly with the accompaniment in measure 142.

The Text

Literal Translation

Recitative

1. What fire he-had in-the look! The eyes I-lowered
2. for fear that-he might-read the my thought secret!
3. Oh, if-he me were-to-surprise, brutal as he is!
4. But enough, come-now. Are these dreams fearful and foolish!
5. Oh, what beautiful sun of mid-August! I am full of life,
6. and completely languid with secret desire; not know-I what I-desire!
7. Oh, what flight of-birds, and how-many cries!
8. What do-they-seek? Where are-they-going? Who knows?
9. The mother my, who the good fortune predicted,
10. understood the their song, and to me child thus sang: Hui! Hui!

Aria

11. They-cry up-there, freely launched in flight.
12. in flight like arrows, the birds. They-defy the clouds,
13. and-the sun burning, and they-go through the paths of-the sky.
14. Let-them wander through the-atmosphere,
15. these thirsting for-blue and for splendor:
16. follow too-they, a dream, an illusion, and they-go through the clouds of-gold!

17. That mounts the wind and howls the storm,
18. with the-wings spread they-know-how everything to-defy;
19. the-rain-the lightning, nothing never them-stops,
20. and they-go over-the abysses and the seas. They-go, far-off,
21. toward a country strange that they-dream-of, perhaps,
22. and that they-seek in-vain. But the gypsies of-the sky
23. follow the-secret power that them drives, and they-go-on!

Idiomatic Translation

Recitative

1. What fire in his gaze! I lowered my eyes
2. for fear that he might read my secret thoughts!
3. Oh, what would he do if he surprised me, brutal as he is!
4. But that's enough, come now. How fearful and foolish those dreams are!
5. Oh, how beautiful the mid-August sun is! I am full of life,
6. and completely languid with secret desire; I don't know what I desire!
7. Oh, look at that flight of birds! How they cry!
8. What are they seeking? Where are they going? Who knows?
9. My mother, who was able to predict good fortune,
10. understood the songs of the birds, and when I was a child, used to sing to me like this: Hui! Hui!

Aria

11. How they cry up there, flying freely,
12. flying like arrows, those birds. They defy the clouds,
13. and the burning sun, and they fly through their paths in the sky.
14. Let them wander through the atmosphere,
15. those birds, thirsting for blue sky and for splendor;
16. they, too, follow a dream, an illusion, and they fly through clouds of gold!
17. Though the wind mounts and the storm howls,
18. with their wings spread, they defy everything;
19. neither the rain nor the lightning stops them,
20. and they fly over every abyss and every sea. They fly, far off,
21. toward a strange country that they dream of, perhaps,
22. and that they seek in vain. But these gypsies of the sky
23. follow the secret power that drives them, and they go on!

The Scenic Picture

The action takes place at an intersection of roads outside the village. The only piece of scenery mentioned in the score is the "theatre" on Stage L.*

* The score says: "On the right a travelling theatre," but this, as is usual in scenic descriptions, means "right" as seen by the audience. In our terminology, from the point of view of the actors, this means stage L.

It is quite possible to imagine a permanent theatrical structure outside a small Calabrian village, but since the composer himself, in the letter quoted on page 133, spoke of "players putting up their tents and booths," it seems more logical to think in terms of a troupe of players who live and perform as a self-contained unit. This "theatre" therefore need be nothing more than a simple platform enclosed by some crude scenic flats and by a curtain that is drawn open only for the commedia del l'arte — the play within the play — which is the major event of the second act of the opera.

We can imagine Canio owning two large carts drawn by horses and donkeys. One of these functions as a house trailer for Canio and Nedda while the other, occupied by Tonio and Peppe, has a removable wall and doubles as a theatrical platform. Both carts also serve as dressing rooms. Nedda changes her clothes in the house trailer and the men use the "theatre" cart or the area behind it. By positioning both carts on Stage L at right angles, and by providing them with step units, one obtains a compact arrangement where the onstage and offstage activities of the principal characters can be readily accommodated.

The wall, over which Silvio makes his entrance later in the first act, is located on the R. In addition, it is advantageous to have, to R of CC, a tree with a circular bench around it. Other trees are imagined in the wings and their branches are visible hanging down at the stage corners nearest the audience.

The Stage Actions Explained

During the first half of the Chorus Scene with bagpipes and bells, the comedians who participated in the earlier parade are changing their clothes: Canio and Peppe in the "theatre" cart and Nedda in the house trailer.

Some thirty or forty measures before Nedda's solo scene begins, Canio and Peppe emerge from their cart dressed in everyday clothes. They join the villagers and, Xing above the theater, proceed to the tavern which is located about a mile down the road toward the UL.

Nedda went inside her trailer soon after Canio kissed her on the forehead. Later, having changed her dress, she appears on the threshold of the cart and watches the men leave. She has been wondering all along if Canio's remarks warning the villagers not to try to make love to her might mean that he has begun to suspect her of infidelity. The thought of what would happen should her husband catch her with Silvio makes her shudder with apprehension.

Toward the end of the Chorus Scene, when the stage is already empty, she descends the steps and goes R and U around the theater, to gaze in the direction where Canio and the others have gone.

When the Recitative begins, she stands there with her back to the audience, looking over her R shoulder.

Recitative

Measures

1. She turns Clw and looks at the spot, downstage center, where her husband was standing when he made the ominous remarks to Tonio and the villagers.

4. She looks away and goes slightly DL.

7. After "segreto," she gives another quick look at the place where Canio was standing earlier, and with the next sentence takes a few rapid steps to DL.

9. She shudders, remembering the threatening sound of Canio's voice.

10. She turns Clw to face DR.

13. She walks R to below the bench.

15. She stretches her arms voluptuously and turns slowly Cclw to face the afternoon sun in the DL sky.

17. She sits down on the bench.

20. She reclines on the bench resting on her R elbow and stretching her legs toward L.

21. After "illanguidita," she strokes her R arm with her L hand and looks at the sky, enjoying the sunshine.

25. The twittering of the birds attracts her attention and she looks into the branches of the tree over her head.

26. Noticing that the birds have flown to DR, she rises and turns Clw to look in that direction.

29. She turns Cclw. The memory of her mother makes her look far away toward DL.

31. After "annunziava," she looks over her R shoulder to catch another glimpse of the birds.

32. After "canto," she looks again toward DL as if reliving the episode when her mother sang to her.

35. Since the orchestral answer to her first trill seems to have come from the birds sitting in the branches to her R, she turns Clw and takes a few steps in that direction.

36. She directs her second trill to the birds in the R trees. The answering twitter makes her laugh with pleasure.

Orchestral Introduction (10 measures)

As the orchestral introduction* begins, the imaginary flock of birds darts from the trees on the R, passes below Nedda to the treetops in the L wing, and then suddenly veers toward UR, sailing over the roof of the strolling players' stage, toward CC. Finishing their enormous aerial circle, the birds now turn toward DR and continue for a while in that direction.

Never taking her eyes off this imagined flight, Nedda duplicates its pattern on a much smaller scale. She was facing DR, but now, as the

* The measures of the Ballatella are numbered independently from those of the preceding Recitative.

introduction begins, she turns Cclw and moves DL well past CC; she then continues to turn Cclw and goes UR to CC, remaining there until the ninth measure, when she finishes her Cclw circle by turning once more to look toward DR.

From here on, the outline of the Ballatella's action adheres very closely to the form of the poem.

> Stridono lassù, liberamente
> Lanciati a vol, a vol come frecce, gli augel.
> Disfidano le nubi e il sol concente,
> E vanno, e vanno per le vie del ciel.
>
> Lasciatelli vagar per l'atmosfera,
> Questi assetati d'azzurro e di splendor:
> Seguono anch'essi un sogno, una chimera,
> E vanno, e vanno fra le nubi d'or!
>
> Che incalzi il vento e latri la tempesta,
> Con l'ali aperte san tutto sfidar;
> La pioggia, i lampi, nulla mai li arresta,
> E vanno, e vanno sugli abissi e i mar.
>
> Vanno laggiù verso un paese strano
> Che sognan forse e che cercano in van.
> Ma i boëmi del ciel seguon l'arcano
> Poter che li sospinge . . . e van!
> E van! e van! e van!

Each of the four quatrains has a distinctive mood. The first is the least personal; the next three are increasingly emotional.

The common feature of the four stanzas is the repeated "e vanno" that appears, refrainlike, at the end of each quatrain. It is important that this recurring verbal "event" be exteriorized by an appropriate physical movement.

First Quatrain (mm. 11–42)

During the first two lines of the poem, Nedda continues to watch the birds as they dart "like arrows" in the August sky. To illustrate the "clouds" and the "boiling sun" in the third line, she turns Cclw and looks toward the sky DL, as if gazing after a few birds that have strayed in that direction. With "e vanno, e vanno," Nedda turns RSB and backs UL while pointing toward the birds circling around in the DR area.

Second Quatrain (mm. 43–74)

The backing movement at the end of the first stanza brought Nedda closer to the DR corner of the traveling theater, so that now, in the beginning of the second stanza, she can go L (or slightly DL) and sit on one of the risers that lead to the apron of the stage. (If there are no risers, or other convenient place to sit, Nedda must of course remain standing.) The decrease in musical energy — indicated by the dolce and the poco allargando — should nevertheless be acted out by leaning against the corner of the structure or by some other form of relaxation in Nedda's posture and attitude.

With "questi assetati," Nedda looks over her R shoulder in the direction of the birds' flight. The words "un sogno, una chimera" are crucial in emphasizing her own dream of freedom. She should therefore turn away from the birds and gaze toward some unattainable goal in the far distance. With the second "e vanno, e vanno," she rises and moves excitedly toward DR.

Third Quatrain (mm. 75–101)

This "stormy" stanza is directed toward DL. It begins with an LSB turn coupled with a backing movement toward UR. This opens up a long diagonal line toward the DL corner and makes it possible to execute a series of walks in that direction. These can occur with the orchestral chords on "tempesta" (m. 80), "sfidar" (m. 86), "pioggia" (m. 88), and "mai" (m. 91). The earlier "l'ali aperte" (mm. 82–83) permits an illustrative gesture imitating the open wings of a bird.

With "e vanno," in the ninety-fourth measure, Nedda turns Clw; on the word "mar" (m. 98), she goes UR toward the DR corner of the theater structure and turns slightly Cclw at the end of the sustained G♯.

Fourth Quatrain (mm. 102–142)

This entire stanza is sung in the direction of the "paese strano," the strange land of Nedda's dreams which she imagines as being located toward DR beyond the walls of the auditorium. She is drawn there by the "arcano poter," the magic power of her love, and her first walk in that direction is timed to coincide with the wistful "cercano in van" in measures 114–118.

In the context of a full production of this opera, the malformed Tonio must overhear the end of Nedda's song without, however, being noticed by her. He enters from UL and becomes visible near the DR corner of the theater. This can happen as early as measure 118, but if Nedda is not to notice him, it is essential that her walk, which begins in measure 114, be energetic enough to take her to the R portion of the stage, well past the CC line. When this scene is done separately without involving Tonio, all this, of course, becomes much less important.

During the final series of "in van" exclamations, Nedda moves farther and farther to DR, ending the Ballatella in the DR corner of the stage.

Contrary to custom, Gilda here wears a dress of the late Italian Renaissance, appropriate for the setting of this opera.

"Caro nome"
from *Rigoletto,* Act I, Scene II
by GIUSEPPE VERDI

The Drama

Verdi's Rigoletto, composed in 1850 and first performed in 1851, is based on Victor Hugo's drama *Le Roi s'amuse,* a title usually translated as *The King's Amusement.* Slated to be premiered in Venice, the opera immediately ran into difficulties with the Austrian authorities who were then ruling the greater part of Northern Italy. In view of the revolutionary spirit that was stirring at the time, the Austrian censor saw no point in inflaming the passions of local patriots by permitting a presentation of an opera that dealt with a plot to assassinate a French king. He undoubtedly felt that if the Italian composers insisted on putting to music the killing of rulers, they should concentrate on their own people. The action was therefore refashioned to take place in Italy, and Francis the First of France was transformed into an unspecified Duke of Mantua.

From Victor Hugo's point of view, this transformation was nothing short of sacrilege. The great French poet and dramatist put enormous emphasis on verisimilitude of local color and exactness of period. His "king" lives among courtiers bearing the most noble and authentic French names, and "amuses" himself in circumstances of the most painstaking historical accuracy.

As a matter of fact, Hugo tried his utmost to prevent Paris audiences from hearing *Rigoletto,* and it took several years of wrangling and a decision of the provincial court before the opera could be mounted on the boards of the Théâtre Italien.

One readily agrees that the story is more convincing if it takes place at the court of a ruler with the unlimited prestige and authority of a sixteenth-century French monarch. But opera goers are quite willing to grant the necessary degree of high-handed despotism to a head of even a small Italian duchy. To make room for musical expansion, most of the historical niceties so dear to Hugo would have been omitted from the opera in any event. It took quite a bit of prodding before Hugo could be persuaded to attend a performance of *Rigoletto,* but it is pleasant to be told that having once heard and seen it, he became one of Verdi's, and the opera's, most fervent admirers.

In the process of transformation, many details of the story had to be changed, but Hugo's original play still contains a number of features that can help us toward a better understanding of the opera's characters. This is particularly true of Gilda, for she is far from being the innocent and pure maiden that most opera goers imagine her to be. Her behavior

147

in the second act conforms well enough with this idea; and her self-immolation at the end of the opera can also be interpreted as an extravagant act of romantically inspired heroism. The events of the third act, however, and particularly her mode of life in the interval between the third and fourth acts, point to a less sugary and more complex personality.

It may be objected that since the "Caro nome" takes place in the second act, the character traits that Gilda displays in the later sections of the opera would not affect the interpretation of that aria. It must be evident, however, that the second-act Gilda must have within her all the qualities and defects that govern her reactions to what happens the next day in the third act, and during the next thirty days that elapse before the last act.

A virtuous girl who is capable of becoming the mistress of a married man; who will live with him for a month, and who will continue to love him in spite of his obvious infidelities; this girl feels and expresses herself differently from a pure maiden who is an innocent victim of malevolent fate. To come to grips with Gilda's personality we will try to assemble and evaluate the available evidence as it is given in the opera as well as in Hugo's play.

Let us spell out what the opera tells us about Gilda and then see to what extent Hugo's drama can help to round out this knowledge.

The Opera

Gilda lives with Giovanna — an older woman who acts as her housekeeper and governess — in a modest house with a little garden surrounded by a high wall. Her mother is dead, but she has a father who loves her to distraction. This father, although he visits her every evening, is very secretive and refuses to tell her anything about himself, not even his name. Although Gilda has been living here for three months, she has seen very little of the city, since she is permitted to leave the house only on Sundays when Giovanna escorts her to church. Gilda is very devoted to her father, but, in view of his morbid preoccupation with her safety, is afraid to tell him that every Sunday a handsome young man has been flirting with her in church and following her home. She finds this mysterious pursuer exceedingly attractive and, in her enforced solitude, thinks and dreams of him constantly.

One evening this young man — who is, of course, none other than the Duke in disguise — succeeds in gaining access to the garden unseen by either Gilda or her father. After the father leaves, Giovanna — who has just pocketed a generous bribe from the Duke — hints to Gilda that her admirer may be a wealthy lord. Gilda assures her that she does not want him to be a prince. The poorer he is, she asserts, the more she will love him, and continues by saying: "Whether awake or dreaming, I am constantly calling him, and my ecstatic soul proclaims . . ." It is at this point that the Duke, having finally ushered out the greedy duenna, finishes Gilda's sentence by saying: "I love you!"

This sudden, totally unexpected and quasi-miraculous appearance of her Prince Charming, coupled with the disappearance of her governess, produces an overwhelming effect upon the girl. She begs the young man to leave at once, but eventually the Duke's eloquent protestations succeed in calming her. She cannot help but be touched by his tender wooing and is forced to admit that she does indeed love him. Now her curiosity is aroused. If he won't tell how he managed to enter the garden, let him at least reveal his name and occupation. Having overheard the girl's conversation with Giovanna, the Duke blurts out the first name that occurs to him — Gualtier Maldè — and claims to be nothing but a needy student.

At this point a noise is heard outside the garden gate. Afraid that her father is about to return, Gilda orders Giovanna to let her admirer escape in the opposite direction, by way of the house. After a hurried and passionate farewell duet, the Duke departs, leaving the girl breathless and completely overcome by her soul-shattering experience. In the "Caro nome" which follows here, Gilda repeats Gualtier Maldè's "beloved name," promising that it will be forever engraved in her heart and swearing to be true to her lover to her dying day ("fin l'ultimo sospir") an oath that, in the final scene, she fulfills to the letter.

The Play

Up to this point, Hugo's drama is by and large in full agreement with the libretto of the opera. There are some minor differences. Gilda — called Blanche in the play — has been with her father for two rather than three months and has gone to church only eight times. This is obviously of very little importance. There are, however, a few details that add to our knowledge of the total situation. Until she joined her father in the big city, Blanche had been living in the little provincial town of Chinon (about 175 miles southwest of Paris) where all her neighbors were under the impression that she was an orphan. Her father is aware that it would have been safer to let her stay there, but he simply could not bear to be separated from her any longer.

This explains why Gilda has been in Mantua for such a short time and also hints that Rigoletto sent for his daughter as soon as she had emerged from childhood. As the girl herself mentions in the last scene of the play, she is not quite sixteen years old.

Producers and makeup artists should note that, in the play, while caressing his daughter's head, the jester remarks:

> Oh! Les beaux cheveaux noirs! Enfant vous ètiez blonde.
> (Oh! The lovely raven hair! Yet, as a child you were a blonde.)
> Qui le croirait?
> (Who would believe it?)

These words do not occur in the opera's text, and, by quoting them here, we do not mean to suggest that all Gildas should have dark hair. We are mentioning this only in order to counteract the once so prevalent conventional notion that Gilda *must* be a blonde whether or not it suits her complexion and personality.

Tenors, stage directors, and conductors will be interested in Hugo's dialogue and stage direction at the very end of the King's scene with Blanche:

LE ROI — THE KING

Un seul baiser, Blanche, sur tes beaux yeux!
(A single kiss, my Blanche, upon your lovely eyes!)

BLANCHE

(*faisant quelque résistance*)
(*resisting feebly*)
Non, non!
(No, no!)
(*The King kisses her and follows the duenna into the house.*)

A passionate kiss — the first she has ever received — is the best possible motivation and explanation for Gilda's breathlessly ecstatic state throughout most of her aria. The orchestral postlude of the "Addio, addio" duet that precedes the aria is, unfortunately, quite short. There is just enough time for the Duke to kiss and run off stage; but *only* if both singers honor Verdi's notated duration of the last note of the duet — a half note which, at the prescribed tempo, lasts less than half a second. Every conductor knows how difficult it is to persuade singers that final tones of this type need not be sustained for several measures. These singers should be made to realize that the dramatic effect of the duet and the aria is greatly enhanced by a short final note, a passionate kiss, and a hurried departure.

In the drama, Blanche remains for a while gazing after her lover, but the only words she utters thereafter are:

> Gaucher Mahiet!* Dear name of my beloved . . .
> I shall engrave you in my heart!

It is upon this meager foundation that Verdi constructed his immortal aria. No wonder that a great opera survives longer than a great play.

To continue with our recital of the events of Gilda's life, we know that after the "Caro nome" she goes inside the house and retires for the night, and that a while later the courtiers, who are under the impression that she is Rigoletto's mistress, kidnap her and take her to the Duke's palace. Left alone, in a sumptuously decorated room and presumably under lock and key, she spends the rest of the night in worry and agitation. Next morning this room is entered by the young man who, the evening before, told her that he was a humble student, but who now is attired as a nobleman. Somewhat later — and this is her first appearance in the opera's third act — she runs on stage into a room full of strangers, sees her father wearing a most ridiculous outfit, and rushes into his arms shaken by sobs.

---

* Gaucher Mahiet is the alias the King gives to Blanche. Since it is unpronounceable in Italian, Verdi's liberettist changed it to Gualtier Maldè.

When her father asks why she is weeping, she whispers to him that she is much too ashamed to speak of it in the presence of others.

Although this is never spelled out, either in the opera or in the play, everyone — her father, the courtiers, and the audience — knows that this girl has just been seduced.

We have no intention of prying into the details of what happened inside that room. Even so, there are at least two legitimate questions which puzzle many opera goers and which are of real concern to the singer who must impersonate Gilda: What was her reaction when she discovered the true identity of her Gualtier Maldè? When and how did she learn of her father's profession and of the fact that he is a part of the Duke's household?

Fortunately, Hugo's drama helps to answer these questions. Instead of the opera's opening aria of the Duke and the Chorus in which the courtiers tell of the abduction of Rigoletto's mistress, the third act of the play opens with a scene in which the kidnapped girl is brought before the man whom she knows as Gaucher Mahiet, and is informed of his true identity. The King — when he realizes that it is Blanche and not Tribou-let's mistress who stands before him — sends the courtiers away and remains alone with the girl. Here, in greatly condensed form, is what transpires in that scene.

THE KING

My Blanche!

BLANCHE

Gaucher Mahiet! Oh, Heaven!

THE KING

I declare, the tricks of fortune are indeed amazing!
My Blanche! My beautiful! My heart's delight!
Come to my arms!

BLANCHE

The King? Forgive me, Sire . . . Whoever you are,
I beg you to have mercy . . .

THE KING

Mercy on you, whom I adore?

He proceeds to tell her how unreasonable she is to prefer a needy student to the King of France. The idea makes him laugh.

BLANCHE

Oh, how he laughs! While I would die for shame!

The King then enunciates his philosophy of life, ending with:

For this is wisdom: honor Heaven above,
Eat, drink, be merry, and crown all with love!

He describes to Blanche the absolute power of a French monarch, adding:

I am the King, my Blanche, and you will be my Queen!

BLANCHE

Your queen? But what about your wife?

THE KING

Good Lord! She's just my wife! You'll be the one I love, the mistress of
my heart!

BLANCHE

Your mistress? Never! My father shall protect me!

THE KING

My buffoon! My poor buffoon, my fool, my Triboulet? He's mine,
he is my property, my slave! He wishes what I wish!

BLANCHE (*crying*)

O, my poor father!

THE KING

Come, dry your tears and say again, you love me!

BLANCHE

I love you not! You frighten me, my Lord!

THE KING (*embracing her*)

Are you afraid?

BLANCHE (*resisting*)

Have pity!

THE KING (*embracing her more passionately*)

Well, at least one tender kiss!

BLANCHE (*struggling*)

No! No!

THE KING (*aside, laughing*)

A curious case!

BLANCHE

I beg you, let me go! (*She sees the door to the King's room, rushes
in, and closes it violently.*)

THE KING

What luck, I've got the key!
(*Taking a key from his key ring, he opens the door with an energetic
push and locks it behind him.*)

Clearly, Blanche has neither the energy nor the will to resist the King
for long. It is only after the lover has had his way, and the deed is done
that, seized by panic, she rushes out of the room and runs directly into
her father's arms.

The next episode in the drama, where Blanche confesses all to Triboulet,
is in most respects identical with the Gilda-Rigoletto scene as we know
it from the third act of the opera; except that when Triboulet asks God
to destroy the King in punishment for his unspeakable crimes, Blanche,
in a pathetic aside, lifts her eyes heavenward, saying:

Grant it not Heaven! For I love him still.

As the curtain falls on the third act of the opera, Rigoletto and Gilda leave the stage and presumably the palace. Neither Verdi nor his librettist saw any reason to offend the sensibilities of the operatic audiences by suggesting that the "dishonored" maiden would remain in the palace and continue to share the bed of the man who had treated her so cruelly. Victor Hugo did not have these scruples. His drama spells out quite plainly what is only hinted at in the opera; namely, that both father and daughter remain at court; that Blanche becomes the King's mistress; and that Triboulet continues to play the fool, and pretends to be quite content with his daughter's semiofficial status as his Highness's current favorite. All this becomes abundantly clear as we compare the opening conversation of the next act of the opera with the corresponding episode of the play.

The Opera

RIGOLETTO

You love him?

GILDA

Always . . .

RIGOLETTO

And yet, I have given you enough time to recover from this folly.

GILDA

I love him!

RIGOLETTO

A woman's heart is unfathomable! O, the vile seducer! But you shall be avenged, my Gilda!

GILDA

Have mercy, father!

RIGOLETTO

And if you were certain that he deceives you, would you still love him?

GILDA

I don't know, but I am sure that he adores me.

RIGOLETTO

He? Well then, come here and watch . . . (*takes her to a crack in the wall*)

The Play (*in slightly condensed form*)

TRIBOULET

You love him still?

BLANCHE

Forever . . .

TRIBOULET

Yet I gave you sufficient time to waken from this dream!

BLANCHE

'Tis true.

TRIBOULET

Who can explain a woman's heart?
How can you love him?

BLANCHE

That I cannot know.
There is no reason, father. Let me tell you this: Though he is cruel,
    and you are always kind, I'd die for him as surely as for you!

TRIBOULET

You say yourself, he's cruel . . .

BLANCHE

But he loves me!

TRIBOULET

Come, come!

BLANCHE

He told me so! He swore a solemn oath!
He is a valiant King, so brave . . .

TRIBOULET

He is a scoundrel!

BLANCHE

You said that you forgave him . . .

TRIBOULET

I was lying! I needed time to set the trap for vengeance . . . but
    soon . . .

BLANCHE

It's now a month, and during all this time you seemed to love the
    King!

TRIBOULET

It's easy to pretend while one is plotting . . .

BLANCHE

Please have mercy, father!

TRIBOULET

And if you were to see with your own eyes that he deceives you?

BLANCHE

No, this cannot be! For just last night he told me he adored me!

TRIBOULET

Last night, you say? What time?

BLANCHE

About this hour.

TRIBOULET

Then look inside and witness your disgrace . . . (*takes her to a crack
    in the wall*)

The Music

The sixty-seven measures that constitute the main body of this aria are
cast in the shape of an extended song form — A-B-C-A — and are framed
by an Introductory Recitative and a Coda. The complete eighty-five
measures are thus divided into:

This fairly conventional arrangement is complicated by some rather unusual aspects of its B section, several portions of which repeat and elaborate musical material that was heard earlier. The main subject of the aria consists of a sequence of four descending scales which are presented in the sixteen measures of Section A, first in a variation by the orchestra and then in their unadorned form by the voice.

Section B begins with a contrasting, ascending theme, but, quite surprisingly, culminates in the same final scales as Section A. One might say that this phrase

forms a refrain that appears twice in Section A (first in the orchestra, then in the voice), three times in Section B (in vocal variations), and again twice when Section A returns (first in the orchestra, then in the voice). Except when this refrain is first sung each vocal and orchestral repetition presents it in a different version — a remarkable demonstration of Verdi's skill in devising exciting vocal and orchestral embellishments for a tune of utmost simplicity.

The musical function of the Introduction is to serve as a bridge from the D-flat major of the preceding passionate love scene to the E major that dominates the mood of the aria like an idée fixe. While vocal and orchestral variations provide much of the musical charm of this scene, its dramatic climax is reached in the second part of Section C with Gilda's

* Be sure that you do *not* count the upbeat at the Allegro Moderato as a measure.

solemn oath of "fidelity to the grave" accompanied by harmonies of almost religious intensity and ending in one of Verdi's most extended vocal cadenzas.

sa - - - - - - - rà!

The Vocal Aspects

Gilda, whose contact with members of the opposite sex has been almost nil except for her father, has just been wooed in a most passionate fashion by a skillful and determined lover. He has given her what is surely her first nonplatonic kiss. Left alone, she is still very much shaken by the experience. Verdi indicates her excitement and breathlessness in this aria by putting breaths in the middle of words, and between words in a phrase — and then combining the end of a phrase with a following one *without* a breath. All too often this aria is sung solely as an exercise in precise, florid singing, and not as an expression of the feelings of a young girl whose first contact with sexual love is an almost shattering experience, whose emotions are almost beyond her control, and whose breath comes in little gasps. But that is what Verdi meant in writing the vocal line of this aria in such an unorthodox fashion.

It is entertaining and informative to compare various artists' interpretations of the aria. Let us take but two of the many recordings: that by Maria Callas (Angel 35518) and that by Reri Grist (Angel 3718). Though to many ears they may sound totally different, there are similarities. The Callas recording employs more pronounced Italianate portamenti (mm. 20, 22, 24, 26, 32, etc.). She also sings the aria more as Verdi wrote it, and she does not fear the low notes in the cadenza in measure 46. Both ladies sing the cadenza in measure 60 identically, interpolating a high D♯ and a long high B. One might say that the Callas recording seems to be more of a dramatic rendition, showing Gilda's excitement and confusion more than the Grist recording, which is more subdued.

To indicate Gilda's breathlessness and excitement to the fullest extent, one can insert very tiny catch breaths during the rests in measures 19, 21, 23, 25, 27, and others. The binding together of phrases is enhanced by a delicate portamento, as Miss Callas has done. The danger lies in the temptation to overdo this device. Every singer must make a decision as to how much to "scoop."

Measure 41 is often sung with a rearrangement of words to permit the high C to be sung on an *ah* vowel, like this:

no - me, ah,   ca - ro no - me tuo sa -

The cadenza in measure 46 can be performed in the following fashion by those sopranos who do not wish to sing the low B and C♯:

rà,   ah, _____

The ornamental vocal line in measures 47–49, with its insistent upward leaps of a sixth for almost three measures, must again reflect in some way Gilda's inner turmoil and agitation. A slight ritardando in measure 49, (not indicated in some piano-vocal scores), followed by an a tempo in measure 50, is useful to make the high skips easier, and to give the aria a new impetus with the unrelenting sixteenth-note figures that follow.

Measures 54–55 are often performed with a slight alteration of the words, an *ah* (instead of "ca–") being sung beginning with the third six-teenth-note of measure 54. Then "ca-ro" is sung on the lower octave A♯ and B in measure 55, with one note for each syllable instead of "–ro" on both notes as printed. There does not seem to be any particular advantage in this, since the *ah* vowel appears on the same notes in either instance.

Measures 60–61 are almost always sung very much like the following, instead of Verdi's cadenza:

tuo _____ sa -   -   -   -   -   -   -   -

-    -   -   -   -   -   -   -   - rà!

When Gilda is sung by a coloratura soprano, the addition of the high D♯ may be desirable.

The many little trills on short notes (mm. 29, 34, 35, 74, 76) are best not even attempted by a singer who cannot execute a short, fast, clear trill. They are another indication of Verdi's desire to show Gilda's state of mind — she is so excited she cannot keep her voice steady. The long trill for two and a half measures on the last note presents a challenge — many sopranos find it difficult if not impossible to sustain a trill for that long a time without letting it become a rather uneven shake. A poor trill is less desirable than no trill at all.

One final word about tempo seems appropriate: sung too slowly, only as a showpiece, this aria tends to seem overly long and almost tiresome.

The Text

Literal Translation

Recitative

1. Gualtier Maldè! Name of him so beloved,
2. yourself engrave in-the heart loving!

Aria:

3. Dear name that the my heart made first to-beat,
4. the delights of-the-love to-me you-must always remind!
5. With-the thought the my desire to you always will-fly,
6. and even the-last sigh, dear name, yours will-be.
7. The my desire to you always will-fly,
8. even the-last sigh yours will-be. Gualtier Maldè!

Idiomatic Translation

Recitative

1. Gualtier Maldè! The name of him so beloved to me,
2. your name is engraved on my loving heart!

Aria:

3. Dear name that first made my heart beat,
4. You must always remind me of the delights of love!
5. In my thoughts my desire will always fly to you,
6. and even with my last breath, I will speak your name.
7. My desire will always fly to you.
8. and even my last breath will be yours. Gualtier Maldè!

The Scenic Picture

Gilda's house and garden are on Stage R and a narrow street on Stage L. They are separated by a high wall which features a gate in its downstage portion. There is a second storey terrace on the garden side with access stairs near the wall. When Gilda stands on the left side of the terrace she is visible to the people in the street. A door leads from the terrace into the second storey of the house. Another door, leading from the garden into the lower floor of the house, is located in the UR wall of the house. A garden bench, Stage R, and a lighted lantern suspended from the UR wall of the house complete the setting.

The Stage Actions Explained

Recitative (mm. 1–10)

For a few seconds Gilda stands completely stunned at the foot of the

terrace steps and gazes as if transfixed at the DR door through which her
lover departed a moment earlier. She feels that something quite miracu-
lous has just happened to her. The man of whom she had been dreaming
has just appeared out of nowhere and his tender caresses made her head
spin. Just as she was hoping, he turned out to be a poor student; and
then, before leaving her, he placed on her lips a passionate kiss, a kiss
that made her feel as if all the stars were coming down from heaven.

It is only with the enharmonic change in the third measure of the
recitative (when the F♭ changes into the E♮) that she is able to take a
few steps toward DR and to utter his name, the dear name she knows she
will cherish the rest of her life.

Aria (mm. 1–85)

Three ideas will now occupy Gilda's mind: the name of her beloved,
the delight of being loved by him, and the all-consuming determination to
belong to him until her last breath. This last thought does not occur to her
immediately, but once it is enunciated (in measure twenty-one of the
aria) it quickly becomes the dominant idea which she repeats again and
again. One almost feels that Gilda has a premonition that before too long
she will, in fact, breathe her last breath to save her lover's life.

Measures

11–18. During this orchestral section, each of the four phrases featuring
the descending scales receives a separate acting interpretation.
There are four "moves" each lasting two measures.

11, 12. Gilda goes DR toward the door through which her lover departed.

13, 14. She turns Cclw and, stretching her arms behind her back, leans
against the door.

15, 16. She takes several steps toward UL, retracing her way and contemplating the area near the terrace steps where she was kissed by
Gualtier Maldè.

17, 18. She turns Clw, goes to above the bench, and sits on its UR corner
while supporting herself on her outstretched L arm.

19. She looks DL toward heaven.

22. With the portamento (from low E to high G♯), she turns slightly
Clw to look toward DR, as if imagining "love's delights" to hover
in that direction.

26. She rises to the R, turns LSB, and backs slightly toward UR.

30. With the crescendo on the long F♯, she turns RSB to look in the
direction of the door.

31–33. This is the first appearance of the "Fidelity to death" idea. The
words "l'ultimo sospiro" and "tuo" should be reinforced with
some gentle, girlish gestures.

35.   *(3rd quarter)* She turns Cclw and goes slowly DL, Xing above the bench.

36.   She continues to move DL while singing.

37.   She reaches the area near the garden gate during the long F♯.

38.   With the G♯ she turns RSB as if again trying to visualize her lover beyond the DR door.

42.   *(3rd quarter)* She goes R, timing herself so as to arrive below the bench by the end of measure 44.

45.   During the sustained high F♯ she turns Cclw as if following in the sky (from R to L) the "flight of her desire."

47.   She sits down facing toward DL.

51.   Still seated, she turns Clw and repeats the preceding measure with more emphasis, as if addressing it more directly to her Gualtier Maldè.

52.   She rises and takes a few steps to the R, stopping just beyond the R edge of the bench.

54.   With the ascending scale, she turns LSB and backs slightly.

56.   She goes L, Xing above the bench, to CC.

58.   *(4th quarter)* She turns RSB so as to face DR.

59.   This is the most emphatic sentence of the aria. It must be sung and acted as if Gilda were pronouncing a sacred oath.

60.   The cadenza must be sung not as a purely vocal display, but as an ecstatic affirmation: "tuo sarà." Yes, my last breath will indeed "belong to you!"

61.   *(3rd quarter)* She turns Clw and goes UR to the lighted lantern which was hung on the wall earlier by Giovanna.

63.   Gilda takes the lantern with her R hand, and while turning Cclw (to face DR) passes it into her L hand.

64.   She utters the "dear name" in the direction of the DR door.

65.   *(3rd quarter)* She turns Cclw and goes L to the edge of the steps leading to the terrace.

67.   She turns Clw to sing toward DR.

70.   She turns Cclw.

71.   She starts ascending the steps.

73.   Having reached the top of the terrace, she turns Clw and passes the lantern into her R hand. In complete productions of *Rigoletto,* when the chorus is present, Gilda must be sure to stand near the terrace wall so that her left profile is clearly visible to the courtiers.

79.   She goes R a few steps along the front railing of the terrace, always looking toward DR.

81.   After she stops singing, she remains for a while gazing at the DR door.

83.   She turns Clw and exits through the center door of the house.

The fashions of the 13th century are not complimentary to the figure of the average Elisabeth. The costume depicted here is more flattering. The decorative design was adapted from an infant's swaddling clothes of that time.

"Dich, theure Halle"
from *Tannhäuser,* Act II
by RICHARD WAGNER

The Drama

Elisabeth, the niece of the reigning Landrave Hermann of Thuringia, is a young woman of unusual self-assurance and candor. These qualities manifest themselves in her frank avowal of personal feelings in the duet with Tannhäuser, as well as in her spirited defense of him later in the second act. We note also that even when she ventures outside the confines of the castle in the third act, she is not accompanied by a duenna, or any female servant or confidante.

Elisabeth's age is not mentioned either in the score or in the libretto of the opera, but judging by her independent behavior, one can imagine that, unlike most other operatic heroines, she is closer to twenty-five than to eighteen.

The action of the opera takes place at the beginning of the thirteenth century, at a time when singing competitions conducted by minstrels and knights were a favorite form of courtly entertainment. The "theure Halle," (the beloved hall) which Elisabeth greets so joyfully in this aria, is located in the Wartburg, the Landrave's sumptuous castle near the Thuringian city of Eisenach. At the festivities held there in the past Elisabeth had been functioning as the official hostess. Among the singers who took part in these contests was Heinrich Tannhäuser whose personality and eloquent singing made a powerful impression on Elisabeth, and who in turn was strongly attracted to the young woman.

We are not told why Tannhäuser decided to leave the Wartburg and to seek his fortune elsewhere. We can only guess that he saw no prospect of satisfying his sensual desires in the rather austere atmosphere of the Thuringian court and that he got bored with the insipid virtuous love songs of his fellow minstrels. Tannhäuser's departure was a severe blow to the lovely Elisabeth. She soon lost interest in the musical entertainments sponsored by the court, and the reason for her absence from the singing competitions was readily guessed by her uncle, as well as by his guests and the other participants. Tannhäuser, in the meantime, found his way to the Venusberg and to the sinful embraces of the heathen goddess.

How long Tannhäuser remained in the Venusberg is a matter of conjecture. The medieval legends give us two versions: one speaks of one year and the other of seven years. In the opera almost everyone remarks on the "long time" that absence had lasted. Even so, seven years appear excessive and if a choice is to be made, one year would seem to be the more likely.

At the end of the first act, Tannhäuser is told of Elisabeth's love for him. He is stunned by the mention of her "sweet name," and is overjoyed at the prospect of seeing the girl whose feelings for him are so clearly apparent to the entire Thuringian court.

At some point before the second act begins, Elisabeth discovers that the minstrel-knight whom she missed so acutely has returned to the Wartburg. Her reunion with Tannhäuser occurs in the Duet that follows immediately upon her aria.

The exact timing of the second act in relation to the first cannot be given with absolute precision. Considering the natural impatience of the young lovers, one would expect this to take place at the earliest opportunity after Tannhäuser's return. The arrangements in connection with the singing contest, however, present certain difficulties. The contest itself is not the problem since it was probably planned long before Tannhäuser's unexpected reappearance. But one wonders how the Landgrave's guests have learned that Elisabeth, who has not been seen at these events for many months, would again be "des Festes Fürstin" (the queen of the festivities). For that is the reason, as the Landgrave tells his niece, why on this occasion the realm's nobles are flocking to the Wartburg in such unusually great numbers. In the beginning of the thirteenth century, it must have taken at least several days before the startling news of Elisabeth's presence at the contest could have reached Eisenach and the country estates of the various Thuringian nobles.

The Music

This aria of 123 measures begins with the rise of the curtain in the sixty-seventh measure of the orchestral introduction to the second act.* To end this aria one adds, as an extra measure, a fortissimo G-major chord.

It is in binary form — two Stanzas followed by a Coda — and is highlighted with great emphasis by the restatement of its main theme in the seventy-seventh measure. The two stanzas are by no means identical, for not only is the second one much shorter than the first — forty measures as against seventy-four — but there are a number of other points of asymmetry and divergence. These are best studied in the following schematic presentation.

Stanza 1–74 measures

1. Orchestra
   Introduction (mm. 1–2)
   Main theme (mm. 3–10)
2. First connecting link:
   Declamatory vocal phrase
   (mm. 11–17)

Stanza 2–40 measures

1. Voice and orchestra
   Introduction (mm. 75–76)
   Main theme (mm. 77–84)
2. (Omitted)

* Measure one begins ten measures before the entrance of the voice.

3. Orchestra
   Second section of the
   main theme leading to
   D major (mm. 18–25)
4. Second connecting link:
   Declamatory vocal phrase
   leading to E minor
   (mm. 26–34)
5. Voice and orchestra
   Sustained half of the
   subsidiary theme in E
   minor (35–54)
   Orchestra bridge (mm. 55–60)
6. Voice and orchestra
   Agitated half of the
   subsidiary theme in E minor
   leading to the dominant of
   G major (mm. 61–74)

3. Voice and orchestra
   Second section of the
   main theme leading to
   A minor (mm. 85–92)
4. (Omitted)

5. (Omitted)

6. Voice and orchestra
   Agitated subsidiary theme
   in A minor leading to the
   G major Coda (mm. 93–115)

7. Orchestra
   Coda (mm. 115–123)*

The first thing we notice is that Stanza 2 does not have the two declamatory sections featured in Stanza 1, but Wagner compensates for this
by adding a vocal line to both sections of the main theme. Even more
significantly, the first section of the subsidiary theme appears only in
Stanza 1. But there is a good reason for this. This portion of the music and
text provides the only contrasting episode in what is essentially an ecstatic-
ally jubilant scene. Wagner obviously felt that a return to the unhappy
mood would not be justified either from a psychological or musical point
of view. To compensate for it, he elongates the agitated section of the
subsidiary theme in Stanza 2. He also makes certain that the orchestral
Coda provides a counterweight to the instrumental opening of Stanza 2,
thus restoring the equilibrium in the duration of the various episodes of
the aria.

Turning to the words and their musical setting, we find a surprisingly
asymmetrical distribution of the four rhymed quatrains among the various
structural parts of the aria. The first quatrain is carried in an almost recitative fashion by the two declamatory sections; the second one — with
its recollection of past unhappiness — is quite logically entrusted to the
cantabile E-minor portion of the subsidiary theme. It is with the third
quatrain that the surprises begin. This quatrain is the only one that is
sung twice; first during the agitated section of the subsidiary theme and

* The music of the Coda repeats the musical phrase that ended the first act. It
refers to Tannhäuser's joyful anticipation of his reunion with Elisabeth.

then immediately after (and quite unexpectedly) with the restatement of the main theme. The fourth quatrain — with its repeated exclamations of "Sei mir gegrüsst" in the più mosso A-minor section, adds still further to the emotional excitement and helps to give the ending of this aria a strong flavor of what the Germans call *Schwärmerei:* an almost hysterical and certainly exaggerated aura of romantic exaltation.

The Vocal Aspects

One of the snares into which most singers fall is the desire to sing too heavily in the middle voice. Lighter voices are especially prone to this tendency. When a lyric soprano attempts to perform arias that require a more robust quality, her temptation is to sing everything that lies in the middle range too heavily and this takes its toll when higher notes appear. A cursory examination of "Dich, theure Halle" would lead one to think that it is not difficult vocally. Yet it is not often that one hears the *last two phrases* of the aria sung well. Why? Even when the optional high notes are sung (thus requiring the singer to sing a B in the penultimate phrase), one would not expect this to be difficult for the average soprano with a normally developed high range. But what is so often forgotten is that it is not the high notes that cause the difficulty, but those many E's, F's, and G's that come before it. These notes are often sung too heavily, and the combination of having many of these notes in the upper middle range, and having to hold some of them a rather long time, tires the singer to the point where the last two phrases become fiendishly difficult. The above remarks are borne out in the recording of the aria by Elizabeth Grümmer (Angel 3620), in which it is sung more than adequately until the end, where the singer's stamina fails her for the crucial high note.

From the very beginning, the singer who attempts this aria must pace herself. The first phrase, sung unaccompanied except for one forte chord in the strings, need not be shouted fortissimo. It is more free in tempo than the long introduction, and the singer is not required to give her all. Measures 25–28 should be sung in tempo, so that a steady tempo is established by the singer before the orchestra enters. Since the accompaniment is piano and pianissimo, all the E♮'s and D's from measures 25 to 50 can be sung without using full voice.

The F♯ in measure 69, and the G's in measures 72 and 74 need not be sung with full power, either. From measure 78 to the end, there is little rest for the voice, and it is here that care must be taken to hold back a little. The exciting rhythmic drive of the accompaniment tends to lure the singer into singing too heavily, and at this point she must not give way to temptation. Wagner was careful to arrange his dynamic markings so that the orchestral outbursts come either between the vocal phrases or only when the singer is given a note high enough to be heard easily over the orchestra. Where the voice could easily be covered, the dynamics in the accompaniment are almost always mezzo piano or piano. A sympathetic conductor can do much to prevent the singer from being overwhelmed, especially in the two "Sei mir gegrüsst" phrases (mm. 93–96 and 97–100), even though the addition of wind instruments and the crescendo will produce considerable increase in volume. When the singer can exhibit enough self-discipline to give a little *less* voice throughout, she can, like the long-distance runner who must pace himself, reach for the end with enough stamina left for a glorious finish.

The Text

Literal Translation
1. You, dear hall, greet I again, joyously greet I you, beloved room!
2. In you come to life his songs and waken me from gloomy dream.
3. When he from you departed, how desolate appeared you to-me.
4. From me fled the peace, the joy went out to-you!
5. As now my bosom high itself lifts, so appear you now to-me proud and exalted;
6. he-who me and you so newly revives, not lingers he far more!
7. Be to-me greeted, be to-me greeted!
8. You, dear hall, be to-me greeted!

Idiomatic Translation
1. I greet you again, dear hall; joyously I greet you!
2. His songs come to life in you and awaken me from a dismal dream.
3. When he departed from you, how desolate you seemed to me.
4. Peace of mind fled from me; joy went out of you!
5. As now my spirit rises, so you appear to me proud and exalted;
6. he who puts new life in both of us now no longer lingers far away!
7. I salute you, I salute you!
8. Oh, dear hall, I salute you!

The Scenic Picture

The scene represents the Hall of Minstrels, a large auditorium in the Wartburg, the residence of landgrave Hermann of Thuringia. A flat floor space down stage is left free to serve as the performing area for the forthcoming contest of the singers. Immediately above this, several rows of seats, separated by two wide sets of steps, ascend in amphitheaterlike fashion over an intermediate platform to a terrace upstage. Beyond the terrace one can see the courtyard of the castle and in the distance a valley. Toward UL the terrace continues behind the last row of seats and leads to the inner apartments. The throne-like seats reserved for Elisabeth and the landgrave are placed near the down left corner of the stage.

The Stage Actions Explained

Elisabeth expects to meet Tannhäuser in the Hall of the Minstrels. We must assume that Wolfram told her (or sent word) that before the arrival of the guests he would bring Tannhäuser to see her. She knows that he will ascend the main staircase that leads to the hall in the UR corner of the stage. After making certain that he is not in the Hall (mm. 3 and 4), she will look for him in the UR direction during the four orchestral sections: measures 5–8, 19–24, 56–61, and 116–123.

When apostrophizing the hall, she will sing toward DL, and when thinking of her own past sadness and present joy, she will turn to DR. She must be very excited at the prospect of seeing the man whom she loves, yet her movements should not be hurried and her walking on stage should not cover too much space.

Measures

1. Elisabeth enters from UL and goes R along the terrace U stage.
3. She stops and turns Cclw to inspect the hall, wondering whether Tannhaüser is there waiting for her.
4. *(4th quarter)* Seeing that the hall is empty, she continues to go R along the terrace and looks to UR to see if perhaps Tannhäuser is approaching from that direction.
8. *(3rd quarter)* She turns Cclw and goes DL, descending the steps to the lower platform. She stops well UR of the throne elevation in the DL corner of the stage.
11. She addresses the hall facing DL.
15. She lets her eyes roam from DL and DR.
18. She goes DR to the floor level and continues in a Clw circle, admiring the hall and also looking UR hoping that Tannhäuser is approaching.
25. She ends her Clw circle with a final Clw turn, so that she again is facing DL.
29. She turns Clw gaily, but immediately recalls her despondency when Tannhäuser left her uncle's domain.
32. With the words: "aus düsterm Traum," she lets her head sink and looks down.
36. With "dir" she addresses the hall over her L shoulder.
39. With "öd" she again looks at the ground.
42. She looks to heaven DR.
50. She turns Cclw to address the hall and goes slowly DL.
56. She continues in a Cclw semicircle to return to the same place on the platform where she stood during measures 11 to 18. While moving U, she looks toward UR wondering how soon Tannhäuser will arrive at the hall.
61. She completes the semicircle with a final Cclw turn to face DR.
66. With "so scheinst du" she looks over her L shoulder to address the hall.
68. With "stolz" she looks to heaven DR.

75. She again descends the steps to the floor level and goes slightly R, looking over her R shoulder in the UR direction.

77. She stops and looks toward heaven DR.

82. Addressing the hall, she turns LSB.

92. She turns Clw.

95. She goes slightly DR.

99. She continues DR for a short distance.

103. She turns LSB to address the hall.

108. She goes DL to CC.

111. With the high B, she backs up slightly.

115. As the orchestra intones Tannhäuser's theme, she turns Cclw and begins a Cclw semicircle that leads her up the steps by which she originally descended to the hall. She goes beyond the point where she sang in measures 11–18 and 61–75, and is ready to welcome Tannhäuser when he appears in the UR area at the end of her aria.

PART TWO

Introduction

In order to perform the fourteen arias discussed in Part II, the soprano will need the help of partners. The importance of these supporting actors cannot be stressed too much. Not only must they listen intently to what is being sung but they must interpret it in terms of what it means to their own stage personalities. The true supporting actor functions almost like a prompter by helping to elicit and stimulate the succeeding words and actions of the singer.

Seven of the following "ensemble" arias include vocal lines sung by partners, either just before or during the aria proper. If a competent tenor is not available, the soprano will be wise not to attempt Donna Anna's "Non mi dir" or Violetta's "Sempre libera." The short tenor lines in the two *Bohème* arias and Louise's "Depuis le jour" can be uttered by almost anyone capable of singing in tune. They could even conceivably be omitted. The Countess's and Susanna's lines before Cherubino's "Voi che sapete" and Masetto's sentence before Zerlina's "Batti, batti" should offer no problems to the supporting singers. One aria, Pamina's "Ach ich fühl's," is preceded by a spoken dialogue, and in the remaining six selections the partners are mute. But whether the participating actor is vocal or silent, it is preferable to enlist the help of a singing actor or a person who not only can act believably but who can so familiarize himself with the succession of all musical events that he can predict their occurrence with great precision. Anticipating vocal and instrumental events so as to be able to synchronize one's actions with them is essential in opera.

Like all midinettes, Mimi makes all of her own clothes and is dressed in the latest fashion (about 1830). A sheer black apron and shawl embroidered with "lillies and roses" completes her costume. (She wears the same outfit in the aria of Act III, except for a heavy black shawl.)

Si, Mi Chiamano Mimi

from *La Bohème,* Act I

by GIACOMO PUCCINI

The Drama

In the score of *La Bohème* each of the four acts is preceded by an introduction featuring thumbnail sketches of the characters and other relevant information. From these vignettes we learn, among other things, that the third act takes place at the end of February, and the fourth act three or four months later. The text of the opera makes it clear, of course, that the first two acts take place on the preceding Christmas eve.

Although the score mentions that the opera is set "around 1830," the historical characters referred to in the text enable us to set the time more precisely.

In the first act, Rodolfo observes that the silver coins scattered on the floor by Schaunard bear the likeness of King Louis Phillippe; in the last act, Colline jokingly assures his companions that the King has summoned him to a meeting of the Cabinet where he will meet Guizot. Since Louis Phillippe did not become King of France until August, 1830, the action cannot take place before Christmas of that year. Guizot, however, resigned as minister in November, 1830, and did not rejoin the Cabinet until October, 1832. The summer of 1833 is therefore the earliest possible date for the last act and Christmas of 1832 the closest we can get to "around 1830."

In the introduction that precedes the first act, we are given a charming portrait of our heroine:

"Mimi was a graceful girl with a special affinity for the artistic and poetic ideals of Rodolfo. She was twenty two years old, small, and delicate. Her face, the features of which had a marvellous refinement, reminded one of an artist's sketch of some high-born beauty. The blood of youth coursed warmly and quickly through her veins and gave a rosy tint to her white skin that had the velvety transparence of a camelia."

The events that precede Mimi's first-act aria can be summarized in a few words. It is Christmas Eve. Mimi, a fragile and gentle seamstress, knocks at the door of her neighbor's garret room to ask for a light for her candle. After a sudden attack of dizziness she leaves, but returns at once to look for the latchkey which she had dropped during her fainting spell. Partly by accident and partly by design, both Mimi's and Rodolfo's candles become extinguished and the young people must continue their search in the darkness.

Rodolfo soon hides the key in his pocket, pretending not to have found it. Mimi — who, as she confesses in the last act, is aware of the deception — plays along with him and accepts his suggestion that they should wait for the moonlight before continuing their search.

To pass the time, Rodolfo tells Mimi of his poetic pursuits, of his "gay poverty" which is relieved mostly by building castles in the air, and of his hopes for romance with a girl as lovely as his neighbor. Impressed and flattered, Mimi agrees to reciprocate and tell Rodolfo something about her own life.

The intimate charm of this scene emanates not so much from what is actually said as from what is implied. Rodolfo hints that he hopes he may be permitted to make love to Mimi, but makes it quite evident that he cannot offer her much material comfort. Mimi, on the other hand, is anxious to convey to Rodolfo that she has "higher" inclinations and is worthy of a poet's attention. She also makes it clear, that she is not a girl who will flirt with the first stranger whom she meets. Her "finer" feelings are revealed in her love for flowers, springtime, and all things poetic. As for being a "good" girl, she impresses upon Rodolfo that although she does not always go to Mass, she says her prayers quite regularly.

The soprano who studies or performs this aria should keep in mind that she is telling the story of her life to a very handsome and romantically inclined young man who is sitting near her in almost total darkness. Although total darkness is not possible on the stage, except for a very short time,* it is nevertheless essential that the performers of this scene try to capture the tingling sense of delicious panic that comes from being alone in the dark with an attractive member of the opposite sex.

In this situation, Mimi is half hoping that Rodolfo will soon start making love to her, but at the same time she is more than a little afraid that his caresses will come too soon, with the result that he would lose respect for her. This nervousness is reflected in the shortness of her musical phrases, in her constant hesitation, and in the succession of inconsequential topics. Mimi knows that if she is to discourage Rodolfo from making amorous advances, she must keep on talking. If she can think of nothing new to say, she might as well — as in measures 26 to 30 — repeat what she had already said a moment ago. And when, more or less accidentally, she brings up matters that sound like invitations to aggressive courtship, she catches herself and makes an effort to correct this impression.

The subtle tempo variations which Puccini notates on these occasions must be justified by Mimi's embarrassment and her desire to set things straight. Notice, for instance, in measures 14 to 20, the sequence "che parlano d'amor, di primavere," where the mention of "love" leads to a slowing down and is then turned into "springtime." Similarly, the suggestive "first kiss of April" in measures 54 and 55 becomes a more hurried "first sunshine" in measures 57 and 58.

---

* It stands to reason that theatrical events should be "visible" in the sense that music must be "audible" no matter how softly it is played.

The most telling of these quasi-Freudian slips is Mimi's revelation that she lives "alone, all alone." This "vivo sola, soletta" reassures Rodolfo that he need not worry about such complications as brothers, cousins, or other meddling relatives.

The Music

Puccini's extraordinarily keen theatrical sense prompted him to take advantage of every conceivable musical device to create the impression of a spontaneous, unpremeditated progression of vocal and scenic events.

In Mimi's arias (this and the next, page 182) we can notice two excellent examples of his flexible and almost capricious style of composition and notation. Observe, for instance, how both these arias begin with a single tone sustained in the orchestra. In the first aria it is the long E played pianissimo by the first violins; in "Donde Lieta" the low F♯ of the first clarinet. The listener may expect these tones to continue in the keys of the preceding pieces; but the violin's E is not the lowered sixth (F♭) of Rodolfo's A-flat major aria, nor is the F♯ of the clarinet the third degree of Marcello's excited D-major comments.

It will take several phrases until Mimi makes up her mind, so to speak, that her first aria is in D major, and her second in D-flat major. And it is only in retrospect that it becomes apparent that this initial note is a pivot tone which, in the first aria, turned out to be the dominant of the dominant, and in the third-act aria was in reality a G♭, the seventh of the dominant.

Furthermore, in his quest for a quasi-improvised vocal line, Puccini made a heroic effort to indicate the precise convolutions of a supple tempo rubato and, for this purpose, did not hesitate to pile up one descriptive term on top of another. We find here not only a kaleidoscopic variety of meter signatures and metronome markings, but also an unusually large assortment of minute qualifying terms: rallentando, ritardando, poco rallentando, poco ritardando, molto ritardando, a piacere, senza rigore di tempo, animando, con molta anima, agitato un poco, agitate appena, sostenendo, as well as both long and short fermatas.

The profusion of these notations is often more confusing than helpful, especially when the main tempo mark and the minor qualifiers appear to contradict each other. Observe, for instance, the forty-ninth measure of the first-act aria, "Si, Mi Chiamano Mimi," where along with the molto sostenuto we find a con molto anima. It is difficult to see how these terms, which normally indicate opposite effects, can coexist in the same musical utterance.

But in spite of all these markings, one is somehow left with the impression that Puccini was not quite certain whether a slowing down or speeding up, whether a crescendo, or a diminuendo would produce the total expressive result he was seeking to achieve.

Doubts regarding the "right" tempo or the best manner of executing a given passage are not so rare among composers as one might imagine.

While drastic reversals of speed indications are unusual,* uncertainties
and vacillations are by no means uncommon.

Singers, coaches, and voice teachers who wish to become better acquainted with the traditional treatment of the vocal line in Puccini's operas
will find much valuable information in Luigi Ricci's book† to which reference will be made occasionally in this volume. However, although these
and other interpretative details quoted by us are presumably based on
authentic statements by the composer, they should not in our opinion be
given too much consideration. It is very likely that Puccini was not averse
to changing his mind and, more often than not, tended to accede to the
wishes of the various artists who at the moment were interpreting the
leading roles of his operas.

The formal structure of Mimi's first-act aria is somewhat unusual. It
consists of two uneven stanzas, the second of which is almost twice as long
as the first: forty-six as against twenty-five measures. The stanzas begin
and end alike, but their inner development follows quite different paths.

By referring to the opening phrase as A and to the closing section as E,
the total shape of the aria can be presented in the following scheme:

Stanza I	A	B	A1	E
Measures	1–5	6–10	11–14	15–25

Stanza II	A	C	D	E
Measures	26–30	31–48	49–59	60–71

The opening fourteen measures of the first stanza are elaborated into a
miniature song form: A-B-A1. The second stanza dispenses with the B and
A1 episodes of the opening section, but to compensate for it presents two
completely new sections: C and D. The closing sections of both stanzas
have different words, but are almost identical from the musical point of
view. In spite of this asymmetry, the total impression is one of tightness
and excellent balance.

The Vocal Aspects

There are four high A's in this aria, and many sopranos feel compelled
to hold each one of them a very long time. It is true that the first one has
a ritardando marked above it, that the second is at the end of a measure
marked "con grande espansione," that the third is at the end of a measure
marked "allargando," and that the fourth has tenuto above it; but it is
also true that each A comes on the fourth beat (or after it) in the measure,
and in three cases it is set to either an unstressed syllable or to an unim-

* Probably the most dramatic example of a complete reversal is found in Chopin's
E-flat minor Prelude (Op. 28, No. 14) where — as Edouard Ganche pointed out in
the Oxford University Press edition of Chopin's works — the composer crossed out
"Allegro" and replaced it with "Largo."

† Luigi Ricci, *Puccini, Interprete di se stesso* (Milan: G. Ricordi, 1964).

portant word in the sentence. Thus it does not seem necessary to put a fermata on each of these high notes.

The aria begins simply, and the first phrase must be sung artlessly to indicate Mimi's ingenousness and her slight embarrassment at being caught in an awkward situation. Puccini's characteristic way of indicating a slight portamento on the last two eighth notes of measure 2 and the first two eighth notes of measure 5 should be carefully observed. When these two phrases are repeated, the same portamenti (mm. 11 and 14) also appear.

Characteristic of Puccini's method of setting recitative sentences is his repetition of a single note, as in measures 6 through 8. Here the singer must be careful to give proper stress to the correct syllable in Italian: on "sto–," "bre–," "te–," and "se–." Most sopranos do not seem to experience difficulty with the *ee* vowel on the high A in measure 18. It should not be held too long; in spite of col canto in the accompaniment, there is only a ritardando in the vocal line. The portamenti at the end of measure 21 and at the beginning of measure 23 should be executed delicately and without excess. The same portamento that appeared in the first phrase of the aria appears again in measure 27 when that phrase is repeated.

The Allegretto moderato at measure 31 is often sung too slowly. From a dramatic point of view we can justify the more rapid tempo as Mimi's babbling to prevent Rodolfo from making love to her too soon. Our acting directions give ample justification (after poco rallentando and a piacere) for the return to this same tempo (marked "a tempo") at measure 41: Mimi is apprehensive because of Rodolfo's quiet but determined amorous advances.

The custom of holding the A in measure 48 for a very long time and of beginning the next phrase with a portamento to the B without a breath does not seem justified. Again, the suggested stage directions provide a very sound dramatic reason for singing the note just as it is notated. Although there is at least one piano-vocal score in existence with permission for this change in Puccini's handwriting, it is most likely that Puccini made concessions for major changes of this kind to certain artists but did not intend to set a precedent. The authors recommend that measure 48 be sung as written.

The climax of the aria, beginning in measure 53, is marked "con grande espansione." Many singers stretch out measures 53–57 so that at least two breaths are necessary. It is preferable to breathe after "aprile" (but not after "bacio") if the entire phrase cannot be sung in one breath. Measures 57–59 should be sung in one breath.

The phrase, "Cosi gentil il profumo d'un fior" is best sung without being broken after "gentil," and should present no difficulty unless the singer holds the A on "–mo" too long. The last portamento in the aria occurs on "faccio" in measure 68; the fermata on "–cio" should be observed. The final three measures, in Puccini's repeated-note style, need not be sung pell-mell, since they are marked "senza rigore di tempo con naturalezza."

Slight elongations of the syllables italicized here are desirable to achieve the natural inflection of the Italian language: "Altro di *me* non le sa*prei* nar*ra*re: *s*ono la *su*a vi*ci*na che la *vien* fuori d'*o*ra im*por*tu*na*re." The breath after "narrare" is a natural one; beyond that point the singer has the choice of singing the long final phrase in one breath, or taking a short breath after "vicina."

Musicians often joke that no two measures in Puccini's music are performed at a steady tempo, and this aria would tend to bear this out. Careful attention, without exaggeration, to the many marks that indicate tempo variations is demanded of any singer who attempts this aria; without such careful attention, much of its charm and subtlety will be lost.

The Text

Literal Translation
1. Yes, me they-call Mimi, but the my name is Lucia.
2. The story my is brief. On linen or on silk I-embroider at home and outside.
3. I-am tranquil and happy and it-is my recreation to-make lilies and roses.
4. Me please those things that have such sweet enchantment,
5. that speak of dreams and of fancies, those things that have name poetry.
6. You me-understand? (Rodolfo: Yes.) Me they-call Mimi, the reason not I-know.
7. Alone, for-myself I-make the dinner by me myself.
8. Not go-I always to Mass but I-pray often the Lord.
9. I-live alone, all-alone; there in a white little-room,
10. I look-out on-the roofs and into sky,
11. but when comes the thaw, the first sun is mine,
12. the first kiss of-the April is mine. The first sun is mine.
13. Grows in a vase a rose . . . Leaf by leaf it I-observe!
14. How pleasing the perfume of-a flower!
15. But the flowers that-I make, alas, not have fragrance!
16. Other of myself not to-you would-I-know to-tell;
17. I-am the your neighbor who you comes outside of-hour to bother.

Idiomatic Translation
1. Yes, I am called Mimi, but my name is Lucia.
2. My story is a short one. I embroider on linen and silk, either at home or away from home.
3. My life is quiet and happy, and for recreation I like to embroider lilies and roses.
4. Those things that have such sweet enchantment please me,
5. those things that speak of dreams and fancies, that are called poetry.

6. Do you understand? (Rodolfo: Yes.) I am called Mimi, but I don't know why.
7. I prepare and eat my dinner all by myself.
8. I don't always go to Mass, but I often pray.
9. I live all alone; there in my little white room,
10. I look out onto the rooftops and into the sky,
11. but when the first thaw comes, the first rays of the sun are mine,
12. the first kiss of April is mine. The first rays of the sun are mine.
13. A rose blossoms in a vase . . . I observe the petals unfolding, leaf by leaf.
14. How pleasing is the perfume of a flower!
15. But the flowers that I embroider, alas, do not have fragrance.
16. I don't know what else to tell you about myself;
17. I'm just a neighbor who comes at an inopportune time to bother you.

The Scenic Picture

The scene represents the garret room of the Bohemians in the Latin Quarter of Paris. The main entrance is to UR, a large window is set into the L wall, and a small stove stands near the DL corner. The furniture consists of a table to L of CC, a sofa near the DR corner of the room, and a chair which is standing near the table. As the aria begins, Rodolfo carries the chair forward and places it DL of the sofa. A waterglass holding a single rose (brought in earlier by Schaunard) stands on the table. Mimi wears a shawl embroidered with lilies and roses.

The Stage Actions Explained

Mimi is seated near the L corner of the sofa facing L. She looks over her L shoulder at Rodolfo who is standing UL of her. Having just told her about himself, he has asked her to reciprocate. Mimi nods her head, and Rodolfo picks up the chair by the table in the center.

Measures

1. Rodolfo places the chair slightly DL of the sofa and sits down facing Mimi. The E♮ in the accompaniment must be sustained long enough to permit this action to be completed before Mimi begins to sing. She turned slightly Clw while Rodolfo was carrying the chair and is now facing DL.
12. Mimi takes off the shawl that she is wearing around her shoulders and shows Rodolfo the flowers which are embroidered on it.
14. After "rose," Rodolfo takes the shawl from Mimi's hands, so as to inspect the embroidery more closely in the darkness. She is slightly embarrassed.
18. After "amor," Mimi turns Clw to sing the next two phrases toward DR.
19. After "primavere," she seems to be listening to an imagined twittering

of birds in the trees. At the same time, Rodolfo inhales the perfume that exudes from the shawl.

21. Rodolfo folds the shawl gently and hangs it on the back of the chair, DL of him. This action makes him turn slightly away from Mimi.

23. With the fermata on "cose," Mimi turns Cclw to face Rodolfo and notices that he is not looking at her. With "poesia," Rodolfo turns Clw toward Mimi.

25. After "m'intende?" Rodolfo gets up and, while singing his "sì," moves the chair closer to the sofa.

26. When Rodolfo sits down again, his knees are almost touching Mimi's skirt. This proximity makes her nervous and, glancing toward UR, in the direction of her own room beyond the entrance of the garret, she edges away from Rodolfo to the R.

34. She turns Cclw to impress Rodolfo with her moral upbringing.

38. She looks over her R shoulder.

39. After "sola," she throws both arms gently into the air.

40. As Mimi's L hand is about to return, palm down, to her lap, Rodolfo puts his R hand under hers and catches it. Mimi is surprised by his boldness but, while she is pleased with the gentleness of his touch, she feels that she must not let him move too rapidly to his goal. The a piacere and col canto at measures 38, 39, and 40 justify a considerable delay in attacking measure 41. Mimi rises, turns slightly Cclw, and backs away toward the R, along the edge of the sofa.

41. Rodolfo keeps holding Mimi's hand and she succeeds only in pulling him over to the R.

45. By this time, both of them are seated side by side on the sofa.

46. 47. Rodolfo passes Mimi's hand into his own L hand and puts his R arm around her waist. With the short "–lo" of "cielo," Mimi disengages her L hand and rises, so as to stand to the R of the sofa. Rodolfo edges to the R and manages to catch her L hand with his R hand.

49. Mimi backs slightly toward U. Rodolfo, still seated and holding her L hand, turns Clw so as to face her.

50. Rodolfo kisses Mimi's hand.

51. She pulls her hand away and goes L, Xing above the sofa, to UL of it. Rodolfo follows Mimi with his eyes and, turning Clw, gets up and backs slightly to DR while facing her.

52. After "mio," Mimi turns RSB to face Rodolfo.

55. With the last note of this measure — which can be sustained quite a bit longer as part of the poco allargando — she turns Cclw to look toward the window in the UL wall of the room.

56. After "mio," she again turns RSB to face Rodolfo and to correct any misapprehension he may feel about the meaning of the "kiss of April."

59. As she looks over her L shoulder toward the window, Mimi notices the rose in the water glass on the table.

60. She goes L to above the table.

61. She picks up the glass with the rose.

62. She holds the glass in her L hand, goes slightly DR toward the chair which is standing DL of the sofa.

64. After she finishes singing, Mimi lifts the glass and inhales the perfume of the rose.

66. She goes DR to UL of the chair.

67. With her R hand she lifts the shawl from the back of the chair so as to look at the embroidery.

69. She drops the shawl on the seat of the chair, turns Cclw, and retraces her steps to the table.

70. After she replaces the glass with the rose on the table, she turns Clw to face Rodolfo.

"Donde lieta"
from *La Bohème,* Act III
by GIACOMO PUCCINI

The Drama

The events of the third act of *La Bohème* take place about two months later. Since that memorable Christmas Eve of the first two acts, Mimi and Rodolfo have been living together. They were quite happy at first, but lately Rodolfo's fits of jealousy have been making Mimi's life miserable. When after a particularly violent quarrel Rodolfo leaves her in the middle of the night, Mimi decides to turn for help to their friend, Marcello. She knows that this indefatigable painter and his chanteuse girl friend, Musetta, have been plying their respective trades in a tavern near La Barrière d'Enfer, one of the old Parisian toll gates. Mimi arrives here on this snowy and gloomy February dawn to ask Marcello to plead with Rodolfo and help to arrange for an amicable separation. Since Rodolfo had also appeared at the tavern a few hours earlier, Marcello agrees to have a man-to-man talk with his friend, but asks Mimi to go home in the meantime, so as not to make a scene in front of strangers. Mimi leaves, but returns a little later and — hidden behind some trees — overhears Rodolfo confessing to Marcello that his supposed jealousy is only a disguise for his feelings of guilt and desperation. In his abject poverty, he cannot heat their garret room properly and, in this dismal situation, cannot bear to see the rapid deterioration of Mimi's health. Rodolfo is convinced that unless Mimi can soon find a wealthier protector, she does not have long to live.

This revelation is a shock to Mimi and she realizes that a separation from Rodolfo has now become a physical as well as an emotional necessity.

Marcello hears Musetta's flirtatious laughter and, distracted by his own jealousy, returns to the tavern; the lovers are now left alone on the square.

It is at this point that Mimi embarks on her gentle farewell aria. Here again, as in the first act, the words sung are less important than the unspoken emotional interplay between the lovers. The performers must keep in mind that by the end of this act Mimi and Rodolfo do not separate, but decide to remain together. It is Marcello and Musetta — who were presumably getting along so famously — whose furious quarrel culminates in a more or less permanent "divorce."

Mimi's and Rodolfo's behavior must reflect the strength of their attachment. They recognize the necessity for a separation but their emotional need for each other is too great to allow it. This tug of war between leaving and remaining is made visible in the blocking of the action which consists of a series of attempted caresses and gentle rejections, of tentative departures and half-hearted returns.

The Music

Mimi's thoughts and feelings are expressed not only by the words she sings but also — and perhaps to an even greater extent — by the musical associations between the various vocal and orchestral phrases and the ideas and events of the first two acts. When acting this aria, the singer must be fully aware of the "meaning" of these musical reminiscences. The following is the order in which they occur in this aria.

Measures*

A — 4–13   is the music of Mimi's entrance in the first act which incorporates the episode of her coughing fit (mm. 9–13). It serves as a reminder of the seriousness of her illness.

B — 14–16   is a quote from section C of the first aria ("Si, mi chiamano Mimi," mm 41–44) which is related to the "bianca cameretta," the little white room in which Mimi lived "all alone" before she met Rodolfo and to which she now plans to return.

C — 18–21   This phrase, with its leap of a seventh, bears a definite resemblance to the "quelle cose che han nome poesia" passage in section E of "Si, mi chiamano Mimi" (m. 23). It relates to the "poetic notions" the lovers have in common and to the romantic joys of their first encounter.

D — 21–23   is the motive of the Café Momus, reminding Mimi of the happy hours that she and Rodolfo spent there.

E — 23–25   (same as mm. 14–16).

F — 26–29   (same as mm. 18–21).

G — 29–30   is a second and different quote from the "romantic affinity" sequence in section E, harking back to "mi piaccion quelle cose" (mm. 15–16), and "germoglia in un vaso una rosa" of the first aria (mm. 60–61).

H — 32–33   is the motive of the "pink bonnet" that Rodolfo bought for Mimi on the evening of their first meeting.

I — 39–42   is the third appearance of the "things that attract them to each other" motive, as in measures 18–21 and 26–29.

These reminiscences show that the repeated "little white room" phrase

* The numbering of the measures begins two measures before the Lento Molto in 2/4:

in A-flat major (mm. 14–16) and the D-flat major "poesia" section that occurs three times (mm. 19–20, 27–28 and 39–40) are the main musical building blocks of this aria.

These two opposing musical ideas are symbolic of Mimi's indecision. Should she leave Rodolfo and return to her lonely A-flat major life, or should she remain with him and once more share their D-flat major affinities? She is painfully aware of Rodolfo's feelings of guilt, and of his disappointment that he could not provide a more acceptable environment for their life together. Mimi feels that if they are to separate, then let it be "senza rancor" (mm. 17–18), without bitterness; but Rodolfo's attitude does not make her task any easier. His silence is that of the hurt lover. After Mimi's first "Addio" (mm. 1 and 2), his reaction is one of surprise: "Che! Vai?" (m. 3) (What! You're leaving?) And his first words when the aria is finished are: "So, it's really all over?"

Thus what finally determines the form of the aria is not Mimi's thinking or behavior — she is much too confused for that — but rather Rodolfo's ostensible acceptance of the separation, the two occasions when he seems ready to leave and has to be stopped by Mimi.

The moments of formal subdivision are thus governed not only by the A-flat major and D-flat major cadences but even more directly by Mimi's "Ascolta, ascolta," (m. 18) and again by her "Bada," (m. 31).

In other words, counting the two introductory measures, we are dealing here with a musical "stream of consciousness" numbering forty-one measures and divided into three sections.

1. The first section (mm. 3–18) ends with "Addio, senza rancor" in the "loneliness" key of A-flat major;
2. The second section (mm. 18–30) hesitates between D flat and A flat, and ends in D flat, just before the change of key signature; and
3. The third section (mm. 31–41) features the climactic vocal ascent to the high B♭ and ends with another "Addio, senza rancor," which is now raised a fourth higher to end the aria in D flat, thus showing Rodolfo that although the words say "Farewell!" the message reads: "Let us stay together!"

The Vocal Aspects

This aria makes only modest vocal demands: it is short, lies within a comfortable vocal range, and has only one climax with a high note. Since the accompaniment is delicately scored, there is absolutely no necessity for using a heavy chest tone for the lower pitches, for the tone quality that results will contradict Mimi's feeling of indecision.

Scrupulous attention must be paid to all the markings that indicate small changes of tempo. Some singers have difficulty with the rhythm in measure 8. This is usually caused by a lack of coordination between the voice and the accompaniment in determining just how much the measure will slow down. The new tempo and meter signature in measure 9, combined with agitando un poco, indicate a sudden acceleration. Measures

9–12 are often sung too slowly. In spite of the sixteenth rest at the end
of measure 12, the sentence "Ritorna un'altra volta a intesser finti fior!,"
should be thought of as one phrase, even if a catch breath is necessary
during the rest. Measures 16 and 17 can be sung freely and simply. Although the first "ascolta" in measure 18 is marked "ritenuto," the a tempo
at measure 19 indicates that the second one is to be sung much faster.
After the second "ascolta," the singer should take sufficient breath so
that "Le poche robe aduna che lasciai sparse" can be sung in one breath.
Similarly, there is adequate time for a good breath so that "Nel mio
cassetto stan chiusi quel cerchietto d'or" can be sung without a break.

Many singers fear that it is not possible to sing measures 26–29 in
one phrase. But it is suggested that an earnest attempt to do so should
be made and that the poco ritardando in measure 27 should not be overdone. There is adequate time for a deep breath before this long phrase.

Singers who experience difficulty in finding the correct pitch for the E♮
in measure 31 would do well to think of the previous D♭ enharmonically
as C♯. The word, "Bada," should be sung with a delicate portamento. In
spite of the molto ritardando in measure 32, the phrase, "sotto il guanciale
c'è la cuffietta rosa," should not be broken. The first "Se vuoi" is marked
"forte" in the accompaniment and should be sung accordingly; the second
"se vuoi" should be sung somewhat more timidly, and the third one in a determined fashion. Mimi is here treading on thin ice with her reminiscences
of happier times. She blurts out the first "If you wish . . . ," she loses her
courage when she sings the second one, and she sings the third one firmly,
yet tenderly, and immediately reaches the vocal climax of the aria. There
should be no need to break the phrase after "ricordo" in measure 37. The
last phrase of the aria should be sung in one breath, but with a slight pause
after "addio," as indicated by the composer. A slight portamento from
"ran–" to "–cor" seems to have become common practice; it is certainly
quite permissible.

The Text

Literal Translation

1. From-whence happy she-left at-the your call of-love.
2. returns alone Mimi to-the solitary nest.
3. She-returns another time to weave artificial flowers!
4. Goodbye, without bitterness. Listen, listen,
5. the few things gather that I-left scattered.
6. In-the my drawer remain shut that little-ring of-gold and the book
   of prayers.
7. Wrap everything in an apron and I-will-send the concierge.
8. Wait, under the pillow there-is the little-bonnet pink.
9. If you-wish . . . if you-wish to-keep-it as keepsake of-love . . .
10. Goodbye, without bitterness.

Idiomatic Translation

1. From where she left, when your love called her,

2. Mimi now returns alone to her solitary nest.
3. She returns once again to embroider her artificial flowers!
4. Goodbye, without bitterness let us part. Listen —
5. Gather up the few things I left behind.
6. In my drawer are that little gold ring and my prayer book.
7. Wrap everything together in an apron, and I will send the concierge for them.
8. Wait — under my pillow there is the little pink bonnet.
9. If you wish, keep it as a remembrance of our love . . .
10. Goodbye, without bitterness let us part.

The Scenic Picture

The action takes place on a winter morning at the intersection of streets outside the Paris tollgate known as the *Barrière d'Enfer*. On the right is a tavern, on the left a stone bench.

The Stage Actions Explained

Introduction (mm. 1 and 2)

Mimi is sitting on the U side of the bench near its R corner and is facing UL. She has been crying and her head is buried in her arms. Rodolfo is standing to the R of the bench (near Mimi's L shoulder). He is leaning over her and is embracing her.*

Measures

1. Mimi rises and turns LSB, disengaging herself from Rodolfo's embrace. He backs away slightly to DR, but continues to face her. Although Mimi's vocal line is marked with a legato slur, her voice must betray that she had been crying. Note that her first word, "addio," is sung on the same pitches as the final "addio" in measure 40. She is trying to find the right inflections and explanations with which to soften the impact of this word, and it takes her the full length of the aria to accomplish this. By then, of course, she has no longer the strength to go through with the separation.

Section 1 (mm. 3–18)

3. Mimi is fighting back her tears and answers Rodolfo's question by nodding her head. He turns Clw and walks away from her toward DR. Not being certain just how much of his conversation with Marcello was overheard by Mimi, he does not know what to do or what to say. He keeps walking until Mimi begins to sing. Then he stops

---

* If Rodolfo happens to be so much taller than Mimi that this embrace makes him look awkward, it is better to have him kneel or to have Mimi stand rather than be seated.

and turns RSF to face her. Mimi remains standing above the bench until measure 9.

9. With the change in meter and the increase in tempo, she gathers her courage and goes DR to UL of Rodolfo.

14. During Mimi's long "fior," Rodolfo comes closer to her.

15. He takes her R hand and tries to kiss it. Afraid that a display of affection would make their separation even more difficult, Mimi backs slightly to UR and pulls her hand away from Rodolfo.

16. Upset by Mimi's rejection of his tenderness, Rodolfo turns slightly Cclw and looks away from her.

17. With "rancor," Mimi turns Cclw and takes a step or two toward UL.

Section 2 (mm. 18–31)

18. Rodolfo starts walking U toward the tavern. Mimi glances over her R shoulder, notices that Rodolfo is leaving and turns RSB, stopping him with "ascolta, ascolta." The half note A♭, specifically marked "ritardando col canto," must be held long enough to permit these actions to take place. Too much delay at this point, however, would be unpleasant.

21. The orchestra tells us that Mimi is recalling their happy excursions to the Café Momus, and this brings to her mind the "cassetto" and the "cerchietto d'or." Neither the little box — a jewel case? — nor the golden circlet — an engagement ring? — have been mentioned before in the opera. (They may have appeared in one of the preliminary versions of the libretto.) We can only guess that the little box — since it also contains Mimi's prayerbook — has been in her possession all along; the ring could be a present from Rodolfo, purchased on one of their strolls through the city.

25. With the repetition of the music heard in measure 14, Rodolfo attempts the same action and takes a step toward Mimi. She again stops him with a gesture.

29. Rodolfo looks at Mimi imploringly, as if to say: "Will you be able to forget how happy we were together?" After "il portiere," Mimi turns Cclw and again begins to walk toward UL. She wants to do something that will show Rodolfo that she will always love him, and decides to present him with the little pink bonnet† which he bought for her when they went to the Café Momus on Christmas eve.

30. Rodolfo takes another step toward the tavern.

Section 3 (mm. 31–41)

31. Mimi turns RSB to face Rodolfo.

34. and 35. Each of the three "se vuoi" phrases should be given a different interpretation. On the first one, Mimi approaches Rodolfo with great

---

† Since this "cufietta rosa" is kept under the pillow it must certainly be a lacy, soft nightcap rather than the stiff hat which is so often paraded by Mimi in the second act of the opera.

warmth of expression. He responds to it by attempting to come closer to her. This again alarms Mimi, so that with the second "se vuoi" she backs away slightly. On the third "se vuoi," she turns Cclw and takes a few steps to the L.

37. The high B♭ is combined with an RSB turn and slight backing to UL.

39. After "addio," Mimi comes a little closer to Rodolfo to sing her final sentence.

40. and 41. With the last word of her aria, she turns Cclw and starts to leave the stage. She slows down, however, hoping that Rodolfo will say something to make her feel better.

The singers will observe that the actions in each of the three sections of this aria unfold along diagonal lines running from UL to DR.

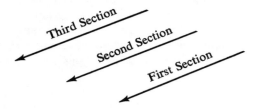

The Rodolfos must take care to remain at all times slightly below their singing partners and the Mimis must learn to gain enough depth in the transitions from section to section to permit the Rodolfos, in measures 18 and 30, to take a step or two toward the tavern.

"Voi lo sapete"
from *Cavalleria Rusticana*
by PIETRO MASCAGNI

The Drama

Santuzza, a simple Sicilian village girl, has fallen in love with the handsome young soldier, Turiddu, who has promised to marry her. After seducing her, he seems unwilling to keep his word, having been lured away by his former passion, Lola. The feelings which Santuzza expresses in her Romanza are presented even more clearly and fully in Verga's play, on which the opera is based. Here, slightly condensed, is what Santuzza tells Turiddu's mother in the play:

Before Turiddu went to the army, he had an understanding with Lola. Then, when he returned, he found her married to Alfio, and at first he put her out of his mind. But she did not forget him. She managed to walk by every time she saw him at my door, and the trollop stole him away from me with her pagan eyes. She would always start a conversation with him: "Friend Turiddu, what are you doing in the neighborhood? Don't you know that it was not the wish of God? Now leave me alone, for I am a married woman!" The "wish of God" was to tempt him! He started courting me just to spite her, because she had married someone else. How true it is that an old love is never forgotten! When he purred sweet words to me, with those honest eyes of his, I felt my heart would jump out of my breast! I was crazy, yes! How could I refuse him when he begged me: "Let me in, Santuzza; let me in if it is true that you really care for me!" How could I refuse him? But I said to him: "Listen, Turiddu. Swear first, swear before God that I shall be your wife!" He swore! Then, when that wicked woman found out, she became insanely jealous and took it into her head to steal him away from me. She changed my Turiddu just like that . . . He denies it because he is sorry for me, but he does not love me any longer. And now I am in this condition . . . I think my brothers would kill me with their own hands if they knew . . . But this is not important. If Turiddu didn't love her, I would die happy. Yesterday evening he came and said: "Goodbye, I am going on an errand." His face was so kind . . . Oh God! Is it possible with a face like that to have the treachery of Judas in one's heart? Later, a neighbor who was going to confession told me that she had seen Turiddu in our vicinity, in front of Lola's door.

The Music

The seventy-nine measures of this Romanza are cast in a simple song form (A-B-A), of which the second A section is a greatly shortened variation of the first.

191

A — 44 measures
Instrumental introduction (mm. 1–10)*
Vocal section (mm. 11–37)
Instrumental postlude (mm. 38–44)
B — 18 measures (mm. 45–63)
A — 16 measures
Instrumental interlude (mm. 63–66)
Vocal section (mm. 67–79)

*   *   *

In its full operatic sequence, the Romanza leads directly into a twenty-nine measure-long Scena for Santuzza and Lucia. When the Romanza is sung separately, it ends quite abruptly, and it seems advisable, therefore, to round it out by adding as a postlude the concluding four measures of the following Scena.

The first measure of this postlude should then overlap the final measure of the Romanza.

In the Italian editions of this opera, the melody of the final words of the Romanza is printed as

In the German and American editions the long F♯ is raised to an A.

This change — which probably began its existence as a typesetting error

---

*Important dynamic markings are missing at this point in most piano-vocal scores. The opening should be marked piano; forte should be added in the fifth measure, followed by another piano on the second eighth-note of the seventh measure; then a crescendo on the next three eighth-notes and a diminuendo in the ninth measure.

— has by now become the standard interpretation. While the original version seems more "correct," the melodramatic ascent to the seventh of the chord has great expressive power and is in keeping with the highly emotional character of the situation.

The Vocal Aspects

This aria, with its repetitions of seven phrases of text, provides the singer with a challenge: to make so many repeated sentences meaningful by the use of varied tone color and dynamics. Sometimes these repetitions merely reiterate more emphatically what has been sung the first time; sometimes they are echoes of the past, filled with a sense of futility and hopelessness, as if Santuzza were talking to herself. The meaning of each repetition will be apparent from the staging of the aria. What the singer must keep in mind is that the vocal colorings and dynamic shadings must match the stage actions that are prescribed: generally, the repetitions which Stantuzza sings facing away from her partner are sung more emotionally and emphatically.

This aria is not considered vocally very difficult, for it contains but a few high notes, a limited vocal range and short phrases. But a word of caution to the singer — do not sing too heavily in the middle range — is applicable to this as well as to other dramatic arias in this volume.

Measures 36–37 can be sung in two different ways. One can start the high A rather quietly and make a crescendo; or one can make a crescendo on "l'amai" with a fortissimo attack on the high A. Maria Callas has recorded it (Angel 3509–3S) as indicated in the piano-vocal score. On an older recording (Vic. LM 6106) Zinka Milanov has chosen the more cautious approach, attacking the high A gently and swelling it with a crescendo after the attack. Milanov also sings "ah! l'amai" unbroken, whereas Callas makes a break after the "ah!" One must not breathe after "invida" in measure 47, but rather make an expressive portamento from "invida" to "ogni."

After the portamento of a tenth down to the low E (mm. 60–61), it is possible for dramatic purposes to express Santuzza's feelings about having Turridu stolen from her by singing "me l'ha rapito" with a heavy chest quality, almost an ugly one. Measures 67–68 must be sung hesitantly; then measures 69–70 must be somewhat more vehement, with a continued increase in intensity and tempo leading to the climax on "pian–" in measure 75. The final "io piango" (mm. 77–79) can present difficulties. The singer will wish to use a full chest tone on the low B. To avoid an abrupt change in quality from the F♯ to the A, it is wiser *not* to sing the F♯ with a chest tone, so that the portamento to the A will not be marred by a crack or break. This is the way it has been recorded by Milanov. Obviously preferring, for dramatic reasons, the heavy chest tone on the F♯, Callas does not sing the A at all, thus making it possible to sing all of the last "io piango" with a chest tone.

The Text

Literal Translation

1. You it know, O mamma, before to-go soldier
2. Turiddu had to Lola eternal faith sworn.
3. He-returned, her he-knew married, and with a new love he-wished to-extinguish
4. the flame which to-him burned the heart.
5. Me-he-loved. Him-I-loved. Ah, him-I-loved.
6. That-one, envious of-each joy my, of-the her husband forgetful,
7. burned with jealousy, from-me him has stolen.
8. Deprived of-the honor my, of-the honor my I-am-left;
9. Lola and Turiddu love-each-other; I weep!

Idiomatic Translation

1. You know, Mamma Lucia, that before going away to serve in the army,
2. Turiddu swore eternal constancy to Lola.
3. When he returned, he found that she was married, and with a new love he hoped to extinguish
4. the flame that still burned in his heart for Lola.
5. We loved each other. Ah, how I loved him!
6. Lola, forgetful of her husband and envious of my every joy,
7. burned with jealousy, and stole Turiddu from me.
8. Now I am left, deprived of my honor;
9. While Lola and Turiddu love each other, I weep!

The Scenic Picture

The action takes place on Easter Sunday morning. The setting represents a square of a Sicilian village, with the church on stage L and Mamma Lucia's tavern and house on the R and UR up toward the right. To R of CC, below the house is the garden of the tavern with tables and chairs for outdoor eating and drinking. The table and chairs used by Santuzza and Mamma in this aria are the ones nearest the center of the stage. Lola's dwelling must be imagined as being located behind the church in the UL direction.

The Stage Actions Explained

When the action begins, Santuzza and Mamma Lucia are standing at CC, with Lucia DL of Santuzza.

Measures

1. Santuzza motions Lucia toward the table. Lucia goes R, Xing Santuzza and table, and sits on R chair.
4. Santuzza turns Cclw to look in the direction of Lola's house UL.

5. She turns Clw, violently, close to tears.

6. She runs toward L chair, stands there for a moment.

8. She then collapses in chair; puts her R arm on table, and weeps with head on R arm.

11. She straightens up to address Lucia.

18. After "giurato," she turns Cclw to look UL, toward Lola's house.

22. She turns Clw to address Lucia.

31. She leans forward.

33. She moves still closer to Lucia.

35. She rises.

36. With "Ah," she turns Cclw and goes DL.

39. She glances toward Lola's house.

40. She turns Clw and goes to the table, then collapses in the chair, and weeps, her head on the table. Lucia strokes Santuzza's head.

45. Santuzza turns toward Lola's house.

47. (Use portamento from "invida" to d'ogni," but no breath.) With the portamento Santuzza turns Clw to address Lucia.

50. She turns again toward Lola.

52. She sings this sentence toward heaven, DL.

54. She turns toward Lucia.

57. Santuzza rises.

59. She turns Cclw and goes L.

62. She turns RSB to address Lucia.

64. She goes R, Xing above table to UL of Lucia.

67. Standing close to Lucia, Santuzza sings her confession softly.

68. Lucia shakes her head, as if not believing that her son would seduce and dishonor a girl.

69. Santuzza shakes her head in the affirmative.

73. She turns Cclw and goes L past CC.

74. With the high A, Santuzza sprays Clw.

76. She goes DR to L of L chair.

77. She kneels down at L of L chair.

"Batti, batti"
from *Don Giovanni*, Act I
by WOLFGANG AMADEUS MOZART

The Drama

Zerlina is a young Spanish girl who has promised to marry the peasant lad, Masetto. Although this is the very day chosen for their wedding, she cannot resist the temptation of flirting with Don Giovanni, and thus gets into serious trouble with her betrothed.

The "Batti, batti" aria is a dramatic duet scene depicting the lovers' quarrel and reconciliation. The quarrel results from Zerlina's gullibility. Trusting the Don's sincerity in offering to marry her, she is nearly seduced by him. Having realized her mistake, she is now desperately trying to win back her disgruntled fiancé. Here is the sequence of events beginning with her first appearance on stage.

1. Zerlina and Masetto, along with a group of peasants, invade the area outside Don Giovanni's palatial estate to dance and sing of the joys of young love.

2. The Don, who is forever in search of amorous adventures, finds Zerlina very much to his taste and offers the young couple his "protection." Anxious to make love to Masetto's charming bride, the Don invites the peasants to his palace garden and tells his servant Leporello to be sure to entertain everyone, most especially Masetto. Zerlina, impressed by the attentions of a nobleman, is only too willing to remain alone with the Don, and assures her fiancé that she will be quite safe "in the hands of a cavalier." The bridegroom has his doubts, however, and refuses to leave without Zerlina.

3. This leads to a scene where Masetto becomes quite rebellious, calls Zerlina a good-for-nothing flirt, remarks that she has "always been his undoing," and suggests sarcastically that her "cavaliere" will soon make a proper "cavaliera" out of her. His protests are of no avail. Threatened by the Don and ignored by Zerlina, he is taken off forcibly to rejoin the other peasants.

4. Remaining alone with Zerlina, the Don first flatters her by telling her how attractive she is. Then, assuring her that she can trust a nobleman's word, he promises to marry her forthwith. Zerlina is stunned by this offer and is naïve enough to take it seriously. She admits feeling sorry for Masetto, but cannot resist the dazzling prospect of becoming a noble lady. It is only by the providential intercession of Donna Elvira that Masetto's bride is saved from becoming the thousand and fourth entry in the Spanish section of Don Giovanni's catalogue of amorous conquests.

5. Elvira, who is probably the most aggressive of Don Giovanni's former "wives," enlightens Zerlina regarding her noble protector's true intentions and leads the girl back to her offended fiancé.

6. While the audience does not witness what takes place when Zerlina rejoins Masetto in the garden, we learn some of it from Leporello's lips and can readily guess the rest of it. As Don Giovanni's faithful servant reports to him — in the Recitative before the "Finch'han dal vino" — Elvira enters with Zerlina and says some dreadful things about the Don. We can imagine Masetto's indignation as he listens to a description of the Don's attempt to seduce Zerlina. When Elvira is finished with her "raving," Leporello leads her gently to the garden gate, deposits her in the street, and locks the door behind her. Since we ourselves see the lady emerge into the square to join in the quartet scene, we can vouch for part of Leporello's report. And while we do not have direct knowledge of what happens at this point between Zerlina and Masetto, we can easily guess that it is the beginning of the altercation, the end of which we witness in the Recitative that precedes the "Batti, batti." The aria itself consists of Zerlina's strenuous efforts to apologize for her behavior, to placate Masetto, and to convince him that she is worthy of his love. But while in the past she has always been able to wind her fiancé around her little finger, his strong resentment now enables him to resist her blandishments. It takes the entire first part of the aria — the sixty measures in 2/4 — before Masetto is ready to forgive his bride. The second, somewhat shorter, portion of the aria — the thirty-nine measures in 6/8 — is then devoted to the joys of reconciliation beween the clever lass and her adoring swain.

The Music

The aria of ninety-nine measures,* marked "Andante grazioso," is in two parts.

Part 1: Song form (A-B-A) with a transition (60 measures in 2/4)
                    Section A — mm.   1–16
                    Section B — mm. 16–36
                    Section A — mm. 37–52
                    Transition — mm. 53–60

Part 2: Two episodes plus Coda (39 measures in 6/8)
                    Episode 1 — mm. 61–78
                    Episode 2 — mm. 79–96
                    Coda — mm. 97–99

---

* The numbering of the measures begins after the vocal upbeats; with the second "batti" in the initial 2/4 section, and with the second "pace" in the 6/8 portion.

The continuous accompaniment passages entrusted to the solo cello must be taken into account when choosing the tempo for this piece. We recommend ♪= 92 for Part 1 of the aria and ♩.= 63 for Part 2. A gradual slowing down from 92 can begin in the fifty-eighth measure when the cello doubles its articulation. This provides a transition to the new tempo of ♩.= 63. The fermata at the end of the first part can receive a vocal embellishment in the form of

co - - re.   pa - ce,   pa - ce *(etc.)*

The Vocal Aspects

The correct pronunciation of the Italian seems to present difficulties to many sopranos who sing this aria. One often hears the words "tua" and "tue" mispronounced so that the stress falls on the "–a" and "–e" instead of on "tu–". Where more than one syllable occurs on a note, there is often a tendency to sing the first syllable *ahead* of the note instead of combining the two syllables *on* the note to which they are attached.

Like most clever women, Zerlina is able to manipulate her adoring lover in a rather shameless manner, and this must be evident not only from her acting but from her tone of voice and vocal delivery.

The sixteenth rests in the middle of words (mm. 25, 26, and 27) must be executed as tiny little sobs, as if Zerlina can hardly control her tears because she is so contrite at having hurt Masetto's feelings. The appoggiaturas indicated by the composer on the first beat of measures 28, 30, 31, and 33 must in all cases be executed so that the small note comes *on* the beat, and so that the time for it is taken from the dotted quarter that follows, changing the actual time given to the dotted quarter to an undotted quarter. The same principle is applied in measure 39: the appoggiatura is sung *on* the third beat, and the rhythm of the last two beats in that measure is as follows: ♪ ♪ ♪

The words "in contento ed allegria" (the last half of m. 64 through the first half of m. 66) should be sung as one phrase. An ample breath after this phrase should make it possible to sing "notte e dì vogliam passar" without the necessity for a breath before "passar." The two repetitions of this phrase (the last half of m. 70 through the first half of m. 73, and the second half of m. 73 through the first half of m. 76) can also easily be sung without a break. Since there are no rests for breaths in measures 91–96, it is wise to plan breaths after "–sar" in measures 92 and 94. A singer with fine breath control may even find it unnecessary to take a breath in both places.

The Text

Literal Translations

Recitative

1. Zer: Masetto, listen a little! Masetto, I-say!
2. Mas: Not me touch.
3. Zer: Why?
4. Mas: Why me you-ask? Faithless-one! The touch bear must-I of-a hand unfaithful?
5. Zer: Ah, no: be-silent, cruel-one, I not merit from you such treatment.
6. Mas: What? And you-have the-impudence to excuse-yourself? To-remain alone
7.   with a man; to-abandon-me the day of-the my wedding — to-place in forehead
8.   of a countryman of-honor this mark of-infamy! Ah, if not would be,
9.   if not would-be the scandal, I-would-like —
10. Zer: But if blame not I-have, but if by him deceived I-remained:
11.   and then what do-you-fear? Calm-yourself, my life:
12.   not to-me he-touched the tip of-the finger. Not me it you-believe?
13.   Ungrateful-one, come here: pour-out; kill-me,
14.   do everything to me that which to-you it-pleases:
15.   but then, Masetto my, but then make peace.

Aria

16. Beat, beat, O handsome Masetto, the your poor Zerlina;
17. I-will-remain here like little-lamb, the your blows to await.
18. I-will-let tear-out-me the hair; I-will-let scratch-out-me the eyes;
19. and the dear your little-hands happy then I-will-know-how to-kiss.
20. Ah, it I-see, not you-have heart! Peace, peace, O life my!
21. In contentment, and merriment, night and day we-wish to-pass.

Idiomatic Translation

Recitative

1. Zer: Masetto, listen a moment! Masetto, please!
2. Mas: Don't touch me.
3. Zer: Why?
4. Mas: Why do you ask me? Faithless woman! Must I bear the touch of your unfaithful hand?
5. Zer: Ah, no, be quiet, you cruel man. I don't merit such treatment from you.
6. Mas: What? You have the impudence to make excuses? To remain
7.   alone with a strange man; to abandon me on the day of our wedding — to place on the head

8.   of a man of honor the infamous horns of the cuckold! Ah, if it weren't,
9.   if it weren't for a scandal, I'd like —
10. Zer: But if it wasn't my fault, if I was deceived by him?
11.   What are you afraid of? Be calm, my darling:
12.   he did not touch the tip of my finger. You don't believe me?
13.   Ungrateful one, come here; pour out your anger, kill me,
14.   do whatever you want to me,
15.   but then, Masetto darling, let's be friends again.

Aria

16. Beat her, O you handsome Masetto, beat your poor Zerlina;
17. I'll stand here a little lamb, awaiting your blows.
18. I'll let you pull out my hair and scratch out my eyes,
19. and then I'll kiss your dear hands.
20. Ah, I see you don't have the heart to do it! Peace, peace, my darling!
21. In contentment and merriment we'll spend our nights and days.

The Scenic Picture

The action takes place in a section of the gardens belonging to Don Giovanni's estate. A bench stands near the DR corner of the stage. Masetto wears a stocking-cap on his head.

The Stage Actions Explained

Recitative*

Measures

1. With the opening chord — a second or two before Zerlina's first line — Masetto enters from UL and goes R. He is angry and refuses to have anything to do with Zerlina. She is most anxious to get back into his good graces. Her first "Masetto" is sung from offstage UL. Then she enters, running after him. Both entrance moves should be timed in such a way that Zerlina catches up with Masetto near CC.
2. With "dico," Zerlina clutches Masetto's L arm. On "non mi toccar," he turns LSB, withdrawing his arm and backing slightly to UR.
5. After "dovrei" Masetto turns Clw and goes DR to UL of the bench, brushing from his L sleeve the "touch" of Zerlina's "faithless hand."
6. Zerlina turns slightly Cclw to face Masetto.
8. With "tal trattamento," she runs DR to Masetto's L. With "come?" he turns LSB landing UR of her. She turns slightly Clw to face him.
10. With "star sola," he starts going slowly DL, shaking his L hand at Zerlina, and forcing her to back toward DL. This continues until measure 12.

* The music and text of the Recitative are given on p. 206. Suggested appoggiaturas are indicated in small notes above the staff.

12. By this time Zerlina has landed near the DL corner of the stage. With "nozze" Masetto stops, and with "in fronte" he points to his forehead.
13. With "questa marca" he illustrates, with both hands how large horns are growing out of his forehead.
15. He removes the knitted stocking cap from his head and crumples it into a ball.
16. With "vorrei" he raises his L arm, illustrating how he would like to strike Zerlina. After "vorrei" he throws the cap on the ground near Zerlina's feet, and stalks angrily R, stopping only DL of the bench.
18. After "rimasi" Zerlina picks up the cap with her R hand.
19. She runs R to Masetto's L. In the meantime he has put his hands on his hips. This enables her to offer him the cap by passing it through the crook of his L arm. At the same time, she lifts her L arm and extends her little finger illustrating "la punta delle dita." With "dita," he takes the cap with his R hand and turns violently Cclw to face Zerlina. With "non me lo credi?" she backs away from him to UL.
21. After "credi?" he throws the cap directly at Zerlina. She backs away, facing him, while the cap falls on the ground near the middle of the stage.
22. After "qui," he turns Cclw and goes R to below the bench where he sits down facing D. Zerlina remains in the upper portion of the stage near CC.

Recitative (Shorter Version)

To simplify the task of the supporting partner, this scene can begin in the middle of the fourteenth measure* Zerlina is standing near the DL corner of the stage, DL of Masetto. He is wearing a knitted stocking cap. With the words: "Ah, se non fosse lo scandalo," he removes the cap and crumples it into a ball.

Continue Measures 16 through 22 as above.

Aria Part 1

Measures

1. Zerlina stands center upstage and addresses Masetto, who is sitting near the L corner of the bench and is facing DR.
4. With "staro qui" she moves slightly L and points to the spot (DL) where she will be ready to endure Masetto's punishment.
8. *(2nd quarter)* Surprised at Masetto's lack of response, she turns Clw and goes slightly DR.
9. In the tone color of this "batti, batti" one should hear a touch of impatience.

---

* If the supporting actor cannot sing Masetto's opening sentence, the action can begin in the sixteenth measure with Zerlina's "Ma se colpa io non ho." In this case, Masetto's cap should be left lying near Zerlina's feet, and Masetto should start the scene standing DL of the bench.

10. *(2nd quarter)* Trying to catch a glimpse of Masetto's face, she goes R, Xing above the bench, to UR of him.
11. He turns his head Cclw so as not to have to see her.
12. *(2nd quarter)* She turns Cclw and, pointing toward the L, begins to move toward the spot where — as she indicated in measure 4 — she would be ready to be spanked by Masetto.
15. *(2nd quarter)* She has now reached the spot UL of where Masetto's cap is lying. She turns Clw to look at him. Masetto, in the meantime, has turned his face away and is gazing DR, pretending not to listen to her.
16. During the orchestral interlude Zerlina first shows her exasperation with Masetto's stubbornness, then decides to show her repentance by direct action. First she puts her hands on her hips, then picks up Masetto's cap, and runs to UR of the bench, intending to hand it to him. To synchronize these three actions with the music we recommend the following subtext:

(What's   the ___   mat-ter,   pick   it   up.)

19. Standing UR of Masetto, Zerlina offers him the cap. He turns away to face DL.
20. The sequence of actions in this orchestral interlude is similar to that in the preceding one. However, instead of picking up the cap, Zerlina throws it on the bench to Masetto's R. Following this, she goes L, Xing above the bench, to UL of Masetto. The recommended subtext is:

(What's   the ___   mat-ter,   throw   it   down.)

23. Zerlina kneels down at Masetto's L. He turns away to face DR, but does not withdraw his L arm so that Zerlina can grasp it without having to reach for it.
24. *(2nd quarter)* She picks up Masetto's L wrist with her L hand and places the palm of his hand over her own R palm.
26. *(2nd quarter)* She strokes his hand with her L hand.
27. *(2nd quarter)* She raises his hand to her R cheek.
28. Masetto refuses Zerlina's advances by withdrawing his L arm. She rises in dismay and backs up slightly.
30. To emphasize her annoyance with Masetto — and to justify the orchestral accents — Zerlina stamps her foot on the downbeat of this measure. She then turns Cclw and takes a step or two toward the L.
31. She repeats the stamping action.
32. She looks at Masetto over her R shoulder and then (after turning Clw)

tiptoes gently to the R, so as to stand directly above him and the bench.

34. Turning Cclw she puts her arms around Masetto's shoulders, but he frees himself from her embrace, rises, and goes DL as far as CC. During the following orchestral interlude, Zerlina bends down, picks up the cap with her R hand, passes it to her L hand, and sits down on the U side of the bench.

35. The melodic sequence played by the flute in this and the following measure has often confused singers. To avoid a wrong entrance in the thirty-sixth measure, we suggest that Zerlina's four actions be co-ordinated with the four quarters of the accompanying flute passage, as indicated in the following subtext:

(Bend down,— right hand,—left hand,— sit down._)

36. *(2nd quarter)* As Zerlina begins the second A section of the aria, she addresses Masetto over her R shoulder and, using the cap in her L hand, pretends to wipe a tear from her L cheek.

40. *(2nd quarter)* Still holding the cap in her L hand, she rises and goes first L and then DL to UR of Masetto. As she goes, she passes the cap into her R hand.

44. She touches Masetto's R shoulder with her L hand. He moves away angrily. She turns Clw and goes to the L of the bench.

46. She throws the cap on the bench and then, turning Cclw, returns to UR of Masetto.

49. *(2nd quarter)* With the repetition of "starò qui" she gets a new idea for cajoling her fiancé.

50. *(2nd quarter)* She comes closer to him.

51. She turns Clw, and backs toward him.

52. She stands back to back with him, her L shoulder touching his R arm.

52. *(2nd quarter)* In time with the trills of the violins, she nudges Masetto with her L elbow. He moves away gingerly, at the same time she backs pertly stage L, thus "keeping in touch" with him.

53. Zerlina's third nudge coincides with the down beat of this measure.

53. *(2nd quarter)* With the fourth violin trill, she turns LSB landing slightly UR of Masetto.

54. *(2nd quarter)* She uses the next group of four violin trills to poke the index fingers of her R and L hands alternately into Masetto's back. He goes L trying to keep a straight face, but she follows him.

55. *(2nd quarter)* She leaves him alone while she sings.

56. *(2nd quarter)* Then she tickles his ribs quite vigorously with both hands. He escapes to L, laughing and crouching.

58. When he arrives in the DL corner of the stage, he turns Clw, crouching and facing Zerlina.

58. *(2nd quarter)* She approaches him.

59. *(2nd quarter)* She lifts her arms with the palms up.

60. She lowers her arms, offering her hands to Masetto. He rises, and, with the last note of her vocal line, put his hands into hers.

Part 2

With the two upbeat eigthth-notes of the vocal line, Zerlina and Masetto begin a simple dance.

61. There are two steps to each measure: using the upstage foot *(Zerlina's L and Masetto's R)* on the first beat of the measure and the downstage foot on the second beat, they dance toward UR. This movement continues for seven steps, ending on the downbeat of the fourth measure.

64. *(2 beat)* Here the dance changes. The two R hands come together, and the dancers begin a semicircle. Zerlina dances L, Xing above Masetto, and he X's to the R below her.

66. *(2nd beat)* The dancers separate, turn Clw, join their L hands and embark on a semicircle in the opposite direction, returning to where they started in the fourth measure.

68. *(2nd beat)* The dancers separate again, this time in a Cclw turn, and continue their step movements, facing each other but without touching hands. Zerlina backs slightly to UR, Masetto remains in place.

70. *(2nd beat)* Zerlina goes DL, closer to Masetto.

72. She stops dancing, grasps Masetto's shoulders, and rotates him Clw. He makes a complete Clw circle.

73. He continues by backing away from Zerlina toward the DL corner of the stage.

74. Zerlina resumes her L-R dancing steps backing to UR.

75. She dances in a complete Cclw circle.

76. *(2nd beat)* Then, facing Masetto, she continues to dance backing toward UR. She stops in the UR portion of the stage.

78. At this point, Zerlina and Masetto face each other from opposite sides of the stage.
(2nd beat) Using her L hand, Zerlina beckons Masetto to come closer.

79. *(2nd beat)* Playing hard to get, he shakes his head and does not budge.

80. *(2nd beat)* Zerlina repeats her beckoning action more emphatically, using both hands.

81. *(2nd beat)* Masetto goes UR, almost as far as CC, and kneels down, facing Zerlina.

82. *(2nd beat)* Using his R hand, he beckons Zerlina to come closer.

83. *(2nd beat)* Now she plays hard to get.

84. *(2nd beat)* He puts his hands behind his back, sticks out his head, purses his mouth, and closes his eyes, inviting Zerlina to kiss him on the lips.

85. She goes DL, to just UR of Masetto.
86. With each of the six *si*'s, she slaps him lightly on his L cheek.
87. Delighted by Zerlina's caresses, Masetto jumps up, turns slightly Cclw, and, crouching again, points to his R cheek.
89. Zerlina repeats the slapping action on Masetto's R cheek.
90. He jumps up again and expresses his delight by dancing a few steps toward DL.
    (2nd beat) Zerlina follows Masetto toward DL.
92. She takes hold of his R hand and, turning Clw, goes toward the bench, pulling him with her.
94. She leaves Masetto at CC and continues alone to above the bench.
96. She turns Cclw, picks up the cap from the bench, and returns to Masetto's R.
97. *(2nd beat)* Holding the ends of the cap in her hands, she throws it completely over Masetto's head, so that it encircles his neck.
98. *(2nd beat)* Using the cap as a lasso, she pulls Masetto's head closer to her face.
99. She kisses him on the lips.

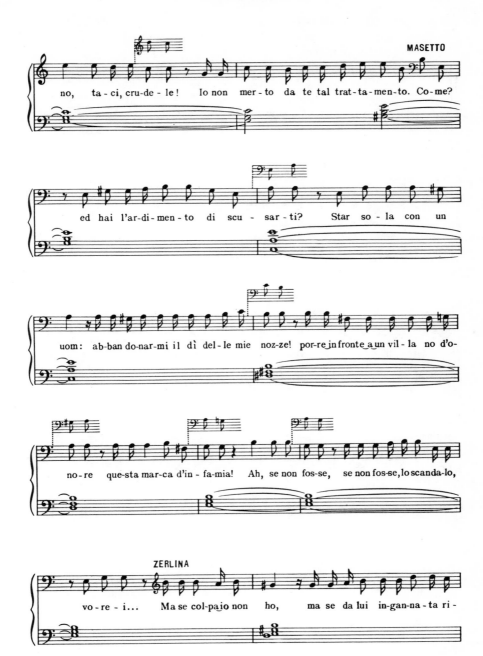

no, ta - ci, cru-de - le! Io non mer - to da te tal trat-ta-men-to. Co-me?

ed hai l'ar-di-men - to di scu - sar-ti? Star so - la con un

uom: ab-ban do-nar-mi il dì del-le mie noz-ze! por-re_jn fronte_a_un vil - la no d'o-

no-re que-sta mar-ca d'in - fa-mia! Ah, se non fos-se, se non fos-se, lo scanda-lo,

vo - re - i... Ma se col-pa_io non ho, ma se da lui in-gan-na-ta ri -

ma - si! E poi che te - mi? tran - quil - la - ti, mia vi - ta: non mi toc -

cò   la pun - ta del - le di - ta: non me lo   cre - di? In - gra - to! vien

qui: sfo - ga - ti,   am - maz - za - mi,   Fa tut - to di me quel che ti

pia - ce;   Ma poi, Ma - set - to mi - o,   ma poi fa pa - ce.

Donna Anna wears a black and silver 17th century Spanish costume with a mourning cap and veil.

"Non mi dir"
from *Don Giovanni,* Act II
by WOLFGANG AMADEUS MOZART

The Drama

This is Donna Anna's seventh appearance in the opera. She was first seen in the second scene of the first act pursuing her attacker. Then, as soon as her father arrived, she left to summon additional help. In her next appearance — as well as in all others from then on — she was accompanied by her fiancé, Don Ottavio. Returning with him in the third scene and discovering her father's lifeless corpse, Anna was prostrated with grief. After she recovered from a fainting spell, she begged her fiancé to join her in finding the culprit and avenging her father's death. Grief over the loss of her beloved father and the desire to find and punish the man responsible for the crime dominated her thinking and her behavior throughout the rest of the first act and during the sextet of the second act.

In the scene containing "Non mi dir," Anna has to deal with a new development: her fiancé's desire to console and distract her by immediately going ahead with their wedding ceremony. Anna's almost hysterical initial reaction to her father's death, as well as her subsequent persistent lamentations, worry Don Ottavio. Throughout the opera he urges Anna to stop grieving and try to forget the tragedy. He feels that marriage will be the best remedy for her disturbed emotions and in the Recitative that precedes this aria he goes so far as to tell her that by delaying the wedding she is being cruel to him.

This accusation makes Anna realize that it is time she started paying more attention to her fiancé, of whom she is very fond. The preceding episodes involving Donna Elvira, Zerlina, and Leporello justified and strengthened Anna's earlier suspicions regarding Don Giovanni. Even Ottavio, who at first found it difficult to believe that his well-born friend could be capable of such monstrous misdeeds, has by this time become fully convinced of Don Giovanni's guilt. Anna is therefore satisfied that the protection of her family's honor and the avenging of her father's death can be safely entrusted to the proper authorities. In the meantime she intends to make it clear to Ottavio that her mourning and grieving should not be interpreted as lack of affection for him.

Ottavio's suggestion that they could be married "by tomorrow," was so shocking to Anna that her vigorous response could well have been interpreted as a downright rejection of his tender solicitude. But now she is going to reassure him of her unchanged feelings for him and yet make it clear that her own grief, as well as the accepted social customs, make a hasty marriage inadvisable.

The Music

Keyboard recitative — 16 measures
Orchestral recitative — 15 measures
Larghetto in 2/4 — 48 measures
Rondo. Allegretto Moderato in 4/4 — 53 measures

Orchestral recitative (mm. 1–15)*

A few musical aspects of this recitative were mentioned earlier (see p. 14) when the notational traditions of the eighteenth century were discussed. It is perhaps useful to repeat that the "Larghetto" mark which Mozart adds in the second half of the third measure applies equally to the other two passages in which the music of the first section of the aria is quoted. There are thus two different tempos here, and we recommend $\downarrow = 76$ for the strictly recitative-like measures and $\flat = 76$ for the portions that quote the music of the Larghetto. Do not forget, also, that the word "Dio" in the tenth measure should be sung at the same speed as "mondo" in the preceding measure, so that the F♮ at the end of "Dio" comes well ahead of the G♮ in the bass of the accompaniment.

Larghetto (mm. 1–48)

Like all of Mozart's slow movements in 2/4, this is conducted in four beats to the measure. The actual tempo will depend on the breath control of the individual singer, but $\flat = 66$ may be considered a sensible point of departure. This section of the aria is shaped in a regular (A-B-A) song form in which the first A is elongated by a four-measure-long orchestral introduction.

Introduction (mm. 1–4)
A — (mm. 5–20)
B — (mm. 21–32)
A — (mm. 33–48)

Rondo. Allegretto Moderato

Opening statement — mm. 1–16
Transition — mm. 17–19
Vocal cadenza — mm. 20–29
Vocal Coda — mm. 30–49
Orchestral postlude — mm. 49–53

The form of this section is rather unusual. It begins with an eight-measure statement by the orchestra which is then repeated almost note

* The measures of each section are numbered separately.

for note by the voice. Beginning with the seventeenth measure there is a three-measure phrase leading to what can only be described as a written-out accompanied cadenza which, beginning with the thirtieth measure of the Allegretto, is extended into a vocal Coda of extraordinary eloquence and beauty. A five-measure-long orchestral postlude balances out the opening four measures of the Larghetto and provides a fitting ending to what is perhaps the crowning jewel of this collection.

The Vocal Aspects

The two recitatives preceding the aria are reproduced here for two reasons: the appoggiaturas preferred by the authors are indicated, and the syllables requiring extra stress or length are underlined to assist the singer with the proper inflection in the pronounciation of Italian.

In measure 2 of the orchestral recitative, the singer may sing "Ah no," after the orchestra has finished the phrase. The same is true in measure 5, where "Troppo" may be sung after the orchestral phrase ends. Though the preceding keyboard recitative can be performed in the usual free fashion, to follow as much as possible the inflection, stress, and length of syllables of the spoken language, this is not entirely true of the orchestral recitative. Measures 7–10 of the orchestral recitative must be sung with close attention to the printed note values, in order to coordinate properly with the orchestra; even measures 11–14 cannot be sung as freely as a typical secco recitative. The B♭ in measure 13 should not be made into a big climax; it can be elongated slightly and the phrase should continue without a break through measure 15.

Measures 5–9 of the Larghetto must be sung as one phrase. The same is true of measures 9–12, even though there is an eighth rest in measure 10; the singer may take a breath during the rest, but should think of "che son io crudel con te" as one phrase. Measure 16 need not be hurried, since the orchestral accompaniment's long note values permit a little relaxation of the tempo. This also applies to measure 18, where the turns must be sung smoothly and without haste. Though some singers do not breathe after measure 32 but carry the fermata on the E into the next phrase, there is neither a valid musical nor dramatic reason for doing so. The inevitable result is a breath somewhere between measures 33 and 36. It is preferable to breathe after measure 32 and to sing measures 33–36 in one phrase.

There are many large skips in the vocal line in this aria; in the slow first section (mm. 39, 43, 46) it is especially necessary for all of them to be sung with delicacy, as legato as possible. A gentle *messa di voce* on the long half-note in measure 47 must not be neglected.

The key to singing the final section of the aria is conservation of vocal resources. The intelligent singer will practice this section without using full voice, because of the agility that is required and because of the extremely high tessitura. Measures 19 through the first three beats of measure 28 are sung entirely on the *ah* vowel. Where notes of the same pitch are repeated, a new attack is naturally required. Where to breathe during measures 23–28 is best left to the discretion of the singer. Perhaps the most logical place is before the A in measure 25. No more than one breath during this phrase should be necessary. The series of B♭'s in measure 26 should be separated, quasi-staccato; this also applies to the series of A's in measure 27. The octave jumps to the upper notes in both instances should be legato. The big leaps in measures 32, 34–35, and 37–38 should also be sung smoothly.

Singers who find it difficult to execute a trill on lower pitches may do well to omit the one in measure 44. Occasionally singers rearrange the syllables in the penultimate measure, a practice the authors find unnecessary.

The Text

Literal Translation

Keyboard Recitative

Don Ottavio

a. Calm yourself, my idol! Of this scoundrel we shall see
b. Punished soon the grave misdeeds. Avenged we shall be!

Donn'Anna

c. But the father, oh God!

Don Ottavio

d. It behooves to lower the eye to the will of heaven.
e. Breathe, oh dear! For your bitter loss may there be to-morrow,
f. If you wish, sweet recompense (in) this heart, this hand . . .
g. Which my tender love . . .

Donn'Anna

h. Oh Gods! What say you in such sad moments?

Don Ottavio

i. And what! Would you wish with new delays to increase my pains?
j. Cruel one!

Orchestral Recitative

1. Cruel-one? Ah, no, my beloved!
2. Too-much me it-displeases to-withhold-from-you a blessing
3. that for-a-long-time the our-soul desire . . . but the world . . . oh, God!
4. Not tempt the constancy of-the susceptible my heart!
5. Sufficiently for you to-me speaks love.

Aria

6. Not to-me say, handsome-idol mine, that am I cruel with you;
7. you well know how-much-I you-loved, you know the my faithfulness.
8. Calm, calm the your torment, if of sorrow not you-wish that-I die!
9. Perhaps one day the heaven yet will-feel pity for me!

Idiomatic Translation
Keyboard Recitative

Don Ottavio

a. Calm yourself, my beloved! This scoundrel shall soon
b. Be punished for his grave misdeeds. We shall be avenged!

Donn'Anna

c. But my father! Oh God!

Don Ottavio

d. We must bow our head before the will of heaven.
e. Take heart, my dear! For your bitter loss, even by to-morrow,
f. If you wish, my heart and my hand shall console you . . .
g. And my tender love . . .

Donn'Anna

h. Oh Gods! What are you saying! At such a sad moment!

Don Ottavio

i. And why not? Would you wish with a new delay to add to my pain?
j. How cruel of you!

Orchestral Recitative
1. Cruel, do you think me? Ah, no, my beloved!
2. It displeases me too much to withhold from you the blessing
3. that our souls have desired for a long time . . . but the world . . . oh, God!
4. Do not tempt the constancy of my susceptible heart!
5. It must be enough for you that I love you.

Aria
6. Do not tell me, my handsome idol, that I am cruel to you;
7. you know very well how much I have always loved you; you know my faithfulness to you.
8. Calm your torment, if you do not want me to die of sorrow!
9. Perhaps one day heaven will yet feel pity for me!

The Scenic Picture

The scene represents a walled-in graveyard the entrance gate of which is located in the UR corner. The statue of the recently slain Commendatore, placed on a three-foot-high socket, stands in the upstage C area. The standing figure's hands are resting on a sword and it is facing toward DR. There are several scattered gravestones including a large one that is placed near the DR corner; a marble bench stands near the DL corner.

The Stage Actions Explained

Before the Recitative begins, Anna and Ottavio appear outside the gate of the cemetery, accompanied by torchbearers. The gate is opened to admit Anna and Ottavio. The others remain outside.

Keyboard Recitative*

Measures

1. Anna, carrying a large bouquet of white flowers, goes DL to R of her father's statue. Ottavio follows but stops a little distance UR of her.
2. Anna puts the flowers on the base of the monument and kneels in a prayerful attitude at R of statue.
4. She raises her head to look at the face of the statue.
7. Ottavio comes a little closer to her.
10. Anna gets up and turns Clw to face Ottavio.
13. *(2nd quarter)* Anna goes DR, Xing Ottavio, to L of gravestone.
14. Ottavio goes D to UL of Anna.
16. *(3rd quarter)* Ottavio goes L to UR of bench.

Orchestral Recitative

1. Anna looks up in surprise. Ottavio continues to go to R of bench.
2. She turns LSB to face Ottavio.
3. *(2nd quarter)* She looks at the statue. Ottavio observes her over his R shoulder.
   (3rd quarter) She goes towards the statue while Ottavio turns Clw to face her.
4. *(2nd quarter)* Having stopped momentarily to look at the statue Anna turns Clw and goes to UR of Ottavio.
7. *(3rd quarter)* Anna extends her L hand toward him.
8. Ottavio takes Anna's hand and lifts it to his lips.
9. He kisses it. Anna backs away slightly withdrawing her hand.
   (3rd quarter) Anna looks over her R shoulder at the statue, then turns slightly Clw, looks DR to heaven, and goes R to beyond CC.
10. She stops, turns LSB, and BU to face Ottavio.
12. *(3rd quarter)* Ottavio turns away from Anna (Cclw).
13. *(3rd quarter)* Anna's high B♭ soothes Ottavio's hurt feelings.
15. *(2nd quarter)* Ottavio turns Clw to face Anna.

Larghetto

1. *(2nd quarter)* Anna extends both arms toward Ottavio.
2. *(2nd quarter)* Ottavio goes to DL of Anna.
4. He takes her hands and places them in his.
8. He releases her R hand and, facing U, kneels to kiss her L hand.
10. *(2nd quarter)* Anna strokes Ottavio's head with her R hand. He releases her L hand and looks up at her.
12. Anna goes slightly UL, Xing above Ottavio and looking at the statue.
13. She turns Clw to face Ottavio. He turns his torso and head slightly Clw to face her.
15. *(2nd quarter)* Anna comes closer to Ottavio.

---

*The music and text of the Recitative are given on pp. 218-220. Suggested appoggiaturas are indicated in small notes above the staff.

17. She carresses him.
20. *(2nd quarter)* Anna turns Cclw and goes L to DL of statue.
22. Ottavio rises and backs slightly toward DR. Anna turns Clw to face Ottavio.
25. *(2nd quarter)* Ottavio goes UL to DR of Anna.
29. *(2nd quarter)* Anna goes DL to DR corner of bench.
31. *(2nd quarter)* To emphasize the repetition of her words, Anna — without turning toward Ottavio — gestures with her R arm in his direction.
    Ottavio goes DL to DR of Anna.
33. Anna sits down on the bench, facing slightly DL.
40. She turns Clw to face Ottavio.
42. Ottavio kneels facing Anna.
45. *(2nd quarter)* Anna rises and goes L to L of bench.
46. *(2nd quarter)* Ottavio rises.
47. Anna turns RSB.
48. She extends both arms to Ottavio. He goes to her (below the bench), places her hands in his, sits down on L corner of the bench, and lifts her hands to his lips.

Rondo. Allegretto moderato

1. Anna goes slightly R and embraces Ottavio by putting her R hand on his R shoulder and her L hand on his L shoulder.
3. She goes R, Xing above him and stroking her L hand along his back until it rests on his L shoulder.
4. *(3rd quarter)* Ottavio rotates slightly Clw and puts his L hand on Anna's L hand.
5. Anna looks into Ottavio's eyes and then turns her head toward heaven at DR.
6. She goes R to CC.
8. *(3rd quarter)* Anna stops to address heaven at DR.
13. She turns slightly Cclw to address Ottavio. He rises but remains standing near the bench.
14. *(3rd quarter)* Anna turns slightly Clw to address heaven DR.
16. *(4th quarter)* She goes a few steps R.
28. *(4th quarter)* She turns LSB to face Ottavio and backs another step or two toward UR.
35. She extends both arms toward Ottavio. He goes UR to DL of her.
39. Anna puts both hands on Ottavio's L shoulder. He embraces her gently.
42. She backs away toward UR.
49. She puts her L hand on Ottavio's R wrist. She then walks around him in a Cclw semicircle while he rotates Cclw. As the curtain closes, they both go toward the gate.

Recitative

DON OCTAVIO

Cal-ma-te-vi, i-dol mi-o! di quel ri-bal-do ve-drem pu-ni-ti in bre-ve i gra-vi ec-ces-si,

ven-di-ca-ti sa-rem.   **DONNA ANNA**   Ma il padre, o Di-o!   **DON OCTAVIO**   Con-

vien chi-na-re il ci-glio   al vo-le-re del ciel.   Re-

spi-ra, o ca-ra! di tua per-di-ta a-ma-ra   fia do-ma-ni, se vuoi, dol-ce com-

pen-so   que-sto cor,   que-sta ma-no,   che il mio te-ne-ro a-

The young widow Norina wears a sheer black negligee over a black satin Empire nightgown.

"Quel guardo il cavaliere"
from *Don Pasquale,* Act I, Scene 2
by GAETANO DONIZETTI

The Drama

Don Pasquale, a rich, old, crusty bachelor, wants his nephew Ernesto to marry a girl whom he has chosen for him. The young man refuses because he happens to be engaged to Norina, whom the uncle has rejected without ever having seen. Ernesto's insubordination makes Pasquale so angry that he threatens not only to disinherit his nephew but to produce new heirs by taking unto himself a young wife. The fact that Ernesto finds this notion completely hilarious infuriates the old gentleman still further, and Pasquale becomes so set on wedded bliss that his friend and physician, Dr. Malatesta, is forced to prescribe some very drastic medicine to cure him of his unfortunate folly. Malatesta tells Pasquale of a beautiful and delightful shy young girl who, so he says, is his sister Sofronia. He then offers her to his old friend as a suitable bride, an offer that makes Pasquale almost delirious with amorous anticipation.

In reality, Malatesta plans to persuade Ernesto's fiancée, Norina, to impersonate Sofronia and — after a sham marriage ceremony — to make the old gentleman's life so miserable that he would be only too happy to relinquish her to his nephew.

The second scene of the opera takes place in Norina's boudoir, and it is here that we meet the young woman, who has not yet learned what is afoot; she is merely expecting Malatesta to come and explain a certain plan for winning Pasquale's consent to her union with Ernesto.

The score describes Norina as "a young widow, quick tempered and impatient of contradictions; yet frank and affectionate."

It is amusing to note that, in this collection of twenty-four heroines, Norina is the only widow. The reason is fairly obvious. No unmarried, innocent, or otherwise inexperienced young lady could be expected to have enough savoir-faire for the wicked game required by the plot of this opera.

Norina's aria, which opens the second scene of the first act, is not, strictly speaking, part of the dramatic plot. The young widow simply introduces herself to the audience by first reading a few sentences from a romantic novel and then saying: "I am quite familiar with all the feminine tricks mentioned in this book. I am quick tempered, and impatient, and yet frank and affectionate." And this, as we have seen, is just how Donizetti and his librettist described her in the cast of characters. But character description is not easy to convert to dramatic action, and, since

223

the words sung by Norina offer so few opportunities for action, one has to look for other clues. We know that it is still the middle of the forenoon and that Norina is expecting a visitor who is well disposed to her and to her fiancé. The first scene of the opera took place a few minutes after nine, and it can be safely assumed that Dr. Malatesta went right ahead with the implementation of his plan. We imagine that his next step was to persuade his cousin, Carlotto, to agree to impersonate the Notary, and by eleven o'clock Malatesta should be well on his way to Norina. Eleven is also a likely hour for an elegant young woman to be putting the finishing touches to her morning toilette. And since it is unthinkable that Norina would live without the services of a personal maid, we arrive at the kernel of our dramatic solution: Norina, with the help of her French maid — whom we shall call Yvette — is getting ready to receive a guest. And a young lady's toilette suggests a great number of activities connected with such objects as shoes, mirrors, fans, cosmetics, flowers, and jewelry.

The Music

The composer has amplified the familiar two-stanza arrangement of this aria by expanding the introduction and adding a contrasting bridge passage between the two verses.

The opening Andante is treated as an independent Arietta based on musical and dramatic ideas not related to the main body of the aria. The Allegretto's bridge passage — with its E-flat major and B-flat minor excursions — provides contrast and adds new vitality to the reappearance of the main subject.

The piece is often shortened, partly because certain ornaments — for instance the leggierissimo G-flat major passages in the Coda — are difficult to execute, and partly because in an aria of this length (202 measures) it is not easy to achieve sufficient vocal and musical variety. It is hoped that the activities of Yvette and other dramatic "inventions" will infuse sufficient theatrical life into this aria and make it unnecessary to keep interfering with its nicely balanced shape.

Andante* in G major (31 measures)
Allegretto* in B♭ major (171 measures)

* To lessen the chance of miscounting, the thirty-one measures of the Andante and the 171 measures of the Allegretto are numbered independently.

Stanza 1:	Orchestral prelude (mm. 1–12)
	Vocal portion (mm. 13–56)
Bridge passage:	(mm. 56–85)
Stanza 2:	Vocal portion (mm. 86–129)
Coda:	Poco più (mosso) (mm. 129–171)

The Vocal Aspects

Don Pasquale was composed at a time (1842) when the art of florid singing was still at its height and when it was taken for granted that singers would adorn the melody with embellishments of their own choosing. The exact places for these vocal embroideries were not, however, left to chance or to the discretion of the performers but were marked with fermatas. Additional fermatas were also used for elongations of single notes and as indications of a slight delay in passing from one tone to another.* A composer would often write out an extended cadenza of his own invention, but when he repeated the same passage in a later stanza he expected the singer to alter it.

Opportunities for such florid extensions and variations in Norina's aria will be found at the end of the Andante as well as in the thirty-sixth and one-hundred and ninth measures of the Allegretto. For the ending of both stanzas, (mm. 81 ff. and mm. 123 ff.) Donizetti wrote out identical coloratura passages. While the first one is best sung as written, the second one certainly deserves to be provided with additional vocal fireworks.

The question of what passages the singer should add at these places is a somewhat delicate one, but, fortunately, we are in possession of authoritative information on this point. In Mathilde Marchesi's book of cadenzas,† this eminent singer and teacher offers a choice of six variations for the embellishment in the thirty-fifth measure of the Allegretto and no less than ten alternatives for the one contained in measures 124 to 129. We decided to reprint all of them here (see pp. 226–227), not only to permit singers to choose from among them but also to demonstrate just what was expected of the impersonator of Norina in the days when vocalists of the caliber of a Grisi, a Pasta, or a Persiani were the reigning prima donnas.

Mathilde Marchesi, who was born in Vienna in 1820, went to Paris in 1845 and soon became the favorite pupil of Manuel Garcia. To quote from the latest edition (1954) of Grove's Dictionary: "There [in Paris of 1845] she had the advantage . . . of hearing all the first singers of the age. . . . Her own aptitude for teaching was already so remarkable that Garcia, while prevented by the effects of an accident from giving his lessons, handed over his whole *clientèle* for the time to his young pupil."

In addition to Marchesi's cadenzas, we include our own suggestions for a short ornament in measure 109 of the Allegretto:

---

* See measure 22 in the Andante and measure 55 in the Allegretto of Norina's aria.

† *Variantes et Points d' Orgue* (Paris: Huegel & Cie, 1900).

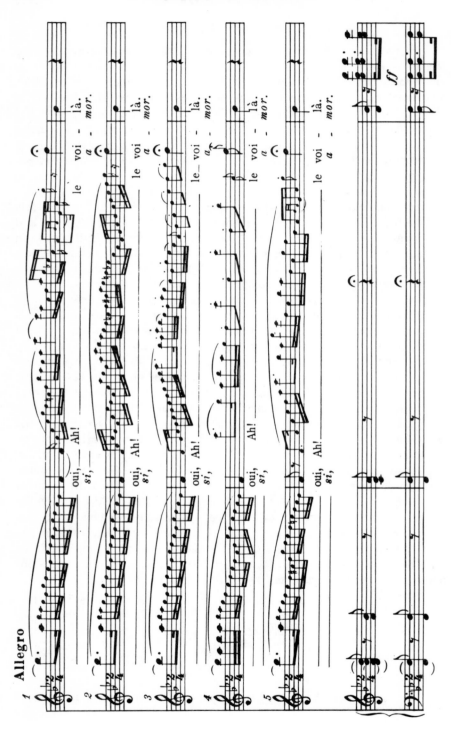

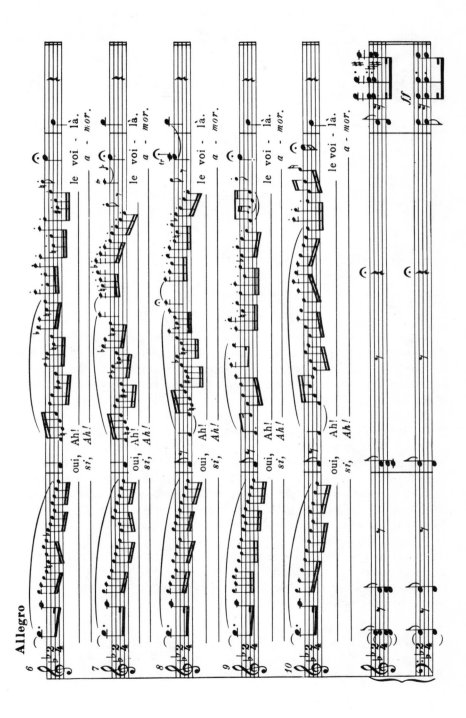

Also, a transcription of the last three measures of the Andante:

The changing meter signatures may, at first, look somewhat confusing, but they are in reality quite simple and have the great advantage of enabling the conductor to count out evenly spaced beats throughout the last two measures. This procedure guarantees a smooth and unhurried execution of the orchestral chords and, incidentally, serves to set up the exact tempo of the coming Allegretto.

Opportunities for discreet portamenti occur in identical places in both verses of the Allegretto: between the first and second notes of measures 16, 20, 24, 30, 32, 40, 42, 48, and 49 in the first verse, and measures 93, 97, 103, 105, 113, 114, 115, 121 and 122 in the second verse. There are also occasions for a slight relaxing of the tempo, as in measures 19–20, 27–28, 41–42, and 48–49 in the first verse, and measures 92–93, 100–101, 114–115, and 121–122 in the second verse. After each of these, of course, an a tempo takes place.

Though not indicated in some piano-vocal scores, it is possible to insert a subito piano on the second beat of measure 151, with a crescendo to forte in measures 155–156. The appoggiaturas in measures 155–158 should be sung as follows:

Measures 164–165 are sometimes sung as follows, with the high B♭ sustained through the first beat of measure 169:

scher - - - zar, ____

In general, the vocal interpretation of this aria can do much to characterize Norina. It can show her clever nature, her coquettishness, her calculating feminine wiles, and her skill as an actress who can bewitch and dupe Don Pasquale.

The Text

Literal Translation

Cavatina

1. That look the knight in middle to-the heart transfixed,
2. he-bent the knee and said: I-am your knight.
3. And so-much was in that look taste of paradise
4. that the knight, Richard, completely by-love conquered,
5. swore that to another never not would-he-turn the thought. Ah!

Aria

6. Know also-I the virtue magic of-a look at time and place,
7. Know also-I how themselves burn the hearts at slow-fire;
8. of-a brief little-smile know also-I the-effect,
9. of deceitful tear, of-a sudden faintness.
10. I-know the thousand ways of-the loving deceptions,
11. the caresses and the-skills easy to entice a heart.
12. Know also-I the virtue magic to inspire love,
13. I-know the-effect, ah, yes to inspire love,
14. I-have head whimsical, I-am alert, vivacious,
15. to-scintillate me it-pleases, me it-pleases to-banter.
16. If I-mount in fury of rare I-remain to-the sign,
17. but in laughter the wrath I-make quickly to change.
18. I-have head whimsical, but heart excellent. Ah!

Idiomatic Translation

Cavatina

1. That look transfixed the knight,
2. he knelt and said: I am your knight.
3. And there was such a taste of paradise in her glance
4. that Richard, the knight, completely conquered by love,
5. swore that he would never think of another. Ah!

Aria

6. I, too, know the magic power of a look at the right time and place,
7. I, too, know how hearts burn with a slow fire;
8. I, too, know the effect of a brief little smile,
9. of a deceitful tear, of a sudden faintness.
10. I know the thousand ways of love's deceptions,
11. the caresses and the easy skills needed to entice a heart.
12. I, too, know the magic power of inspiring love.
13. I know the effect, ah, yes, of inspiring love,
14. I have a whimsical mind; I am alert, vivacious,
15. and it pleases me to scintillate and to banter.
16. If I become angry, I rarely remain that way,
17. but I turn wrath quickly into laughter.
18. I have a whimsical mind, but a very fine heart. Ah!

The Scenic Picture

The scene takes place in Rome; the setting is Norina's boudoir, a very elegant and feminine room. There are two windows in the back wall and three doors in the side walls. The UR door leads to Norina's bedroom, the UL one to other rooms, and the DR one to the hall and the main entrance. A couch in the center and two small tables set by the side walls are the only pieces of furniture used. A hand mirror, an atomizer with perfume, and implements for manicuring are set on the R table; a fan lies on the L table and a small volume on the couch. It is eleven o'clock in the morning. Since the window curtains are drawn, the room is still in semidarkness.

The Stage Actions Explained

Norina's maid is an invented character not provided for in the score. She should be played as a very young, naïve French girl. Although Yvette understands Italian, she does not speak it, and for that reason has nothing to sing.

Yvette worships Norina, tries to imitate her, and is terribly anxious to learn from her and to please her.

Andante (31 measures)

The proscenium curtain opens in silence. Just before the opening pizzicati of the strings, a gentle tinkling of a bell is heard from Norina's bedroom.

Measures

2. Yvette comes in from UL with a flower vase in her hands. She had been arranging a bouquet, but on hearing Norina's bell, tiptoed into the boudoir, still holding the vase.
3. She quickly puts the vase on the L table and hurries to draw open the curtains on the L window.

4. Norina's bell is heard again. Yvette runs to the R window, draws open the curtains, and enters the bedroom, leaving the door open.

6–7. The stage is empty. The following conversation is imagined taking place in the bedroom:
Norina: Listen, Yvette, I want you to hear something I was reading last night. Come with me.
Yvette: But your shoes, Ma'am . . .
Norina: You can put them on out there. Come!

8. Norina, in negligee and slippers, enters from UR and goes to the couch.

9. Yvette, carrying her mistress's shoes, follows Norina and closes the door behind her. Norina picks up the volume lying on the couch, turns Clw, and sits down, reclining so that her legs are stretched out slightly toward the R.

10. Yvette crouches near the DR corner of the sofa. Norina opens the book.

11. She reads from the book. Yvette listens and, at the same time, removes one of Norina's slippers.

13. Yvette puts a shoe on Norina's foot.

15. She removes the other slipper.

17. She puts on the other shoe.

18. Yvette laughs, jumps up and, turning Clw, goes to above the R table where she deposits the slippers on the floor, out of sight. She then picks up a cuticle stick and a nail buffer from the table and goes UL to above the UR corner of the couch.

20. Norina passes the book into her L hand and stretches out her R arm, so that Yvette can take hold of her R hand. Yvette uses the cuticle stick on Norina's R hand nails.

22. Yvette polishes the nails with the buffer.

23. Norina withdraws her R arm, passes the book into her R hand, and lifts her L arm stretching it over her L shoulder behind her head. Yvette goes L, Xing above Norina, to the L of the couch.

24. Yvette uses the cuticle stick on Norina's L hand nails.

26. She polishes Norina's nails with the buffer.

27. She stops working and listens to Norina. Norina withdraws her L arm, sits up a little straighter on the couch, takes hold of the book with both hands, turns a page, and addresses Yvette over her L shoulder.

29. Yvette looks at the picture in the book, pretends to be shocked, and opens her eyes wide.

30. Yvette goes R, Xing above Norina to put the manicuring things on the R table. After her first laugh, Norina throws the book on the couch. After the second laugh, she gets up.

31. Norina goes L toward the L table.

Allegretto (171 measures)

During the first two measures while Norina is walking L, Yvette picks up the hand mirror and turns Cclw to face her mistress.

3. Norina turns Clw and motions to Yvette to come closer with the mirror.

5. Yvette runs L, Xing the couch and kneels (with her back to the audience) DR of her mistress, holding the mirror with both hands so that Norina can admire herself in it. During the four measures beginning with

8. Norina backs away slightly, adjusts her hair with both hands, and then parades DR, Xing above and quite close to the kneeling Yvette. The maid accommodates Norina by moving the mirror in a Cclw arc.

11. Norina looks at Yvette — who is now kneeling to her L — pats her cheek with her L hand, and takes the mirror away from her with her R hand.

12. Norina turns Clw to face R, takes a quick look in the mirror, and then walks quite slowly R to below the couch. Yvette rises while turning LSB and backs slightly to L while facing Norina.

20. Having arrived below the couch, Norina turns Cclw to face D.

25. She passes the mirror from her R to her L hand and, as she does so, notices that she is not wearing any bracelets on either wrist.

27. She looks at Yvette and points to her L wrist.

28. With her head, she motions Yvette to go to the bedroom and get her jewel box. Yvette understands, nods her head, and runs to the UR door, Xing above the couch. As she passes by the R table she picks up the slippers and takes them with her.

30. Norina turns Clw and goes to the R table where she replaces the mirror. She then turns Cclw and goes L as if intending to sit down. Noticing the novel lying on the couch, she cuts short the first note of measure 37* and takes her time in picking up the book. She then opens the volume and sings the cadenza, turning a few pages and laughing as if to make fun of the story she had read earlier.

37. Still holding the book, Norina continues to walk L to the L table.

44. She puts the book on the L table and then turns Clw to face D.

50. Yvette returns from the bedroom carrying in both hands a fairly large jewel box. She runs L and stops above the couch.

52. Norina turns Clw.

53. With the descending scale of the cadenza, she goes UR to Yvette's L.

54. She opens the lid of the box, wondering which piece of jewelry she should wear this morning.

55. She decides to make the choice while sitting down and gestures

---

* The singer who intends to use one of the six variations suggested by Mathilde Marchesi (see page 233) will therefore choose from among her third, fourth, or sixth cadenza, since these are the ones that begin with a short note followed by a rest.

Don Pasquale

toward a point below the couch where she wants Yvette to carry the opened box. Yvette understands.

56. Both women go to below the couch, Norina in a Clw, Yvette in a Cclw arc.

58. Norina sits down; Yvette crouches DR of her mistress, facing her.

59. Yvette puts the box on the couch to Norina's R.

60. Norina lifts a bracelet from the box, looks at it, shakes her head, and puts it back.

62. Norina picks up another piece of jewelry and looks at it. Yvette takes hold of a large necklace, rises, and backs to DR, facing her mistress.

64. Norina shakes her head and replaces the piece of jewelry in the box.

Yvette makes a full circle, holding the necklace in front of her neck, as if modelling it.

66. Norina notices Yvette's action, rises from the couch, and, pretending to be angry, shakes her finger at Yvette.

68. Norina goes DR and takes the necklace away from Yvette. Yvette folds her hands begging her mistress to forgive her.

70. Norina smiles to reassure Yvette that she was not really angry.

72. Norina turns Cclw and, looking at the necklace, returns to the couch.

74. She sits down and holds the necklace to her L, evaluating it.

76. She turns Clw and holds the necklace to her R.

78. She decides to wear the necklace and starts putting it on.

79. Yvette runs UL to above the couch to help Norina and, during the next three measures, manages to secure the clasp.

83. Norina rises. Yvette runs in a Clw arc to DR of the L table from where she can admire Norina.

89. Norina turns Clw and walks to the R table.

93. Norina picks up the mirror so that she can see whether the necklace suits her. Yvette, turning Clw, looks at the vase on the L table and suddenly remembers the bouquet she was arranging earlier.

94. Norina looks at the mirror. Yvette runs out the UL door.

101. Norina replaces the mirror on the table and goes slightly L.

108. Yvette returns with a large bouquet and goes to the L table where she puts the flowers into the vase.

109. During the short cadenza, Norina points at the flowers, which are a surprise to her.

110. Yvette sees the book. She takes it and holds it behind her back as she turns RSB. While Norina goes L to the flowers, Yvette goes R, Xing slowly above Norina to UR of the couch, all the while managing to hide the book from her mistress. Norina remains unaware of Yvette's sly behavior.

118. While Norina adjusts the flowers in the vase, Yvette goes DL to the couch and, turning Clw, sits down facing R and excitedly looks at the book's illustrations.

123. Norina turns Clw and notices what Yvette is doing.

125. She picks up the fan lying on the table, backs away from the flowers and, during the cadenza, goes R to above the couch. Yvette, who is completely absorbed in the book, is not aware of her mistress' approach.

129. Norina gives Yvette's L shoulder a sharp rap with the fan. Yvette jumps up, drops the book on the floor below the couch, turns LSB, and backs slightly to DR facing Norina.

131. Norina points to the book and motions Yvette to put it on the R table.

133. Yvette does so.

135. Norina returns to UR of the L table, and puts down the fan.

137. She picks up the flower vase. Yvette turns Cclw to watch.

139. Norina backs away from the table.
141. Still holding the vase, she makes a full Clw circle. She then returns to the table.
147. She puts the vase down.
148. Yvette picks up the atomizer and checks to see whether it works.
152. She goes a few steps to L. Norina goes R to DL of Yvette.
155. She turns Clw and remains with her back to the audience while Yvette, moving from R to L above her mistress, sprays perfume on her.
158. Norina continues to turn Clw and takes the atomizer from Yvette.
159. She turns further Clw to face D.
161. She sprays some perfume behind her R ear.
164. Then she sprays some behind her L ear.
166. She turns Cclw, hands the atomizer to Yvette and runs to below the couch, Xing Yvette.
170. With the last two chords, Norina turns Clw and collapses on the couch in a picturesque pose. Yvette watches her mistress with adoring eyes.

Like Mimi, Louise was very fashionable and made all of her own clothes.
A chic skirt and blouse are very appropriate for this aria.

"Depuis le Jour"
from *Louise,* Act III
by GUSTAVE CHARPENTIER

The Drama

The plot of *Louise* is very simple. Two young people — a poet, Julien, and a little seamstress, Louise — love each other and wish to marry. The girl's parents, members of the French working class, are opposed to the marriage on the grounds that the young man does not have a respectable profession and a permanent job. Louise's mother, an embittered and rather unpleasant woman, is especially antagonistic toward Julien whom she considers to be a lazy and debauched good-for-nothing. When it becomes clear that the parents' consent cannot be obtained, Julien persuades Louise to run away with him. They live together, unmarried, but otherwise in perfect harmony and contentment until, several weeks later, Louise's mother finds them and begs Julien to permit Louise to return home. It seems that Louise's father, who adores his daughter, has become very ill and that only the girl's return can help him over the crisis. The mother promises that as soon as the older man recovers, Louise will be free to rejoin her lover. Louise, who is very fond of her father, accedes to her mother's plea, but after the recovery takes place, the parents refuse to allow Louise to leave. The girl who is anxious to regain her freedom and the joys of her newly awakened womanhood, becomes so rebellious that her father, seeing that he cannot recapture her love, drives her from the house forever.

Louise's exact age is not indicated, but judging from certain episodes — when her mother slaps her, or when her father rocks her on his knee — she must be quite young: surely not over eighteen years old. The portrayal of a serious conflict between a teenager and her parents — caught in what is known today as the generation gap — was still something of a novelty in the year 1900 when this opera appeared. It had, furthermore, a special poignancy in France where, both by tradition and law, parental authority had always been particularly strict. A very substantial part of the opera is devoted to a depiction of the city of Paris which, like every great urban center, tempts young people by offering them unlimited opportunities for pleasure, and by showing them too many examples of unbridled excesses.

The composer, who also wrote the libretto of the opera, was an advocate of feminine emancipation and used the opera as a platform for his ideas of free love and complete independence for young people of both sexes. It is Charpentier who speaks through Julien, when in the second act the poet argues that most parental love is nothing but selfishness, that every human being has the right to be free, and that every heart has the right

237

to love. What is of special interest to us in connection with Louise's aria is that Charpentier was one of the few opera composers who had the courage to have commonplace and everyday characters sing quite frankly of physical love, a subject that had theretofore always been veiled in heroics and euphemisms. It is true that the purely musical techniques for describing the convolutions of physical love owe their development to Wagner. But it is well to keep in mind that in *Tristan und Isolde* all this is submerged in Schopenhauerian terms of the "night," and the lovers' "union in death"; and in the Prelude to Strauss's *Der Rosenkavalier* the orchestra describes what is taking place behind a closed theater curtain. It is a very different thing to present us with an eighteen-year-old French seamstress who, in the presence of her Julien, openly reminisces on the sexual delights she experienced in her love relation with him.

The Music

Andante (111 measures)
Instrumental introduction (mm. 1–4)
First Stanza (mm. 4–27)
Second Stanza (mm. 27–89)
Coda (mm. 89–111*)

This aria is cast in the familiar two-stanza mold framed by an Introduction and a Coda. The second stanza, however, is so much more elaborate and so much longer than the first that one can perhaps speak of the first as a promise, and of the second as the fulfillment. This, of course, would only be in keeping with the content of the poem; in the beginning Louise believes she is "dreaming . . . her soul still dazzled by Julien's first kiss," while towards the end she is "trembling at the delicious memory of her first day of love."

The high point of both stanzas falls on a sustained high A. We note that the first climax, which occurs after only fourteen preparatory measures, is sung softly and is reached by means of a diminuendo.

In contrast, the second stanza progresses in a gradual, phrase by phrase ascent that lasts forty-five measures and culminates in a much longer high A which, after a prolonged crescendo, is sung full voice.

The Vocal Aspects

There seems to be a great deal of discrepancy in the interpretation of this aria by various performers. It might be suggested that the reason for this is a lack of attention to the many markings that affect the tempo and the dynamics. Though subtleties may be overdone, one often finds that in this aria too little attention is paid to the almost abrupt changes of

---

*In the piano-vocal score, the last measure modulates into G minor. When the aria is performed separately, one of course ends it with a G major chord.

dynamics and tempos. It seems almost superfluous to say that this aria should not be attempted by a singer who does not possess fine breath control, the ability to sing a superb *messa di voce* in the high range, evenness of quality from top to bottom, and effortless control of dynamics.

The first phrase (mm. 5–8) should be sung in one breath; the low D should be sung gently in measures 5 and 7. The second phrase (mm. 11–17), must also be sung in one breath, in spite of the breath mark in the piano-vocal score at the end of measure 12! The marking, "un poco animato" at measure 15 should be scrupulously observed. The next phrase, "Je crois rêver sous un ciel de féerie," should also be sung in one phrase, and the Meno at measure 19 and a tempo at measure 20 should not be ignored. In spite of the difficult skip of a ninth, the word "baiser" (mm. 26–27) must be sung as softly as possible. Then Meno is again indicated at measure 34; there is no a tempo at measure 35 in the score but it is certainly meant to be there.

Though no phrasing is indicated after "Ah!" (mm. 45–46), it seems likely that an exclamation could be followed by a slight pause, and thus a breath is possible before "je suis heureuse!" The più vivo at measure 55 is too often ignored — but here the tempo should pick up noticeably and suddenly. When the voice enters at measure 58, the tempo is slightly slower. Many sopranos put a long fermata on the high A in measure 61; to accomplish this, they must take an akward breath after "coeur" in measure 60. The authors recommend that measures 58–62 be sung in one breath, and that "joie" in measure 61 be held only slightly longer than written, in accordance with the Meno written above it.

If the second più vivo (m. 63) is observed, it is possible to sing "Tout vibre, tout se réjouit de mon triomphe!" in one phrase. Then "Autour de moi tout est sourire" can also be one phrase, with a slight catch breath before "lumière et joie!" The phrase, "et je tremble" (mm. 77–81) should be sung in one breath, with a catch breath before "délicieusement." Another catch breath is possible after "au souvenir charmant," so that "du premier jour d'amour!" can be sung unhurried.

Though the first "Quelle belle vie" (mm. 32–35) is sung quietly, the repetition of this phrase (mm. 92–93), sung mezzo forte, is almost an outburst of joy. The real climax of the aria in measures 96–100 can best be handled in the following manner: measure 96 need not be hurried; after "ah," an unhurried breath permits "je suis heu–" to be sung quietly and carefully; then the high B can be attacked pianissimo and an extended *messa di voce* is possible. The markings "Animato" in measure 97 and "rallentando" at the end of measure 99 should be carefully observed. The breath in measure 100 need be but a short one, almost a little gasp. The low D's in measures 103–107 should not be sung with a heavy chest quality. Although they may be difficult after the extended high B, the singer should not resort to a deep, throaty tone in an effort to be audible. The low notes should be soft, half murmured, half sung. The final phrase should not be sung too softly and should be unbroken.

The Text

Literal Translation

1. Since the day when I myself am given,
2. All flowered seems my destiny.
3. I think to-dream under a sky of enchantment,
4. The-soul still intoxicated from your first kiss!
5. What beautiful life! My dream was not a dream!
6. Ah, I am happy! The-love spreads over me its wings!
7. In-the garden of my heart sings a joy new!
8. Everything vibrates, everything itself rejoices at my triumph!
9. Around of me everything is smile, light and joy!
10. I am happy, too happy,
11. And I tremble deliciously at-the memory charming of-the first day of love!

Idiomatic Translation

1. Since the day when I gave myself to you,
2. my destiny seems strewn with flowers.
3. I think I am dreaming under a magic sky,
4. my soul still intoxicated by your first kiss!
5. What a beautiful life! My dream was not a dream!
6. Ah, I am so happy! Love spreads its wings over me!
7. A new joy sings in the garden of my heart!
8. Everything pulsates, everything rejoices at my triumph!
9. Around me, everything is smiling, everything is light and joy!
10. I am happy, too happy,
11. And I tremble deliciously at the charming memory of the first day of our love!

The Scenic Picture

This aria opens the third act of the opera which takes place on a summer afternoon at the summit of the Parisian hill of Montmartre. The scenic description in the score mentions a one-storey house with an open porch and a little garden enclosed by a low fence. At the back is a hedge beyond which one sees a panorama of Paris.

The house is upstage to the R of center and surrounding the porch is a railing. The door of the house and the stoop leading into the garden are located at the center of the stage near the L corner of the porch. The fence extends on both sides of the house. It encircles the R corner of the garden and all of its L side. There are two chairs — one above the railing to the R of the stoop and the other in the garden DL of the porch. A flower bed is in the DR corner of the garden and a rustic table UL of the flower bed.

The Stage Actions Explained

Louise is sitting on the porch, to the R of the stoop that leads into the garden. With her elbows on the railing, she leans forward and watches Julien, who sits in a rustic chair below the DL corner of the porch. He is facing DL and holds a book in his hands.

Measures

1. Louise smiles as she gazes tenderly at Julien.
5. Hearing Louise's voice, Julien turns his head Clw, puts the book on his lap, and listens over his R shoulder.
9. Louise rises, goes slightly L, and then steps down from the porch into the garden.
11. She continues to face DL and address Julien.
15. With "destinée," she looks heavenward, turns Clw, and goes DR to below the table.
17. After "'destinée," she turns Cclw and, half-sitting on the table, leans back, supporting herself on her outstretched arms.
19. Julien, still sitting, turns Clw to watch Louise.
25. She turns Cclw to look at Julien.
28. She goes L to Julien's R, and kneels by his side.
30.* As Julien sings "Louise" he caresses her head.

Lou - i - - se

36. Louise rises and backs slightly to U.
37. She looks heavenward.
39. With the second "rêve," she looks at Julien.
41. She moves closer to him.
42.† She embraces him from above and caresses his head.
43. She turns Cclw and goes L, halfway to the fence.
47. With the long G♯, she looks heavenward, turns slowly RSB and backs slightly to UL.
50. She looks at Julien.
55. As she ends her vocal phrase, she looks at the flowers in the DR corner of the garden, and goes DR, Xing Julien.
58. She kneels UL of the flower bed.
63. She rises.
65. She looks heavenward.

* Julien's singing "Louise" — the only word he has in "Depuis le Jour" — is omitted in the sheet music and anthology versions of this aria. If Louise's partner is not a singer this may also be omitted in this staging version.

† The third horn's exclamatory ♭ in measure 42 should be added to the piano accompaniment.

67. She turns LSB and backs to UR.
70. She goes L to below the table.
76. She sits on the table and leans back to rest on her R elbow.
90. She straightens into a sitting position.
92. She turns Cclw to look at Julien.
94. She slides off the table toward the L.
96. She turns RSB, backs to U, and with her hands behind her leans against the railing of the porch.
100. She looks at Julien.
102. She goes DL to UR of Julien.
104.‡ After "délicieusement," she touches Julien's R shoulder.
107. After "charmant," she kneels at Julien's R.

‡ The solo viola line should be added to the piano accompaniment after "délicieusement," and again two measures later, in measure 107, after "charmant."

Cio-Cio-San's kimono closes left over right. It is a simple tasteful garment, with two padded rolls at the bottom, completed with the brocaded obi, obi sash, and white tabis.

"Un bel di"
from *Madama Butterfly*, Act II
by GIACOMO PUCCINI

The Drama

Butterfly's celebrated aria occurs near the beginning of Act II. From other sources in the text — Butterfly's conversation with Sharpless later in the same act, and the letter from Pinkerton read by Sharpless — we know that Butterfly has been deserted by Pinkerton for more than three years. The money that Pinkerton gave to Butterfly when he left is now almost gone. Butterfly has had a child, now about two-and-a-half years old, who is the image of his father. During Pinkerton's absence Butterfly has had little companionship. Her family has abandoned and disowned her, and she has had almost no one to talk to except her faithful servant, Suzuki. Butterfly has been waiting for Pinkerton to return, since she innocently believed his idle remark that he would return "in the blissful season when the robin remakes his nest."

But Suzuki has become doubtful that Pinkerton will ever return. Butterfly tries to convince her that Pinkerton's return is certain because he has seen to it that the rent for the house has been paid in his absence, and because he would not have bothered to have locks put on the doors if he did not intend to come back. The purpose of the locks, in Butterfly's words, is "to keep mosquitoes, relatives, and sorrows outside, and to keep his bride, with jealous care, inside." Suzuki says that no one has ever heard of a foreign husband returning. This makes Butterfly furious, and she insists that Suzuki say with her, "He will return." At this point Suzuki breaks into tears and crouches at Butterfly's feet.

The Music

Puccini sought to include an air of authenticity in the music for this opera, and he even went to the trouble of consulting a number of Japanese experts for their advice. There are authentic Japanese melodies, as well as expert imitations, throughout the score. The pentatonic scale (the first, second, third, fifth, and sixth notes of the major scale; or the five consecutive black notes on the piano) is often employed. At the beginning of Act II, before the aria, we find numerous repetitions of a melody utilizing what might be called a "minor" pentatonic scale, employing the notes D, F, A, and B, or their transpositions:

245

This theme, especially with its sometimes rather shrill orchestral color, demonstrates Puccini's simple and yet telling way of depicting the loneliness and poverty of Butterfly. However, only moments after its numerous repetitions, Butterfly's mood changes to one of confidence, and the present aria is set to a diatonic melody in a major key. Artfully disguised, however, the "minor Pentatonic" scale returns in the harmonic texture and the melody at the climax of the aria (mm. 59–61), beginning with the words, "Tienti la tua paura." It is Puccini's way of showing Butterfly's underlying despair even when she is apparently optimistic and confident of Pinkerton's return.

The singing is continuous and the longest period of rest for the voice is two beats. Although there are a number of changes of meter and tempo, the aria is basically slow, with many small rubati so characteristic of Puccini. It is perhaps dangerous to make a sweeping statement that it is often sung too slowly, with too little nuance in tempo, and that many singers tend to disregard the note values and make the ritardandos too drawn-out, yet this is all too often the case.

The aria, without an introduction, is seventy measures long, and can be divided into four main sections:

1. The arrival of Pinkerton's ship into the harbor — 16 measures

2. Butterfly's behavior as a reaction to this — 11 measures

3. Pinkerton's approach and Butterfly's reaction — 20 measures

4. The reunion of Butterfly and Pinkerton — 23 measures

    a. Vocal ecstasy — 9 measures

    b. Butterfly's reassurance of Suzuki — 5 measures

    c. Wordless ecstasy — 9 measures

From a musical standpoint, the aria can be described as an A-B-A form, with measures 1–18 as the first A, measures 19–48 as B, and measures 49–70 as a modified return of A. Actually, the final section (mm. 49–70) is in itself a smaller A-B-A (first A, mm. 49–56; B, mm. 57–61, second A, mm. 62–70).

One should also note Puccini's device of quoting, during the course of the aria, some music that Butterfly has previously sung. It occurs first when Butterfly quotes Pinkerton's remarks just before his departure:

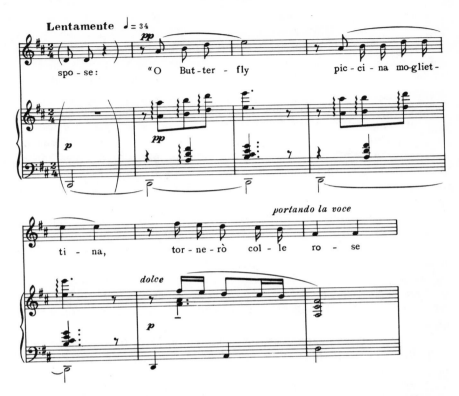

This melody occurs in the aria, in measures 42–47, transposed a half-tone lower in the accompaniment when Butterfly describes Pinkerton's imaginary return.

Special Problems

American productions of *Madama Butterfly* are often criticized for lack of authenticity and a disregard of Japanese customs.

It is well known, for instance, that Orientals do not readily show their emotions and seldom touch each other. Certainly this must have been even more true seventy years ago. Thus it would seem improper for Butterfly and Suzuki to embrace — all the more so because they are mistress and servant, and the caste system at the turn of the century was much more rigid than it is today.

Yet it must be remembered that this is essentially an Italian opera, and that Puccini's musical outpourings at moments of great emotion must be matched by what takes place on stage. The singers must see to it, therefore, that demonstrations of emotion and affection between Butterfly and Suzuki be always initiated by Butterfly. After all, she prides herself on being an American and while she was living with Pinkerton undoubtedly learned to be more demonstrative.

In an effort to be authentic, the mistake is sometimes made of costuming the women in actual Japanese clothing. Westerners, being unaccustomed to these clothes, often find them uncomfortable. The obi (or sash) seems particularly constricting across the chest and bosom. It is probably wiser to choose looser fitting imitations rather than authentic Japanese garb.

The problem of footwear must also be dealt with. Since we know that the Japanese did not wear shoes or clogs indoors, it is necessary for the stage director and singer to arrange matters whereby this custom can be taken into account. In this aria, we can assume that Butterfly and Suzuki are wearing only socks, and that their sandals or clogs have been left on the porch. It can be assumed that Butterfly and Suzuki pass from house to garden and back again without stopping to put on or take off footwear.

An attempt should be made to imitate the way in which Japanese women walk. Suzuki and Butterfly should practice walking with their knees together, using only the lower part of the leg below the knee to take a step. This will necessitate — especially when done somewhat rapidly — bringing one foot in front of the other, with the result that each leg swings outward slightly in moving forward. To see Butterfly and Suzuki walking with the long, relaxed stride of contemporary women is indeed incongruous, especially when they are wearing kimonos.

Singers portraying Japanese women must also learn to kneel gracefully on both knees simultaneously, even if their leg muscles at first resist. Care must be taken that the hands are not used to help keep one's balance while kneeling. Sometimes it is necessary for singers to wear knee pads under their costumes.

We try to be authentic, but we are forced to adjust occasionally for the sake of good sense. And since *Madama Butterfly* is performed mostly for Western audiences, it is hoped that our Oriental friends will forgive an occasional transgression.

The Vocal Aspects

The role of Butterfly cannot be successfully attempted by an immature singer. Butterfly is onstage during most of the opera, and the vocal demands in every act are considerable. Yet this aria remains one of the favorite teaching pieces in many a vocal studio. Even though arias can be studied without considering the singer's suitability for the entire role, there still should exist in the mind of every vocal teacher the demands that the aria alone makes upon a young voice. To make it easier to sing, liberties are often taken with phrasing that violate the composer's intent and that break up the text into brief, unintelligible fragments. Even though in measure 2 Puccini indicates an eighth rest, and a breath is possible, it should be taken in such a way that the phrase does not seem to stop and so that the first six measures of the aria are considered as one phrase. In measure 4 there is indeed, from the standpoint of text, a possibility for a breath (after "fumo"), but Puccini has written a slur which negates this possibility. Measures 9 through 12 should also be sung in one breath, although many singers divide this passage into two phrases. Although there is a comma after "pesa" in measure 24, it is better to sing measures 22 through 26 in one breath. Even if a catch breath is necessary, the second beat of measure 31 through measure 37 should be sung in one phrase.

Since Butterfly is acting out what she imagines will happen when Pinkerton returns, the tone quality the singer employs need not always be a full, opulent sound, which often tends to obscure the meaning of the words. This is a "cantabile" aria, and it should be sung somewhere between an "enunciated" cantabile and a "full" cantabile; but the text is important enough so that the words must be understood. The aria is rather ambiguous: Butterfly's most impassioned mature utterances are combined with a naive explanation and demonstration of what will happen when Pinkerton returns to her. This ambiguity must be reflected in the variety of tone color the singer displays.

The ending of the aria presents a problem to most singers. Although the last syllable of the final word ("l'aspetto") is meant to be sung on the lower octave Bb, the alternate high Bb is also given as an optional note, with the result that almost all singers refuse to sing the lower note. However, the vocal difficulties of singing the syllable "–to" on the repeated high Bb are self-evident. The alternate ending given here, requiring the alteration of a few words of the text, was (as Puccini's friend, the conductor Giorgio Polacco, assured Mr. Goldovsky) highly approved by the composer.

Tien-ti la tua pa-u-ra,   io ne son si-cu-ra, ver-ra.——

The Text

Literal Translation

Introduction

 1. You weep? Why? Why? Ah, the faith to-you it-lacks! Listen!

Aria

 2. One beautiful day, we-shall-see raise-itself a thread of smoke
 3. on-the-farthest edge of-the ocean. And then the ship appears.
 4. Then the ship white enters in-the port, thunders the its salute.
 5. You-see? He's come! I not to-him go-down towards, I not.
 6. Myself I-place there on-the brow of-the hill and I-wait,
 7. and I-wait long time and not me weighs, the long waiting.
 8. And . . . gone-out from-the crowd city, a man, a tiny speck himself-starts up the hill.
 9. Who will-it-be? And when he-will-be arrived, what will-he-say?
10. He-will-call, "Butterfly," from-the distance.

11. I without giving answer myself from-him will-stay hidden,
12. a little for joke and a little in-order not to-die
13. at-the first meeting, and he, somewhat in pain, will-call, will-call:
14. "Tiny little-wife, perfume of verbena,"
15. the names that to-me he-gave at-the his coming.
16. All this will-happen, to-you it I-promise.
17. Keep-you the your fear, I with firm faith him-await.

Idiomatic Translation

Introduction

  1. You're weeping? Why? Ah, you lack faith! Listen!

Aria

  2. One beautiful day we shall see a thread of smoke rising
  3. on the horizon. And then the ship appears.
  4. Then the white ship enters the port, and thunders its salute.
  5. You see? He's come! I do not go down to meet him, not I.
  6. I stand on the brow of the hill, and I wait,
  7. and I wait for a long time, but it does not tire me, the long wait.
  8. And . . . leaving the crowd of the city, a man, a tiny speck in the distance, starts up the hill.
  9. Who will it be? And when he has come, what will he say?
10. He'll call, "Butterfly," from a distance.
11. I won't answer, but will stay hidden from him,
12. to tease him a little, and in order not to die
13. at our first meeting, and he, somewhat worried, will call:
14. "Tiny little wife, perfume of verbena,"
15. the same names he used to call me when we first met.
16. All this will happen, I promise you.
17. Go on, be afraid. I'll keep waiting with unwavering faith.

The Scenic Picture

The entire opera takes place in and around the house that Pinkerton leased when he married Butterfly. Constructed in typical Japanese style, it has no doors or windows, but sliding panels ("shosi" in Japanese) that can open the entire house to the out-of-doors or close it up completely. In this scene the panels are placed so that the entire house, except for the rear wall, is open; thus the house and garden are one unit, and passage from one to the other is made effortlessly. In the DR corner of the house is a Japanese shrine where Suzuki has prayed at the beginning of the act. Upstage of the shrine is a folding screen. In the center of the room is a low Japanese table, and to the R of it, a Western-style chair that Pinkerton has left behind. Upstage of the low table against the back wall is a cupboard which normally houses a large beautifully framed photograph of Pinkerton. This important prop, which was used earlier in this act, is now standing on the low table.

The house is surrounded by a garden that occupies the L third of the stage and extends in a narrow strip below the house on stage R. The house has a porch surrounding its L and D side. To pass between the inside room and the garden when the house panels are open, one needs only to X above the DL corner post that supports the roof of the porch. The house and the porch are raised to a level six inches above the stage floor. While this higher level is advantageous, the staging of the aria functions just as well if everything is played on the stage floor. A path or walk of pebbles or sand runs below the D edge of the porch and it is on this walk that Suzuki is kneeling. The rest of the house is presumed to be offstage R.

The harbor of Nagasaki is imagined being located at the bottom of the hill toward DL and supposedly visible from the DL corner of the garden. This is also the direction from which Pinkerton would arrive, were he to return.

The Stage Actions Explained

Since there is no orchestral Prelude, it is advisable, in lieu of an introduction, to utilize the eighteen measures that precede the aria.* Before the start of this introduction, Suzuki was forced, at Butterfly's insistence, to say "Tornerà" (He will return). Now the weeping Suzuki is kneeling on the D stage garden walk facing UR. She remains on her knees during the rest of the aria. She changes her position occasionally so that she can look at the various locations that Butterfly indicates (the house, the shrine, etc.). When Butterfly is addressing her, she looks at Butterfly, but all her changes of position while she is kneeling must be made unobtrusively with her back always to the audience.

Butterfly sings "Piangi?" standing on the garden path UR of Suzuki. She kneels, addressing Suzuki, on the second "Perchè?" (Why?) and sings "Ah la fede ti manca! Senti." (Ah, you lack faith. Listen.) while kneeling.

Measures
1. Butterfly remains kneeling, addressing Suzuki.
2. Butterfly rises (*2nd quarter*) and BU slightly to UR of Suzuki (*still slightly below platform*).
3. Butterfly points to the harbor, DL offstage.
9. She goes L slightly, Xing above Suzuki, onto the platform, visualizing the arrival of Pinkerton's ship into the harbor.
15. (*1st quarter*) Butterfly turns Clw to address Suzuki.
   (*3rd quarter*) Butterfly looks in the direction of the harbor.
17. Butterfly, looking into the distance downstage, sings to herself.
18. She sings "io no" to Suzuki.
19. Butterfly turns Cclw and points DL to the place where she will stand to watch for Pinkerton's return.
22. She turns Clw to address Suzuki.

* This music is given on page 252.

26. Butterfly turns Cclw and goes L off the platform a short distance into the garden. She looks DL offstage, standing on tiptoe, just as she expects to do when Pinkerton returns.

37. (*during the rest with the fermata*) Butterfly turns Clw and goes R onto the platform, UL of Suzuki, to address her.

38. On the second "Chi sarà" Butterfly looks in the direction of the harbor.

40. She sings the second "Che dirà" to Suzuki.

42. Butterfly looks towards harbor on "dalla lontana."

44. She goes UR to above the low table, pointing to the folding screen above the shrine to indicate where she will hide when Pinkerton arrives.

49. She turns LSB and BU UR so that she lands just UR of the low table, her eyes raised heavenward in excitement and anticipation.

51. Butterfly indicates to Suzuki the DL corner of the stage, from which Pinkerton will appear.

54. (*3rd quarter*) Butterfly turns Clw, almost shyly, as she recalls the endearing names that Pinkerton once called her, and looks at Pinkerton's photograph on the table.

55. Suzuki begins to weep again, in remorse for having hurt Butterfly.

56. Butterfly looks at Suzuki.

58. Butterfly goes DL slightly towards Suzuki.

62. Butterfly looks heavenward with confidence and exultation.

63. Suzuki gets up, hesitates a moment, and then runs UR onto the platform and into Butterfly's embrace, Xing above the low table.

65. They separate; Butterfly dimisses Suzuki, who X's above Butterfly and exits UR above the screen.

68. Butterfly goes to above the low table, kneels facing DR.

69. She picks up Pinkerton's photograph, admires it, and embraces it.

To visit the Countess in her boudoir Cherubino wears the square-cut coat, breeches and a vest of the mid-18th century. A lace jabot and powdered wig complete his costume. The dress sword is an integral part of any cavalier's dress of this period.

"Voi che Sapete"
from *Le Nozze Di Figaro,* Act II
by WOLFGANG AMADEUS MOZART

The Music and the Drama

Annoyed at having caught Cherubino making love to both the gardener's daughter, Barbarina, and to his wife's personal maid, Susanna, and angry that the boy's adoration for the Countess has become an item of common gossip among his servants, Count Almaviva has granted the pageboy an officer's commission and ordered him to leave the castle at once.

Countermanding this order, the Count's valet, Figaro, persuades the youngster to disobey the Count and to delay his departure. Figaro has conceived the idea of dressing Cherubino in Susanna's clothes, and having him keep her rendezvous with his Lordship. It is in this situation that the Countess would appear, catch her husband red-handed, teach him a much-needed lesson, and keep him away from Figaro's bride.

The Countess and Susanna are foolish enough to cooperate in this harebrained scheme. But before disguising Cherubino they decide to cajole him by letting him recite — or rather sing — his latest love poem to the Countess. The scene begins just before the entrance of the love-sick pageboy.

COUNTESS

Where is the song?

SUSANNA

Here it is. We'll make him sing it to us at once. I hear someone coming. It is he. *(opens the door for Cherubino)* Come in, come in, gallant soldier!

CHERUBINO

O, do not call me by this hateful title. It reminds me that I must leave my Godmother, who is so kind!

SUSANNA

And so lovely!

CHERUBINO

She is . . . truly!

SUSANNA *(teasing him)*

She is . . . truly! You big hypocrite! Hurry up and sing to Milady the song you gave me this morning.

COUNTESS

Who wrote the song?

SUSANNA

Look at him! Look how he blushes!

255

COUNTESS

Take my guitar, Susanna, and play the accompaniment.

CHERUBINO

I am so nervous . . . but if Madam wishes.

SUSANNA

She wishes it indeed! Let's have none of your excuses. (*Susanna strums the introduction on the guitar.*)

The text of Cherubino's poem consists of eight four-line stanzas. It is an appeal to women who — since they are experts in these matters — can tell the young poet whether or not what he is experiencing is really love. "I will describe to you my condition," he tells them. He then proceeds to list his symptoms, and finally repeats the appeal he voiced at the beginning of the poem. This simple sequence — appeal, description, appeal — corresponds to the musical form of the Arietta with its A-B-A structure: Exposition (mm. 1–20), Middle section (mm. 21–61), and Recapitulation (mm. 62–79).

This conventional pattern, followed in thousands of similar compositions, acquires a special charm when Cherubino gets carried away and, instead of parading the customary amorous aches and pains, becomes almost embarrassingly personal and specific. To appreciate the subtlety of Mozart's treatment of this piece, the singing actress should keep in mind that the "normal" procedure would have been to set the two A sections in the tonic key of B-flat major — and the middle section in the dominant key of F major. This is just how Cherubino's Canzona evolves until measures 33 and 35 when the contrast between "diletto" (delight) and "martir" (torture) — is echoed in the juxtaposition of F major and F minor. At this point, the boy goes off the deep end, harmonically speaking, and his "freezing and burning" sensations take him to the faraway key of A-flat major. Attempting to maintain the fiction of poetic detachment, he finishes this stanza with a melodic formula he used in the A section,* but the heat of the passion carries him on to ever more personal avowals.

When describing his search for "un bene fuori di me" (the desired and remote treasure) (mm. 45–48) Cherubino lands in the "remote" key of C minor, and his pretense not to know what "it" is and who possesses this "treasure" is unmasked as a lie by the modulation into the "sensuous" key of G minor (m. 52). The climax is reached in the next stanza where, with unexpected violence, the sixth and seventh quatrains of the poem are compressed into one single nine-measure musical phrase. Here, the breathlessness of the hurried sentences, the "involuntary sighing, moaning, palpitating, and trembling," coupled with the chromatic ascents in the flute and oboe, and the "pleasure of delicious longing" in measures 59 and 60, make it perfectly clear that what the boy describes so graphically

---

* Compare the melody of "ed in un momento," etc., in measures 41 and 42, with that of "donne vedete," etc., of measures 17 and 18.

is not "love," but the self-gratification of adolescent sex!*

At this point, Cherubino realizes the impropriety of telling this to the Countess; and especially in the presence of Susanna which makes it all the more embarrassing. He quickly returns to the formality of the initial stanza and ends the song in the same polite and aristocratic posture with which he started it.

The Vocal Aspects

As has already been mentioned, Mozart did not use the time signature of 4/8. Although many of his Andante's are notated in 2/4, they are in fact meant to be sung with four beats to the measure at a moderate tempo. This aria is one which is often sung too fast, for the singer mistakenly believes that it is an Andante in *two*.

Even with a slower tempo (four beats to the measure), it should be easy for any singer to sing four-measure phrases — and this holds true even when there is an eighth rest at the end of the second measure. Thus measures 9–12 should be one phrase, as well as measures 13–16, even though there is an eighth rest at the end of measure 14. The singer should observe this rest, but have the feeling that the phrase continues over it, and should therefore not take a breath. It is recommended that the entire beginning of the aria, through measure 48, be sung in four-measure phrases. With long two-beat rests at the end of each four-measure phrase, this should not tire the singer. A breath is logical at the end of measure 50. When Cherubino is carried away by his emotions and the short, breathless phrases come with great frequency (mm. 52–56), his excitement can of course be demonstrated by short, audible catch breaths. A good breath after "dì" in measure 58 will permit the singer to continue to the end of measure 61 without the necessity for a breath after "piace" in measure 59. The singing of four-measure phrases can be resumed with measure 62 and continued through the end of the aria.

Though this aria is often sung by high mezzo-sopranos, it is perfectly suitable for sopranos. The role of Cherubino has been performed with great success by many sopranos, the most celebrated of recent years being Jarmila Novotna. To add a touch of humor, by demonstrating that Cherubino is indeed already a man and that his voice is changing, it is possible to use a noticeably deep chest tone at the end of "avvampar" (mm. 39–40) and again on "cor" in measure 73.

The Text

Literal Translation

1. You that know what thing is love, ladies, see if-I it-have in-the heart.

---

* In these nine measures, which are without parallel in eighteenth-century opera, Mozart anticipated musical techniques that were fully explored only much later by Wagner and his successors. An example of this later treatment is found in this volume in the soprano aria "Depuis le Jour" from Charpentier's *Louise* (p. 238).

2. That which-I experience, to-you I-will-repeat.
3. It-is for me new, to-understand not-it I-know-how.
4. I-feel a longing full of desire, that-now is delight, that-now is suffering.
5. I-freeze, and then I-feel the-soul burst-into-flame,
6. and in a moment I-go-back to freezing;
7. I-search-for a blessing outside of me,
8. not know-I who-it holds, not know-I what-it-is.
9. I-sigh and moan without wishing-to,
10. I-throb and tremble without knowing.
11. Not find-I peace night nor day,
12. but yet me it-pleases to-pine thus.

Idiomatic Translation

1. You who know what love is, ladies, see if I have it in my heart.
2. What I am experiencing, I'll repeat to you.
3. It's new to me, and I don't understand it.
4. I feel a longing, full of desire, that is sometimes delight and sometimes suffering.
5. I find myself, in turn, freezing and then burning,
6. and in a moment I'm freezing again.
7. I look for fulfillment elsewhere,
8. but I don't know who can provide it or even what it is.
9. Against my will I sigh and I moan,
10. I throb and tremble without even knowing that I do.
11. Night or day, I do not find peace,
12. but yet at the same time I find pleasure in all this pining!

The Scenic Picture

The setting is the sitting room of Countess Almaviva's apartments. The main entrance to the room is on stage L. The door to the rest of the Countess's quarters, including the room of her maid, Susanna, is on stage R. There is a small dressing table, with a chair above it, on stage L and a sofa on stage R. An embroidery frame stands in the DR corner of the room.

The Stage Actions Explained

The Countess is seated on the couch and watches the pageboy over her L shoulder. She holds Cherubino's poem to the R of her, so that both she and Susanna can glance at it occasionally. Susanna sits sideways on the corner of the couch to the R of the Countess and is facing toward the L. She is holding the guitar in such a fashion that very little of her fingerwork is visible to the audience. Cherubino is standing UR of the table facing toward DR.

Measures

1. When the Introduction begins, he turns away from the two women

(Cclw), adjusts his collar and cuffs, and clears his throat very discreetly.

5. He turns Clw and goes slightly R, to UL of the Countess.

6. He makes an elaborate bow and gets set in a "formal" pose. His weight is on his L foot; the heel of this R foot — which is placed somewhat DR of his L foot — does not touch the floor, and his R knee is bent ever so slightly. He holds his L arm behind his back, while his R hand, palm up, is extended toward the Countess. One must feel that he intends to remain in this position for the duration of the song.

13. The women notice that Cherubino is not following the expected melodic line as it was played by Susanna in the fifth measure of the Introduction. They find Cherubino's newly invented ascending chromatic line quite charming and amusing.

14. The Coutess and Susanna look at each other and laugh silently. This laughter, as well as that two measures later, must not interfere with the orchestral giggles of the flute and the oboe.

16. Cherubino becomes aware that the women are laughing at him. He abandons his formal pose and comes a step or two closer.

17. His return to the "expected" melodic continuation must have the added meaning of: "Of course I know the tune! And please don't make fun of me!" With "Donne," he gestures with both hands toward the two women.

19. With "nel cor," he points gently to his own heart.

21. As the middle section of the Arietta begins, Cherubino abandons all pretense of formality. In these first eight measures (mm. 21 to 28) he acts like a young boy asking for help. He makes very unobtrusive illustrative gestures: with "io," he points to himself; with "voi," to the ladies; with "è per me nuovo," he looks around rather helplessly; and with "capir nol sò," gazes appealingly at the Countess.

28. He takes a step or two downward, and looks heavenward in the DR direction as if expecting to find there the right words to describe his condition.

32. After "desir," his eyes and his head move from DR to DL, as if following some invisible bird symbolizing his desire.

33. The contrast between the F-major phrase (mm. 33 and 34) and the F minor (mm. 35 and 36) represents the difference between the imagined Countess whom the boy caresses in his daydreams, and the real Countess whom he may not and does not dare touch. With "diletto," he still sees the vision of the dream Countess, but

35. With "ch'ora," he turns his head Clw and looks at the real Countess over his R shoulder.

36. The hopelessness of his craving for the Countess, which is reflected in the word "martir" (torture), makes him turn his head away (Cclw) and walk L to below the table.

40. He turns Clw to address the two women.

41. By restating the original melody of the song (compare mm. 5–9 and mm. 17–21) Cherubino tries to assure the Countess and Susanna that he is expressing a purely poetic sentiment.

43. Realizing that it is useless to pretend — he is after all singing a whole tone lower — he turns Cclw and goes L to DL of the table.

45. He turns RSB and backs to UL, so that

46. He can look directly at the Countess.

48. He goes R, Xing above the table, to above its UR corner.

49. By gazing fixedly at the Countess, he makes clear that his words are an utter lie: he knows perfectly well "chi il tiene," who possesses the treasure for which he is pining.

50. After "tiene," he looks directly at the Countess's lap.

51. With "non," he turns away (Cclw) averting his face from the two women. He does not want them to realize that he knows all too well what "it" is.

52. After "cos'è," he turns RSB to face the Countess. The authors feel that the emotional turmoil of the musical phrase that begins here calls for a gradual acceleration of the beat that should continue to the fifty-eighth measure. A ritardando that can set in with "mi piace" will then provide the necessary relaxation so that the tempo can return to its original speed by the time the Recapitulation (m. 62) is reached.

54. After "senza voler," Cherubino goes R, and continues this movement until he has traversed half the distance that separates him from the couch.

56. After "senza saper," he continues in the same direction and stops above the couch, between the Countess and Susanna.

58. With "ma pur," he turns Cclw, so that

59. With "piace," he can look down the décolletage of the Countess's dressing gown.

60. The sight of the Countess's bosom (and the shocked look on Susanna's face) brings the boy to his senses.

61. With "cosi," he catches himself, goes L to UL of the couch, turns Clw, and assumes the formal pose in which, in measure 9, he began his song.

67. The subdued laughter of the women in measures 67 and 69 refers not so much to Cherubino's singing as to his recent passionate effusions.

70. The pageboy comes a little closer to the couch.

73. The descent to the lower vocal register carries something of the meaning of : "You see! My voice is changing!"

77. After finishing his song, Cherubino makes an elaborate bow.

Susanna wears a light summer evening dress (similar to the Countess's) and, as the attributes of her position, a cap and apron. These will later be ex-changed for the Countess's mantilla and fan.

"Deh vieni"
from *Le Nozze Di Figaro,* Act IV
by Wolfgang Amadeus Mozart

The Drama

Young couples in love who are prevented from getting married — or, as in more recent plots, from remaining happily united in an unmarried state — are the most familiar and popular characters of both the spoken and the sung drama.

In comedies, the obstacles to the union are eventually overcome and all ends happily; in tragedy, the story usually ends otherwise, with the death of at least one of the protagonists. Variety of treatment is provided by the nature of the obstacles that lie in the way of the lovers' union.

One of the favorite ploys of the classical theater was the opposition of an older and influential man whose resistance had to be overcome in some particularly entertaining fashion. Beaumarchais's *The Barber of Seville* and *The Marriage of Figaro,* on which Rossini's and Mozart's operas are based, offer typical examples of this basic pattern. In the *Barber,* the dangerous opponent is Rosina's guardian, Dr. Bartolo, and once he is maneuvered into giving his consent to her marriage with the Count the conflict is over. The battle plan of *The Marriage of Figaro* is laid out on a much more ambitious scale and its skirmishes extend beyond the immediate goal of assuring Susanna's and Figaro's union.

Beaumarchais himself* describes the play as a "most light-hearted intrigue," and compresses its essence into a single sentence. The plot, according to him, deals with a "Spanish grandee, enamored of a pretty servant girl whom he wants to seduce, and with the efforts of the young bride, her fiancé, and the nobleman's own wife who, by combining their wits, manage to thwart this seduction project which for a man of Count Almaviva's rank, position, and wealth should be only too easy to accomplish."

This, however, describes only one half of the plot. In the equally important other half — which could be called "A Lesson for Husbands" — Almaviva is punished for his infidelity and Figaro is taught not to question the fidelity of his virtuous young bride, Susanna.

No less than seven other characters are involved in the action. The most appealing of these is Cherubino,† a young scamp who constantly gets

---

* In his Preface to *The Marriage of Figaro.*

† Cherubino (Little Cherub) is the boy's nickname. His real name, Leon Astorga, is mentioned in *The Guilty Mother,* Beaumarchais's third play involving Figaro and the two Almavivas.

with "Oh come par," that Susanna is caught up with the beauty of the night and that her singing genuinely expresses her love for Figaro. The authors recommend the following appoggiaturas in the recitative:

Oh co-me par che all' a-mo-ro-so fo-co l'a-me-ni-tà del lo-co, la ter-ra e il ciel ri-spon-da, co-me la not-te i fur-ti miei se-con-da!

The tempo of the aria may be interpreted with considerable latitude. The authors prefer a tempo that is fast enough to be felt in two beats to the measure by the singer, even though the conductor may wish to conduct it in six to achieve a precise ensemble with the pizzicati of the strings. Too slow a tempo makes this aria tedious and forces the singer to break many of the phrases for a breath. We recommend ♪ = 112 for the beginning and a somewhat more fluent movement for the third stanza where the sustained tones in the vocal line suggest an underlying pulse of two dotted quarter-note beats to the measure.

Since Mozart chose to write out some of the appoggiaturas it is not unlikely that he would have wished some of the other, more obvious ones to be sung as well. Thus it is stylistically correct to sing a G instead of an

F on the first quarter in measure 9, a D instead of a C on the first quarter of measure 18, a B instead of a C on the first quarter of measure 23, and an E instead of an F on the first quarter of measure 32.

Some sopranos dislike singing the low notes in measures 14–15, and in fact some editions print alternate notes an octave higher. Since the role of Susanna was specially created for the English singer, Nancy Storace, who had lost her top voice, Mozart saddled all future interpreters of this role with a conspicuous lack of long, high notes, and with some rather awkward low ones. Even so, the authors feel that the low Bb's and low A in measures 14–15 are better sung as written. The accompaniment, after all, consists of pizzicato notes in the strings and quiet melodic interludes in the woodwinds. The written-out ornaments on the first beat of measure 28 are best sung *on* the beat, not ahead of it, so that the time for them is taken from the dotted eighth.

When this aria is performed at a tempo fast enough to feel two beats to the measure, it is possible to sing "ti vo' la fronte incoronar di rose" (last half of m. 38 through the first half of m. 42) in one phrase, although one will seldom hear this. It is also possible to sing the next phrase (last half of m. 42 through the first half of m. 45) without taking a breath, and to make a gentle *messa di voce* on the long F in measure 44 as well. To accomplish this in both cases all that is required is careful planning of breathing in measures 38 and 42; the effect to be gained is worth the effort. The written-out appoggiatura in measure 47 is *not* to be performed as a short grace note; the A should be an eighth, and the following G a quarter note.

The Text

Literal Translation

Recitative

1. Arrived-has finally the moment that I-will-enjoy without uneasiness
2. in arms to-the-idol my. Timid fears, leave from-the my breast,
3. to disturb not come the my delight. Oh, how it-seems that to-the amorous fire
4. the-pleasantness of-the place, the earth and the sky respond,
5. as the night the deceptions my assists!

Aria

6. Ah, come, not delay, O joy beautiful, come where love to enjoy you-summons,
7. as-long-as not shines in sky nocturnal torch,
8. as-long-as the-air is still dark, and the world is-still.
9. Here murmurs the brook, here plays the-breeze
10. that with-the sweet whisper the heart restores;
11. here smile the little-flowers, and the-grass is fresh;
12. to-the pleasures of-love here everything entices.
13. Come, darling my, among these trees hidden, come, come!
14. To-you I-wish the forehead to-crown with roses.

Idiomatic Translation

Recitative

1. The moment has finally come when I can enjoy without fear
2. the embrace of my beloved. Timid fears, depart from my breast.
3. Do not come to disturb my delight. Oh, how it seems that amorous fire
4. responds to the charm of this place, this earth, this sky!
5. How the darkness abets my deceits!

Aria

6. Oh, come without delay, blessed joy. Come where love and pleasure summon you,
7. while the moon is not yet shining in the sky,
8. while the sky is still dark, and the world is silent.
9. Here murmurs the brook, here plays the breeze
10. that with sweet whispering consoles the heart.
11. Here the little flowers smile, and the grass is fresh.
12. Here everything entices one to the pleasures of love.
13. Come, my darling, among these sheltering trees, come!
14. I want to adorn your forehead with roses!

The Scenic Picture

The fourth act of this opera takes place in a grove of pine trees situated in the gardens of the Almaviva estate near Seville. Most of the center portion of the stage is occupied by an eighteen-inch-high platform whose upper section is filled with a large ornamental fountain. The D section of the base of the fountain must be solid enough to serve as a seat. Steps lead up to the platform on the right and the left of it. Two semicircular pavilions adorned by rose trellises are located on each side of the stage. There are many pine trees, two of which stand slightly DR and DL of the two pavilions. The DL tree serves as a hiding place from behind which Figaro can listen to Susanna. It is late afternoon and the stage becomes darker as the act progresses.

The Stage Actions Explained

Before proceeding with the listing of the actions, two problems must be considered: "What is Susanna wearing in this scene?" and "How can she best interpret the music of the Recitative with its unusual alternation of seemingly contradictory moods?"

Since these questions are dealt with in *Bringing Opera to Life,* a few pertinent excerpts from that textbook will be helpful.

[In] the last act of the *Marriage of Figaro* the Countess and Susanna assume each other's appearance . . . in order to punish their respective husbands. How and when should this exchange of costumes take place? According to the score, the mistress and the maid are already disguised when they enter the stage, but

I have always felt that this is quite illogical. Susanna, who has been forewarned by Marcellina, knows that the jealous and suspicious Figaro is hiding nearby. In order to teach him a lesson, she proceeds to sing a recitative specifically designed to convey the impression that she, Susanna, is rapturously awaiting the embraces of the Count. It is obvious that if Figaro can hear her every word (and if he cannot, then neither Susanna's recitative and aria nor Figaro's subsequent remarks make any logical sense), he can most probably also catch a glimpse of her. Susanna is clever enough to realize that if Figaro saw his bride dressed up as the Countess, her entire elaborately planned scheme would be given away immediately. In my opinion, this scene is meaningful only if Figaro's bride is still recognizable as herself at this point.

A real problem arises after Susanna's aria, when in a matter of seconds the Countess must be able to assume the appearance of her servant. I solve this difficulty by having both women wear a very similar basic dress so that when changing their appearance they need concern themselves only with such minor, but characteristic, accessories as the maid's dust cap and apron and the mistress's fan and shawl. These can be very quickly and visibly exchanged in the corner of the stage opposite the one where Figaro is hiding.*

. . . the romantically languishing recitative sentences and the gaily whispering orchestral passages that precede and follow them are so far apart in mood and energy values that, at first glance, they seem to contradict each other completely. I feel, nevertheless, that this contrast is intentional and that it constitutes a perfectly logical musical equivalent of Susanna's feelings at this moment. The dramatic context makes it abundantly clear that Susanna is about to indulge in a bit of clever teasing. Her yearning for the embraces of Count Almaviva, which she voices here, is obviously an "act" meant to excite Figaro's jealousy and to punish him for his unworthy suspicions. I am convinced that the laughter and amusement portrayed by the orchestra represent Susanna's real feelings, while the passion of her opening sentences is pure pretense. Having been told of Figaro's suspicions by Marcellina, and seeing him hovering nearby, Susanna cannot resist the temptation to play a practical joke on her fiancé. It is then only natural for her to act out her own amusement during the gay orchestral passages and to feed the flame of Figaro's jealousy in her vocal sentences. . . . In the beginning of the recitative the instruments laugh and Susanna's utterances show an exaggerated — and totally uncharacteristic — affection; soon the orchestral laughter subsides, and, beginning with the aria proper, the vocal and orchestral lines coalesce in a completely unanimous expression of amorous tenderness. . . . Treated as an expression of Susanna's love for Figaro, this aria becomes the very epitome of a young bride's amorous impatience.**

Recitative

As the instrumental recitative begins, Susanna and the Countess are standing halfway between the fountain and the R pavilion. Figaro, hiding behind the trunk of a large tree in the DL corner of the stage, sits on the ground so that he is barely visible to the audience. Susanna, who is

* P. 369.
** Pp. 84-85.

standing to UL of the Countess, has just whispered to her mistress that the fun is about to begin and that Figaro is to be punished for his unworthy suspicions.

Measures

1. Susanna runs L and ascends the steps of the platform.
3. She looks toward DL and then, pointing in that direction, indicates to the Countess that Figaro is still sitting behind the tree.
4. She laughs silently, retraces her way down the steps of the platform, and points to herself to draw the attention of the Countess to the romantic ardor of her coming sentence.
5. She begins to sing after the orchestral chord and emphasizes the exaggerated emotionalism of her words with appropriate gestures.
8. She giggles silently, runs up the steps again to look in Figaro's direction. The Countess shakes her head at Susanna's naughtiness, turns Clw, and takes a few steps to R.
12. As Susanna — standing in the center of the platform — starts her second sentence, the Countess turns Cclw to listen to her.
15. Susanna tiptoes down the L steps of the platform and forces herself to become more serious. The Countess withdraws into the R wing with an expression that seems to say: "It is all very well for you to joke about marital infidelities. For me, alas, this is no longer a laughing matter!"
17. Susanna stands DL of the platform and sings in Figaro's direction.
20. With "il ciel," she turns Clw and looks toward heaven DR.
21. She goes R to CC (below the platform).
22. She begins her final recitative sentence facing DR but after "i furti miei" glances over her L shoulder in Figaro's direction. The mention of "stolen pleasures" makes her feel sorry for her fiancé and leads to a feeling of tenderness for him, thus helping her to get into the mood of the aria.

The Aria

1. She looks at the pavilion on her R and goes to the trellis which is attached to it.
2. She picks several roses from the trellis.
4. Arranging the flowers into a bouquet, she turns Cclw and goes UL to the R of the platform.
6. She stands R of the platform and sings facing to DL.
12. *(4th eighth)* She turns Clw and, remarking that the moon has not risen yet, looks at heaven DR.
15. *(4th eighth)* She turns Cclw to face DL.
18. *(4th eighth)* She ascends the platform and sits down on the rim of the fountain's bowl, slightly to R of its center.
21. She faces to DL.
23. She dips her L hand into the bowl and plays with the water inside it.
26. She extends her arms and admires the bouquet of roses.

29. She rises and moves slightly L, singing "piacer d'amor" in Figaro's direction.

32. *(4th eighth)* She moves L to the edge of the platform.

36. She descends the L steps of the platform.

42. She goes L to UR of the tree behind which Figaro is hiding.

46. With the fermata on the fifth eighth-note, she bends down, places the bouquet on the ground, and rises at once.

48. *(3rd eighth)* She blows a hand kiss in Figaro's direction and then runs nimbly R to the DR corner of the stage, ready to exchange her apron and dust cap for the fan and shawl of the Countess.

To complement the light feeling of the music, a sheer fabric has been super-imposed on a brocade gown of the Italian Renaissance.

"Ah! Je veux vivre"
from *Roméo et Juliette,* Act I
by CHARLES GOUNOD

The Drama

The eminent critic Ernest Newman makes a strong case for the contention that *Romeo and Juliet* is unsuitable material for an opera.* He claims
that there is little in the play of the stuff that opera is made of, that the
characters do not develop but rather that events develop. He says that with
the exception of the two main characters, no one in the play is sufficiently
important to warrant musical characterization. Yet the tale of the two
tragic lovers has inspired composers of many eras to write operas, from
Georg Benda in 1776 to Boris Blacher in 1946. Today, Gounod's opera
is enjoying a revival, with new productions not only by the Metropolitan
Opera but by many civic and community opera companies as well.

The librettists of Gounod's *Roméo et Juliette,* Jules Barbier and Michel
Carré, skillfully adapted Shakespeare's tragedy to the operatic stage in a
well-connected and compact manner. To condense it as much as possible,
events that take place in several different scenes in the play were rearranged and included in one scene in the opera.

The conversation that the nurse (Gertrude, in the opera) and Juliet have
just before the Waltz Song occurs much earlier in the play; and in Shakespeare it is a three-way conversation between Juliet's mother (Lady Capulet, who does not appear in the opera), the nurse, and Juliet. Here we learn
Juliet's exact age: she is about two weeks away from her fourteenth
birthday. It is here also that the idea of marriage is first broached. Lady
Capulet says: "I was your mother much upon the years that you are now
a maid." And she proposes Count Paris as a suitor for Juliet's hand.

Shakespeare's play is so well known that it is not necessary to discuss
the details of the plot. The Waltz Song is Juliet's second appearance in the
opera. Earlier in the act, she was introduced to the guests at the ball given
by her father, and it is implied that this is her birthday celebration. She
has already met Count Paris. As the dancing ends, everyone leaves to
seek refreshments. At this point the uninvited guests — Romeo and his
friends — enter, and after Mercutio's celebrated "Queen Mab" song,
Romeo notices Juliet in the distance offstage. He is immediately smitten
by her beauty and, before Mercutio and his friends leave, they chide
Romeo for his volatile attitude toward pretty girls.

* *More Stories of Famous Operas* (Philadelphia: The Blakiston Company, 1946),
pp. 465-466.

The Music

The form of the aria is a modified rondo:

Introduction, A1, A2, B, A3, C, A4

After a short introduction (mm. 1–14) which contains the vocal cadenza, the A section appears twice, A1 (mm. 15–46) and A2 (mm. 47–78), each time beginning and ending in F major. The B section (mm. 79–104) is in a minor, and ends with an ascending and descending chromatic scale, returning to F major. The A section appears for the third time (A3: mm. 105–134) again in F major. The lengthy C section is divided into two parts: the first (Un poco meno Allegro, ma poco) (mm. 135–150) has a continuous pedal point on F over which a number of fleeting modulations appear, and again ends in F major. The second part (mm. 151–182) beginning with the return to Tempo I, contains some of the most florid music in the aria, with several sequential and repetitious figures and an extended trill. Before the fourth and final return of the A section, there is a cadenza of twelve measures (mm. 183–194). The final return of the A (A4) section is entrusted to the orchestra (mm. 195–212).

The music is straightforward in a moderate waltz tempo which slows down only at cadential points. The B section, as well as the first part of the C section, can be taken a little slower. The obviously gay music reflects Juliet's mood of youthful excitement, and her unwillingness to think of anything so serious as marriage.

The Vocal Aspects

Although this aria is often sung by rather light lyric-coloratura voices, the entire role of Juliet requires a somewhat more robust instrument. Gounod's score characterizes Juliet very well. At the beginning of the opera, the lighthearted, florid music she sings depicts her youth and immaturity. But in a very short time, Juliet must change from a young girl to a mature woman. Thus when she reaches the bedroom scene in Act IV, the music she sings is much less florid, has more substance, and is accompanied by heavier sonorities in the orchestra.

The vocal demands of the entire role, then, are somewhat comparable to those of Violetta in *La Traviata*. At the beginning of both operas, the leading lady must sing music that requires flexibility and agility. But later those demands change radically and require a voice of larger size and greater stamina.

In the Waltz Song, the opening cadenza sometimes presents an intonation problem, and the chromatic half steps are difficult to sing in tune. The singer must learn very carefully not only the correct pitches but also the correct rhythms, so that there are three dotted half notes at the end of the cadenza, not four or more! The little grace notes that Gounod uses so tellingly to depict Juliet's lighthearted mood must be sung cleanly, and early enough so that they do not seem to be omitted or become a "smear."

It is easy for the chromatic scale (mm. 101–104) to become blurred at the end of the B section. It is recommended that the singer firmly but lightly accent the downbeat of each measure of the chromatic scale so that no more than six pitches are sung in a measure.

When the A section appears for the third time, the vocal line is usually decorated with variations in measures 117–120 in the following manner:

Since in the acting directions accompanying this aria the singer is asked to twirl, expending considerable physical energy while singing the repeated descending F-major scale passages in measures 159–162, it is wise to consider a breath before the high-trilled A in measure 163, and then to attempt to continue the phrase after the B♭ through "Douce flamme." It is customary for the singer to attack the E in measure 183 *after* the downbeat, both to give the voice a moment of extra rest, and to insure the taking of a deep breath before the final cadenza.

Many singers do not sing words on the final phrase, "Longtemps encor," but only "ah." Although this is not necessarily condoned, it seems to be such an established practice that it will continue as long as the aria is sung. The interpolation of the high C before the final note is also traditional. Though this opera was first performed at a time when vocal extemporizations by singers were becoming a thing of the past, it seems probable that Gounod did not object to an extra high C.

The Text

Literal Translation

Recitative

1. Jul: Let us see, nurse, one me-awaits, speak quickly!
2. Ger: Breathe a moment! Is-it I that-one evades,
3.   or the Count Paris that-one seeks?
4. Jul: Paris?
5. Ger: You would-have there, one-says, the pearl of-the husbands.
6. Jul: Ha, ha! I dream well truly to-the marriage!
7. Ger: By my virtue! I-was married at your age!
8. Jul: No, no! I wish not you-to-listen longer for-long-time!
9.   Leave my soul, leave my soul to its springtime!

Aria

10. Ah, I wish to-live in the dream that me-intoxicates this day yet!
11. Sweet flame, I you keep in my soul like a treasure!
12. I wish to-live in this dream that me-intoxicates this day yet!
13. Sweet flame, I you keep in my soul like a treasure!
14. This drunkenness of youth but lasts, alas only-a-day.

15. Then comes the-hour when the-one weeps, the heart gives in to the-love,
16. And the happiness flees without return.
17. Ah, I wish to-live in this dream that me-intoxicates for-long-time yet!
18. Sweet flame, I you keep in my soul like a treasure!
19. Far from the-winter morose, let-me, let-me slumber,
20. And breathe the rose, breathe the rose before of it-to-pluck.
21. Ah, sweet flame, stay in my soul like a sweet treasure for-long-time yet!

Idiomatic Translation

Recitative

 1. Jul: Hurry, nurse, they are waiting for me!
 2. Ger: Let me catch my breath! Is it that you are getting away from me,
 3.   or looking for Count Paris?
 4. Jul: Paris?
 5. Ger: You would have, as they say, a jewel of a husband.
 6. Jul: Ha, ha! I'll think about getting married — some day!
 7. Ger: Well, I declare! I was married already at your age!
 8. Jul: No, no! I don't want to listen to you anymore!
 9.   Let my soul enjoy its springtime of youth!

Aria

10. Ah, I want to live in the dream that still intoxicates me today!
11. Sweet flame of youth, I will keep you in my heart!
12. I want to live in the dream that still intoxicates me today!
13. Sweet flame of youth, I will keep you in my heart!
14. This drunkenness of youth lasts, alas, only a day.
15. Then comes the time when one weeps, the heart gives in to love,
16. And happiness flees forever.
17. Ah, I want to live in this intoxicating dream for a long time yet!
18. Sweet flame of youth, I will keep you in my heart!
19. Far from the gloomy winter of old age, let me slumber,
20. And breathe the scent of the rose before I must pluck its petals.
21. Ah, sweet flame of youth, stay in my soul like a sweet treasure for a long time!

The Scenic Picture

The setting for the aria is a large hall in the mansion of the Capulets. There is a bench just above the curtain line DL, and another DR. Although the rear of the stage may be spanned by a long platform with steps leading up to it, and although it is possible for the rear wall to be a scrim behind which we can vaguely see figures engaged in eating and drinking, these elements are not essential for the staging of this aria. The sides of the stage are masked by drapes or flats painted to represent masonry walls. Upstage is a row of columns (the tops of which lead to a vaulted ceiling) running parallel to the footlights, behind which Romeo can hide and watch Juliet. Romeo's presence is not essential for the execution of this aria.

The Stage Actions Explained

The acting directions for this aria involve the singer in rather vigorous movements, and their proper execution will require all the physical resources she possesses, especially breath control. The justification for such strenuous action is based upon the character of the music and the dramatic situation; Juliet is highly excited on this memorable evening in her life: a ball is being given in her honor by her father and she is meeting a rather attractive suitor. There are, however, two relatively calm moments when Juliet can sit or kneel.

Recitative

Measures

1. Juliet enters from UR (just below the row of columns) and runs DL a few steps.
3. She stops momentarily, turns Clw and looks impatiently over her R shoulder to see if Gertrude is coming.
5. She turns Cclw and goes a little further DL.
7. She stops, again turns Clw, and goes UR.
8. Gertrude also enters from UR and goes DL toward Juliet. Juliet takes Gertrude's wrists, and while backing, pulls Gertrude DL. This action continues until the first beat of measure 11. They should reach C stage, somewhat U of the benches.
12. Gertrude manages to free her wrists of Juliet's hands and backs away slightly to R.
14. Gertrude turns Clw and goes DR slightly, singing "est-ce moi . . ." in a teasing manner.
17. She turns LSB and goes L to Juliet.
19. Juliet goes R a few steps, Xing Gertrude.
21. *(3rd quarter)* Gertrude puts her hands on her hips and addresses Juliet.
24. *(2nd quarter)* Juliet turns LSB to address Gertrude.
28. She goes L to Gertrude's R.

Aria

Measures

1. Juliet takes Gertrude hands and twirls her in a complete Clw circle, as if Juliet were the center of a clock and Gertrude were the minute hand. As Gertrude completes the circle, Juliet flings her away so that Gertrude lands somewhat DL of Juliet (but UR of L bench) and facing Juliet.
15. Juliet begins the aria (after the cadenza) in C stage, somewhat UR of Gertrude, addressing her.

31. Juliet begins swaying gently from side to side, putting her weight on her L foot on the downbeat of one measure, and on her R foot on the downbeat of the next.

45. She goes DL to Gertrude and takes her hands.

47. Still holding hands, Juliet and Gertrude dance together, taking a small step on each downbeat, beginning with the downstage foot in measure 47, the upstage foot in measure 48, etc. As they dance, they move slightly UR, Juliet moving backwards. Their arms sway slightly D when they take a step with the D foot, and slightly U on the step taken with the U foot.

75. Gertrude tires of dancing turns Cclw and goes DL to L bench.

78. She sits on the U side of L bench and faces DL, away from Juliet.

79. Juliet goes DL to UR of Gertrude and kneels on her L knee beside her.

85. Juliet takes Gertrude by the hands and turns her so as to face her.

93. Juliet releases Gertrude's hands, rises, and backs UR slightly.

98. She goes DL returning to Gertrude, reaches down, takes her hands, and forces her to get up. She pulls her slightly UR.

101. Juliet again wishes to twirl Gertrude in a circle. Gertrude is wary, however, and does not permit Juliet to do so. She escapes (m. 103), turning Cclw, and goes DL to R of L bench, and then turns Clw to face Juliet.

105. Juliet again dances, taking small alternate steps on each downbeat, backing UR. She holds out her hands to Gertrude, imploring her to dance again. Gertrude adamantly refuses, shaking her head and holding her hands behind her. Juliet continus to move UR until she reaches C stage in measure 121.

121. Juliet tires of trying to persuade Gertrude to dance, turns Clw, and dances DR toward R bench.

133. She stops dancing.

135. She sits on DR bench, facing DR.

136. Gertrude goes R to CC, watching Juliet. Seeing that Juliet seems to be daydreaming, she turns Cclw and returns to the L bench.

150. Gertrude sits on U side of L bench; her attention is immediately drawn to what is happening offstage L where the guests are milling around. She turns to face L.

151. Juliet gets up.

152. She begins to dance, moving slightly UL as she does so, but turning her head to face downstage.

159. She twirls in two complete circles while singing the descending scales, always moving toward L.

163. She stops directly UR of Gertrude, who is so engrossed in what is going on offstage L that she does not notice Juliet's approach.

165. Juliet embraces Gertrude around the shoulders from behind.

169. She turns Gertrude's shoulders to face her, takes her hands, and pulls her up.

176. They again dance UR slightly, Juliet moving backwards. They take alternate steps on the downbeat of each measure for four measures, beginning with the upstage foot.

181. Gertrude manages to escape again, turns Cclw, and goes DL slightly. Juliet is somewhat L of CC, UR of Gertrude, who soon turns Clw to face Juliet.

195. Juliet holds out her hands to Gertrude once more. Gertrude relents, runs UR to Juliet, and they take hands.

199. They dance UR, taking alternate steps on each downbeat, with Juliet moving backwards.

207. Juliet flings Gertrude to R, away from her, so that Gertrude X's her. Gertrude's momentum carries her to R bench, onto which she collapses; she fans herself with her L hand. When Juliet flings Gertrude R, she leaves her arms extended and raised, with her R hand almost over her head; she remains in this pose until the music stops. Though this may seem to be operatic posturing, the brilliant ending of the aria, usually performed with a stringendo, seems to call for a flamboyant gesture. Juliet's final position should be in C stage, facing Gertrude, DR.

Though the opera takes place in 1800, Tosca's concert gown is in the more becoming style of 1810. To a gold embroidered light silk gown is added a court mantle, typical of the period.

"Vissi d'Arte"
from *Tosca,* Act II
by GIACOMO PUCCINI

The Drama

It is June 1800, in Rome, where Floria Tosca, the famous opera singer is fulfilling an engagement at the Argentina theater. She is in her early twenties and is involved in a passionate love affair with the painter, Mario Cavaradossi. In the first act of Sardou's play, on which the opera is based, her lover gives the following account of her background and general character:

As an artist she is incomparable . . . but as a woman . . . ah, the woman! This exquisite creature was picked up in the fields, as a little savage, tending goats. The Benedictines of Verona took her in, out of charity, and barely taught her to read and to pray. But she is one of those women who can quickly guess whatever they do not know. The convent organist was her first music teacher, and she profited so well from his lessons that at the age of sixteen she had already become something of a local celebrity. People would come to hear her sing on holidays, and Cimarosa, brought there by a friend, took it into his head to win her away from God. The monks, however, were unwilling to yield her to the devil. It was a fine struggle. Cimarosa contrived conspiracies and the convent resorted to intrigues. All Rome took sides . . . so much so that the late pope had to intervene. He had the girl brought before him and, after hearing her sing, patted her on the cheek, saying: "Go your way, my child! You will move every heart as you have moved mine. You will make people shed gentle tears . . . and this too, is a way of praying to God!" Four years later she made a triumphant debut in Paisiello's *Nina* and, since then she has sung in Milan, in Naples, in Venice . . . wherever she sings, they want no one but Tosca. Our affair began right here at the Argentina where she is singing at present. It was one of those meetings where two people feel they belong to each other on first sight . . . I know of only one fault she has: it is an insane jealousy that cannot help but disturb our happiness. Of course there is also her excessive religious devotion, but love and religion do get along fairly well.

Later, in the same conversation, Cavaradossi gives his reasons for not wanting Tosca to know of his plans to help the escaped political prisoner, Angelotti:

Her participation in this is quite unnecessary, isn't that so? Let's avoid the unnecessary. However little risk there may be in telling her, there is even less in saying nothing, and right away we eliminate questions, worries, nervousness . . . especially her ill humor on seeing me protect a criminal such as you. For, as far as she is concerned — with her royalist tendencies — you would be nothing better than that! And then, supposing your stay in Rome had to be prolonged . . . one blundering word could ruin everything. Above all consider that she is devout, and that the confessional is a most dangerous guardian of secrets . . . . Besides, the only truly discreet woman is one who knows nothing!

As we know from the opera, Cavaradossi's well-reasoned decision not to involve Tosca has the most far-reaching and unfortunate results. The chief of the Roman police, Baron Scarpia, takes advantage of Tosca's two main weaknesses: her violent jealousy and her love for Mario. In the second act, when she is forced to listen to the moans of her tortured lover who is put through a cruel questioning ordeal by Scarpia's henchmen, she gives away the secret hiding place of Angelotti and thereby proves Cavaradossi's complicity in his escape. After her lover is led away to prison and Tosca begs the chief of police to save his life, Scarpia reveals himself as a completely depraved, lecherous blackmailer. The only way Tosca can save Mario, he tells her, is to let him, Scarpia, make love to her. She shrinks back in horror, when the sound of snare drums coming through the open window gives the Baron another opportunity to weaken Tosca's resistance. "Listen to the marching soldiers," he tell her, "they are accompanying the workers who are about to erect the gallows where your lover will be hanged in a very few hours."

It is at this point that Tosca, driven to despair, embarks upon the eloquent lament known as the "Vissi d'Arte" aria.

Special Problems

This Andante Lento Appassionato — known in Italy as "La Preghiera di Tosca," and in this country simply as Tosca's "Vissi d'Arte" — consists of thirty-seven measures and is the shortest aria in this collection. But in spite of its brevity, it poses at least three rather unusual problems: (1) how should Scarpia behave during this piece; (2) how to end the aria; and (3) how to start it?

1. How should Scarpia behave?

According to the direction in the score, Scarpia goes to the corner of the table where he had been having supper earlier in the act. Completely unmoved by Tosca's sorrow, he leans on the table, pours himself some coffee, and sips it while continuing to watch her.

This stage business looks well on paper, but it does not "play" well. If Scarpia continues to "act his part," he cannot help but distract the audience's attention from what takes place on the opposite side of the stage. Neither does total impassivity on his part solve the problem. The audience must necessarily be greatly touched by Tosca's heartbreaking predicament, and a completely unmoved Scarpia injects a disturbing note that is not in harmony with the music and mood of this scene. Situations of this kind are not unknown in opera and are always greatly annoying to both performing participants. It is sometimes possible to take the "silent" partner temporarily off stage, but in this case this does not work. The best approach is to make Scarpia "faceless," by having him stand by the open window, with his back to the audience, and look out during the entire aria. This is not particularly imaginative or exciting, but under the circumstances it works well enough. Background behavior requiring total passivity is easiest to handle when the face of the actor is not seen by the audience. In the thirty-fifth measure, when Scarpia's theme makes its appearance in the orchestra, it is of course necessary to relate it to a fully visible person, and at this point Scarpia must turn around and become part of the action.

Should this musical phrase be omitted in performance — a procedure which we will discuss in a moment — Scarpia becomes completely unnecessary for the execution of this aria, so that when this scene is staged as a separate number (but *only* then, of course), he might as well not be on stage.

2. How to end the aria

In the form in which it was composed, and in which it appears in all published scores, the postlude of the aria introduces three musical, vocal, and dramatic events:

(a) The orchestral enunciation of Scarpia's theme,
(b) Scarpia's "Risolvi!" urging Tosca to make up her mind whether she wants to save Cavaradossi's life, and
(c) Tosca's "Mi vuoi supplice a tuoi piedi?" (Do you want me to beg at your feet?) during which she kneels before Scarpia.

As the opera achieved world success, it soon became apparent that these orchestral and vocal lines could not be heard because they were invariably drowned out by applause.

A loud expression of approval — and occasionally of disapproval — at the end of an aria, is an indispensable ingredient of operatic life in most parts of the world, particularly in Italy. And though contemporary composers may deplore these interruptions of dramatic and musical continuity, there is no doubt that Puccini would have been greatly disturbed and mortified were the "Vissi d'Arte" to be greeted by polite or respectful silence. He craved applause no less than his singers but he was hoping that in "Vissi d'Arte" this sign of approval would be deferred until after Tosca's final kneeling at Scarpia's feet.

It seems that — at least in his soprano arias — Puccini preferred thunderous applause to break out after a quiet ending. He felt, perhaps, that this evidenced a more genuine appreciation than the usual enthusiasm unleashed by loud orchestral chords and the more commonplace high, sustained vocal tones. He had successfully introduced soft endings in his earlier arias for Manon Lescaut and Mimi, and was obviously hoping to duplicate this and to obtain a similar effect in *Tosca*. This, however, turned out to be a miscalculation and, since everything that followed Tosca's sobbing "perchè me ne rimuneri cosi?" was invariably lost in the tumult, conductors soon decided to omit the three musical events mentioned above and skip over the thirty-fifth measure, going directly to the final tonic chord in the thirty-sixth and thirty-seventh measures. It is arguable whether this is the best procedure for the opera itself, but it certainly makes excellent sense when the aria is performed as a separate entity.

3. How to start the aria

Difficulty arises only when this aria is sung as a separate number. In the absence of an orchestral introduction or a preliminary recitative, there is no convenient way in which the soprano can place the pitch of the opening E♭. And what is equally disturbing is that Tosca must embark upon her eloquent lament without the slightest psychological and dramatic preparation.

A somewhat similar problem was encountered in Cio-Cio-San's "Un bel di." The solution we recommended for the *Madama Butterfly* aria was to attach to the beginning of the piece a segment of the preceding scene. In the case of Cio-Cio-San — since the added measures were part of her own music — this method was quite acceptable and the extra measures became nothing more than a form of a recitative-like introduction.

In the present instance, however, this would lead us too far afield. The earlier section of the music is sung, not by Tosca but by Scarpia. It is he who points out to the unhappy Tosca the ominous meaning of the snare-drum tattoo which she hears through the open window of his palatial apartment. Were we to include in the staging of this aria the complete musical and dramatic presentation of these preliminary fifty-six measures, the contribution of the baritone would greatly exceed the amount of supporting vocal "partnership" which we set as a limit for the present volume.

We do not know of any completely satisfactory solution to this problem. We prefer to omit the baritone lines completely, and to add eighteen preparatory accompaniment measures, beginning with the measure when Scarpia normally sings the word "Mario." The snare drum sound is then heard long enough to impress Tosca with its deadly significance and to permit her to act out her horror and despair.

The Music

Preliminary Orchestral Introduction (Allegro in 2/4; 18 measures)

The fast and fairly loud tattoo of the two snare drums continues for ten measures, bcoming gradually much softer but remaining in a strict tempo of $\quarternote = 132$. This is followed by a continuous diminuendo entrusted to two clarinets. During these eight measures the tempo slows down until it reaches $\quad \s:= 80$. By the time the Andante is reached, the tempo becomes identical with the preceding Allegro, except that the beat of 80 is now applicable to the ♪note rather than the quarter (i.e. ♪= 80 or $\quad = 40$ as marked in the score).

Once the soprano has understood clearly this process of slowing down and the correspondence of tempo between the last two measures of the Allegro and the opening measure of the Andante, she will be able to attack her vocal line and to continue singing at the correct speed without the slightest hesitation.

The Aria (Andante Lento Appassionato — 37 Measures)

The thirty-seven measures of this aria are divided into an Introduction of thirteen measures followed by the main portion of the piece, which has twenty-four measures. We find here a fine example of Puccini's special knack of creating neatly balanced forms out of miniature building blocks.

This aria begins with an E-flat minor introduction in 2/4. The thirteen measures of this section are divided into two parts of seven (mm. 1–7) and six measures (mm. 8–13). This leads to the main body of the aria which, although in a different key, is a close approximation of the twenty-three-measure-long Andantino sostenuto that accompanied Tosca's initial appearance in the opera. This portion of the aria is in E-flat major and in 4/4. It is a simple song form, A-B-A. The first A has eight measures (mm. 14–21), the B section (mm. 22–25) is quite short, and the second A section, extended by a vocal climax and a short Coda, has twelve measures (mm. 26–37).

The omission of the thirty-fifth measure — the reason for which we discussed earlier — eliminates the Coda, leaving us with a simple A-B-A, with the second A slightly extended.

The Vocal Aspects

The first three short phrases of the aria — consisting of two measures, two measures, and three measures — should be thought of as a unit. Because of the slow tempo, it is not likely that these seven measures can be sung in one breath. But since they are one connected idea, the singer should conceive of these measures as one long phrase, even if a catch breath is necessary after the second and fourth measure. It should be possible to sing the next phrase of five measures in one breath, without a catch breath after "furtiva." Since the orchestra makes a crescendo on the second beat of measure 9 through the first beat of measure 10, the voice should make a similar increase in volume, and the skip of an octave from "–va" to "quan–" should be negotiated with care, legato but not portamento. The con anima in measure 10 calls for a slight increase in tempo through the first beat of measure 12.

Measure 15 through the second beat of measure 18 should also be conceived of as one phrase, even though a breath is taken after "sincera" in measure 16. Many singers find it difficult to sing a duple rhythm against the triplet accompaniment throughout this phrase. The liberties usually taken here with note values and tempo should be avoided.

Although almost all interpreters of this aria breathe after the last beat of measure 19, the orchestral phrasing begins a new phrase one beat earlier. Since the text seems to indicate that "Sempre con fè sincera, diedi fiori agl'altar" be considered as a unit, some readjustments can be made. In Luigi Ricci's book, *Puccini interprete di se stesso**, it is indicated that Puccini sanctioned the following slight rearrangement of syllables in measure 20:

This makes it possible to sing "Sempre con fè sincera, diedi fiori" in one breath, and then "agl'altar" can be sung with adequate breath control for the crescendo to forte and the decrescendo to piano. Ricci also indicates that in spite of the marking of "con anima" in measure 20, a rallentando is possible, with a return to a tempo in measure 21.

The singer who finds it difficult to sing two against three in measures 16–18 will encounter similar problems in other measures (for instance mm. 29–31). A readjustment of syllables in measure 32 is common, and is suggested by Ricci, as follows:

Such a readjustment will give the singer an opportunity for a sufficient breath before the climax of the aria, and will also facilitate the molto allargando in measure 33. The A♭ should be attacked forte, without forcing the voice and should decrease in volume to piano as a great sigh of despair. The sextuplet in measure 34 is often sung too fast, though it is marked "rallentando." As can be seen in the above musical illustration, Ricci suggests that "perchè" (the second and third sextuplets) be sung lento, and that the singer breathe after this word, continuing a tempo on the remaining sextuplets with another rallentando on "–mune" before the fermata on "–ri." He also suggests a crescendo on "–ri," which continues over the sixteenth rest through "co-" and a lengthy descrescendo on the last note, which is held for almost two measures. As indicated earlier, this is possible only when measure 35 is omitted, and neither Scarpia's nor Tosca's lines are sung.

* See footnote, p. 176.

Since this aria is neither long nor vocally taxing, it is a favorite teaching piece, but it is regrettable that excessive rhythmic liberties are taken so often. Vocal poignancy need not be married to musical inaccuracy.

The Text

Literal Translation

1. I-loved for-art, I-lived for-love, not did-I never evil to soul living!
2. With hand secret how-many miseries I-knew, I-relieved . . .
3. Always with faith sincere, the my prayers in-the holy tabernacles arose.
4. Always with faith sincere, I-gave flowers for-the altars.
5. In-the-hour of-the sorrow, why, why, Lord, why me for-it do-you-reward thus?
6. I-gave jewels of-the Madonna to-the mantle,
7. and I-gave the singing to-the stars, to-the heavens,
8. which because-of-it smiled more beautifully . . .
9. In-the-hour of-the suffering, why, why, Lord, ah . . .
10. why me for-it do-you-reward thus?

Idiomatic Translation

1. I have lived for art and for love, and I did not harm a living soul!
2. Secretly I relieved many miseries . . .
3. Always with sincere faith, my prayers arose in church.
4. Always with sincere faith, I gave flowers for the altars.
5. In this hour of sorrow, why, Lord, am I rewarded like this?
6. I gave jewels to adorn the mantle of the Madonna,
7. and I gave my singing to the stars and the heavens,
8. which, because of my singing, smiled more beautifully . . .
9. In this hour of suffering, why, Lord, ah . . .
10. why do you reward me like this?

The Scenic Picture

The scene represents Baron Scarpia's apartment on the second floor of the Palazzo Farnese in Rome. There are two doors — the main entrance in the center and, in the middle of the left wall, a smaller door leading to the torture chamber. A large window facing the courtyard of the palace is located in the UR corner of the room. A small table set for supper, with an arm chair behind it, stands near the right wall below the window. In the DL corner is a desk with a chair next to it. A crucifix hangs on the wall above the desk. To the left of center, parallel with the footlights, is a fairly large sofa. It is nighttime and the room is illuminated by candles.

The Stage Actions Explained

The score gives only two acting directions: several measures before the

Andante lento appassionato it says: "Shattered by her sorrow, Tosca sinks down on the sofa," and in the twentieth measure of the aria she is told to rise. That is all, except that, as most opera lovers know, Maria Jeritza started the fashion of singing most of the piece lying flat on the ground on her stomach, a flamboyant interpretation that should not be imitated by less flamboyant personalities.

But whether sitting, standing, or lying down, it is by no means easy for the soprano to act out the meaning of this song. A glance at the text will show that the aria deals almost entirely with abstract ideas, and abstractions, as we know, lend themselves only with difficulty to muscular exteriorization.

Tosca sings of her dedication to her art and to her lover. She has never harmed a living soul, she says; on the contrary, without being ostentatious, she tried to help those in need; she has prayed with sincere faith and put flowers on the altar; she has adorned the mantle of the Madonna with jewels, and has gladdened the stars and the heavens with her singing. Why is it, then, that in this hour of sorrow the Lord is repaying her in such a dreadful fashion?

This question is the real point of her lament and she mentions it twice: in the B section of the aria and at the very end.

Except for the jewels of which she sings (some of which she may be wearing herself) and the symbolic direction of the heavens, there is very little suggestion in the words that can be used for a look, a turn, or a gesture — with one important exception. Later in this act Tosca takes a crucifix from the wall and places it on the body of the dead Scarpia. There is no reason why this crucifix could not be located so that Tosca could turn to it on several occasions and give her complaint a much more direct significance.

Orchestral introduction (18 mm. before Andante Lento Appassionato)

Tosca stands by the open window and looks toward R, following with horrified eyes the patrol of soldiers and drummers as they disappear in the distant street below. (When Scarpia is included in the action, he stands — also facing R — well UL of Tosca.)

At the seventh measure, Tosca turns Cclw and goes L, Xing above the table, and then DL (Xing Scarpia) to the UR corner of the couch.

In the fifteenth measure she stops, leans on the corner of the couch, and keeps her eyes riveted on the crucifix, as if accusing it silently: "Why, O Lord, why?" (Scarpia follows Tosca with his eyes, turning his head Cclw as she passes him.)

Aria (Andante Lento Appassionato)

Measures

1. Tosca turns her head slightly Clw and gazes into the distance DL, as if imagining "arte," her devotion to her art, to be located there.
3. She turns still further Clw and finds a different focusing point for the image of her Mario.

4. (On "amore," Scarpia smiles, for he is counting on Tosca's "love" to drive her into his arms. He goes R, to the window, where he remains, with his back to the audience, until the thirty-fifth measure.)

5. Tosca turns Clw to look in the direction of the window. The "anima viva," the living souls whom she has never harmed, include Scarpia, the marching soldiers, and the other wicked people who, for some unfathomable reason, have conspired to torture her. She gestures very gently with her R hand, possibly turning her palm up.

8. She looks at her R hand and, turning Cclw, illustrates "man furtiva" by hiding it for a moment under her L hand.

10. She looks at the crucifix and goes L, Xing above the couch to the L of it.

12. She turns Clw and goes R to below the couch.

14. Tosca sits down on the couch and faces D.

21. She gets up, turns Cclw and goes L toward the crucifix.

26. She turns Clw and goes R, Xing the couch.

28. She stops DR of the couch, and turns slightly Cclw.

29. She looks at heaven, illustrating "agli astri, al ciel."

31. She glances over her R shoulder, at the window, to emphasize that her "hour of pain" and sorrow is connected with the activities that are going on beyond the window. On the first "perchè," she turns LSB.

32. On the second "perchè," she backs slightly to UR facing the crucifix.

33. With "ah," she goes DL, Xing above the couch, to UR of the crucifix.

34. With the third "perchè," she stretches out her folded hands toward the crucifix.

35. (If played) Scarpia turns Cclw and goes DL toward the couch. Tosca must stop singing before the third quarter of the measure. She buries her head in her hands.

35. (If omitted) Tosca holds her last note much longer than in the directions above. After she finishes singing, she buries her head in her hands.

In 1860 the crinoline reached its largest circumference and Violetta's gown
is of that year. Because of its generous dimensions, the dress can be otherwise
very simple and of the exquisite taste for which Violetta was famous.

"Ah, fors' e lui" and "Sempre libera"
from *La Traviata,* Act I
by GIUSEPPE VERDI

The Drama

La Traviata is not the name of an operatic character but is an Italian word which, translated literally, means "wayward" or "fallen" woman. To be even more exact, Verdi's Violetta Valery is a "kept woman" who belongs to the demimonde, a shady world of easy virtue in nineteenth-century France, peopled by young and elegant women who made their intimate favors available to a select company of wealthy and profligate men.

The dramatic recreation of the opera's heroine is made easier by the fact that her prototype — a real person who called herself Marie Duplessis* and who died in Paris at the age of twenty-three — was immortalized as Marguerite Gautier in a novel written by one of her lovers, Dumas fils. *La Dame aux Camélias* was soon dramatized by its author and had an immediate and immense success at its first presentation in Paris in 1852. About a year later Marie Duplessis, alias Marguerite Gautier, came to life in still another incarnation as Violetta Valery, the heroine of Verdi's *La Traviata.*

For a glimpse of the original model of Violetta Valery we are indebted to the French literary and dramatic critic, Jules Janin, whose recollections of Marie Duplessis were added to the second edition of the novel.† A few extracts from these recollections will give the present-day singing actress an idea of the personality she is asked to portray in Verdi's opera.

"The whole of her toilette was in keeping with her young and graceful figure; and her beautiful, oval face fitted to perfection the charm which she radiated like an indescribable perfume. She entered the room and passed through the astonished crowd her head held high. Liszt** and I were very much surprised when she sat down at our table. She immediately addressed the great artist and told him that she had heard him play. We could observe her with the greatest of ease, from the embroidered folds of her petticoat to her gloved hand and to the curls of her black hair which made you think you were looking at a picture. Her handkerchief marvellously trimmed with costly lace, and the two pearls in her ears could have made a queen jealous. All these beautiful objects were as natural to her as if she had been born amidst silk and velvet, beneath some gilded ceiling with a crown upon her head, and a

* Her real name was Rose Alphonsine Plessis.

† An English translation of this *Memoir* appears in the Heritage Press edition of the novel published in 1955.

** Franz Liszt later became one of her lovers.

crowd of flatterers at her feet. Her bearing was in keeping with her language; her thoughts with her smile; her dress with her person; and you would have looked in vain in the very highest circles for a woman more beautiful and one in more complete harmony with her ornaments, her dress, and her conversation. It would be impossible to describe with what art and infinite tact this woman ran through all the usual elegant gossip and small talk of the day.

In spite of Duplessis's beguiling charm — which is attested to by many writers†, the author of *La Dame aux Camélias* was well aware that a kept woman, no matter how beautiful and elegant, could not arouse the sympathy of theater goers of his time unless he could persuade them that, in contrast to her demimondaine sisters, she posessed truly unusual and admirable qualities of the heart. And so he endowed his literary and theatrical heroine with a moral fiber and an unselfish devotion that were quite undreamed of by his real-life mistress. Once the flame of true love invades the heart of Marguerite Gautier and of her operatic successor, they develop a capacity for self-sacrifice and martyrdom that gives them a stamp of greatness and lifts them far above such attractive women who led unconventional sexual lives as Manon, Carmen, Mimi, Gioconda, or Louise.

It is of course true that this does not directly affect Violetta's behavior in the "Sempre Libera." It is only in the second act of the opera that Violetta realizes that for the sake of Alfredo's future she must act in a manner that will make him hate her; and it is only in the third act that she lets him humiliate her before the whole world rather than reveal to him that her actions are motivated solely by her solicitude for his happiness. Throughout the first act — and this naturally includes the aria that ends it — she is, on the surface, almost indistinguishable from the beguiling Marie Duplessis as painted for us by Jules Janin.

Even so, the singing actress must be aware, and must make the audience feel, that beneath her veneer of artificial gaiety and pleasure-seeking, there beats a heart capable of infinite tenderness and protective love.

It is well to keep in mind that both the play and the opera were considered quite scandalous when they first appeared. Women of easy virtue had often been portrayed in books — Balzac, among others, depicted memorable ones — but before the younger Dumas no one had dared to expose on the stage the intimate details of a kept woman's life.

The author was well aware, indeed, that many aspects of the story that could be depicted in a book had to be played down in a play, just as Verdi realized that he had to handle them still more discreetly in an opera. One regrets to say that in this process many important ideas have been obscured to the point of becoming virtually incomprehensible.

Not too many opera lovers, for instance, are able to appreciate the

---

† In his review of the play's première, the famous French critic, Theophile Gautier, allotted more space to Marie Duplessis than to the sensationally successful drama.

importance of the flower which Violetta hands to Alfredo just before he leaves the stage near the end of the first act. In the novel, Marguerite takes from a bunch of red camellias a single flower and places it into Armand's buttonhole, telling him to return it when it has changed color. These camellias which are so prominently featured in the title of both the book and the play* are fully "explained" only in the novel where we read: "During twenty-five days of each month the camellias were white, during the other five days they were red." What a subtle way for a courtesan to indicate her availability to her lovers! Truly, one could not find a more appropriate symbol of the shocking immodesty practiced by the inhabitants of the demimonde, that region of society considered so depraved and immoral by our great-grandparents. Neither the play nor the opera is brazen enough to mention the color of the flower or to hint at the message it conveys.

But this is a minor detail. Much more regrettable is the absence in the opera's first act of any mention of Violetta's lovers, or of the money which she receives from them. As a result, it becomes extremely difficult to illuminate the all-important change which, beginning with the second act, must be shown in Violetta's attitude to love, sex, and money.

Unless the director makes a special effort at the very beginning to highlight the vulgarity of the aging Flora, and to build up Baron Douphol's role as Mr. Moneybags and Violetta's lover of the moment,** the audience has no inkling that, in the first act, it is witnessing a party which, on the distaff side, is composed entirely of kept women.

The aria which is generally known by the first words of its final Allegro section "Sempre Libera" portrays Violetta's inner conflict. Here is a young woman of twenty-two who has become accustomed to a life of luxury and to a continuous round of gay parties, interrupted only by occasional bouts with a disease to which she will eventually succumb. She knows that she is seriously ill, but feels that her feverish activity is all that keeps her going. She has just met a young man whose devotion to her is obviously deeper than that of the many other men whose pleasures she has served, and who have paid her large sums of money. For the first time in her life she is contemplating the possibility that she might be capable of a serious love relationship with a man who is dedicated to her in sickness and in health, both for her attractive exterior and her inner worth. The idea that she might escape from her present environment and find another life is a new and somewhat frightening thought. The vision of an ideal love which Alfredo evoked before her is so startling that she can scarcely dare to take it seriously.

The singer who wishes to master this aria must contrast Violetta's thoughtless abandonment to superficial pleasures with her yearning for

---

* One wonders whether *Camille,* that ridiculously inappropriate English translation of *La Dame aux Camélias,* may not have had its origin in a desire to avoid any reference to an indelicate subject.

** See *Bringing Opera to Life,* p. 365.

a more respectable and profound happiness. It is in the duet scene with Alfredo that the conflict between those aspects of her personality first become apparent.

The operatic conventions of his time prevented Verdi from probing into, or even mentioning, the less attractive "commercial" side of Violetta's profession. It is nevertheless important for the singing actress to realize not only what Violetta would gain but also what she would sacrifice by yielding to a serious love affair. The sections in the Dumas novel and play that deal with the corresponding conversation between Marguerite and Armand establish this side of the conflict more clearly than Verdi is able to do in the opera. We strongly suggest that singers read them in their complete form.*

But for the convenience of our readers, here is a condensation that outlines the main ideas as they are presented, first in the novel and then in the play.

An excerpt from the novel, as related in the first person by Armand:

"Marguerite, let me say to you something which you have no doubt heard so often that the habit of hearing it has made you believe it no longer, but which is none the less real. . . ."

"And that is?" she said, with the smile of a young mother listening to some foolish notion of her child.

"It is this, that ever since I have seen you, you have taken a place in my life; that when I try to drive you out of my mind, you always come back; that now that I know you, and that I know all that is strange in you, you have become a necessity of my life, and you will drive me mad if you will not let me love you."

"But foolish creature that you are, don't you know that I spend six or seven thousand francs a month, and that I could not live on less; don't you know that I would ruin you in no time, and that your family would cast you out if you were to live with a woman like me. Let us be friends, good friends, but nothing more."

"But what the devil are you doing there?" cried Prudence, who had come in without our hearing her and who now stood just inside the door, with her hair undone and her dress unbuttoned. I recognized the hand of Gaston.†

"We are talking sense," said Marguerite; "leave us alone; we will join you soon."

"Good, good! Talk, my children," said Prudence going out and closing the door behind her.

"Well, it is agreed then," continued Marguerite, when we were alone, "you won't fall in love with me?"

"Then I must go away."

"I never met anyone like you."

"That is because no one has ever loved you as I love you." Little by little I

---

* For a list of background texts, see p. 326.
† This naturalistic detail with its broad hint at what was going on at Violetta's parties was omitted from the play and would have of course been completely unthinkable in a nineteenth-century opera.

had drawn closer to Marguerite, I had put my arms about her waist, and I felt her supple body weigh lightly on my clasped hands. "If you only knew how much I love you!" I said in a low voice.

"You really mean it?"

"I swear it!"

"Well, if you promise to do everything I tell you, without a word, without a question, perhaps I will say yes."

"I will do everything that you wish! I will be all that you wish!"

"We shall see."

"When shall we see?"

"Later on."

"Why?"

"Because!" said Marguerite. Releasing herself from my arms, and taking from a great bunch of red camellias a single flower, she placed it in my buttonhole. "Because one cannot always carry out agreements the day they are signed."

"And when shall I see you again?" I said, clasping her in my arms.

"When this camellia changes color."

"When will it change color?"

"To-morrow night between eleven and twelve. Are you satisfied?"

An excerpt from the same conversation as it occurs in the play.

MARGUERITE

How long have you felt this devotion?

ARMAND

For two years. Ever since the day when I first saw you, beautiful, and proud. From that day I have watched you from a distance and in silence.

MARGUERITE

Why do you tell me this for the first time, today?

ARMAND

I did not know you, Marguerite.

MARGUERITE

You should have tried to know me. When I was ill and you called so regularly to enquire after me, why didn't you come up?

ARMAND

What right had I?

MARGUERITE

Is one usually so considerate with a woman like me?

ARMAND

One is always considerate with a woman. Besides . . .

MARGUERITE

Besides?

ARMAND

I was afraid. Afraid of the influence that you might have over my whole life.

MARGUERITE

You love me as much as that?

ARMAND *(seeing that she is laughing)*

If I were to tell you how much, it would not be today!

MARGUERITE

Never tell me!

ARMAND

Why not?

MARGUERITE

Because a woman who spends a hundred thousand francs a year may
suit a rich old man, but not a young man like you. There! We have
been talking nonsense! Give me your hand and let us join the
others.

ARMAND

I'll stay here if I may.

MARGUERITE

Shall I give you a piece of good advice? If what you say is true, go
away at once. Or else, love me as a friend and nothing else. You
are too young and too sensitive to live in this world of ours. Love
some other woman and marry her. *(Prudence opens the door.)*

PRUDENCE

What in the world are you two doing here?

MARGUERITE

Being sensible. We'll be with you in a moment.

PRUDENCE

Prattle away, children *(Exit.)*

MARGUERITE

It is agreed then, that you are not to love me.

ARMAND

Then I must take your advice and leave you.

MARGUERITE

Is it like that?

ARMAND

Yes. Have you ever been in love with anyone?

MARGUERITE

Never!

ARMAND

Thank God!

MARGUERITE

You are a strange boy!

ARMAND

What if I were to tell you that I have passed whole nights beneath
your windows and that I have treasured a glove that you dropped.

MARGUERITE

I should not believe you.

ARMAND

You are right to laugh at me! Good bye!

MARGUERITE

Armand! I don't want you to go away angry.

ARMAND

Angry? How could I be angry with you?

MARGUERITE

Come to see me often . . . we shall speak of this again.

ARMAND

It is too much and not enough!

MARGUERITE

Then ask what you will of me, for it seems that I am in your debt.

ARMAND

I can't bear to hear you laugh at what is serious!

MARGUERITE

I am not laughing now.

ARMAND

Would you like someone to love you deeply and forever?

MARGUERITE

And if I were to believe you, what would you say? What does it matter? If I am to live a shorter time than most people, I must live more quickly, that is all! But be sure of this: however eternal your love, and however short my life, I shall yet live longer than your love! In the meantime since you are sincere, that deserves something. Take this flower. *(She gives him a camellia. Armand kisses it.)* Bring it back to me.

ARMAND

When?

MARGUERITE

When it is faded.

ARMAND

How long will that take?

MARGUERITE

A morning or an evening. And now go! *(Armand goes, looks back, returns to kiss her hand once more. Then leaves.) (alone, looking at the closed door)* Why not? and yet why? That's the way life passes, trying to answer these two questions! *(Gaston appears at the door followed by the others. He goes to the piano.)*

GASTON *(singing and playing)*

"Chorus of villagers!"

OLYMPE

On with the wedding dance. *(They dance.)*

End of Act I

* * *

Nothing illuminates the enormous advantages of musical treatment in the hands of a genius better than the juxtaposition of Marguerite's "Why not? And yet why?" with Violetta's aria that closes the first act of the opera.

The Music

While it conforms to the conventional scheme — Recitative, Cantabile section, and Cabaletta — this aria is the longest and most elaborate of all Verdi's compositions in this genre. Its 252 measures are divided into four main sections and no less than fifteen subsections. (Each of the four sections is numbered separately.) Since each of these episodes plays an important part in the actions of the aria, it is useful to get an overall view of the succession and length of the various events.

I Recitative (22 measures)
*1. "E strano . . ." (mm. 1–22)

II Andantino (94 measures)
Stanza 1
2. Orchestral Introduction (mm. 1–4)
3. "Ah fors' è lui" (mm. 5–28)
4. "A quel amor". (mm. 29–44)

Stanza 2
5. Orchestral Introduction (mm. 45–48)
6. "A me fanciulla" (mm. 49–72)
7. "Sentia che amore" (mm. 73–88)
   Coda
8. "Croce e delizia (mm. 89–94)

III Recitative (20 measures)
9. "Follie! Follie!" (mm. 1–20)

IV Allegro Brillante (116 measures)
Exposition
10. Orchestral Introduction (mm. 1–8) include upbeat
11. "Sempre libera" (mm. 9–35)

Middle Section
Andantino (with Alfredo) and Recitative
12. "Amor, amor" (mm. 36–50)
13. "Follie! Follie!" (mm. 51–57)

Recapitulation
14. "Sempre libera" (mm. 58–86)

Coda (with Alfredo)
15. "Dee volar . . ." (mm. 86–116)

* When this piece is performed as a separate number, the Recitative must be preceded by an A♭ major chord.

The Vocal Aspects

To discuss in detail all of the various vocal matters in this long aria would require a volume in itself and would lead to such minutiae that very few readers would have the patience to cope with it all. Thus some high-lights must suffice. It is hoped that this aria will not be tried by singers with-out considerable command of such vocal resources as flexibility, stamina, above-average breath capacity, and an extremely wide range with an effortless top voice. It is disturbing that this aria is studied by singers too immature to meet its extensive challenges.

Though some changing of notes and placement of words are indulged in, this aria is most often sung pretty much as Verdi wrote it, without the tampering that is done to music of an earlier era. We still feel the influence of Arturo Toscanini, whose interpretations of Verdi and Puccini were closer to the intentions of these composers than those of many of his predecessors and contemporaries. The reverence and respect with which the musical world regarded him have had a healthy and lasting effect on the performances of many standard operas. When one hears again the recording of the memorable broadcast of *La Traviata* made in December, 1946, with Licia Albanese in the title role, one can even now sense the tremendous drive and excitement imparted to his singers by that renowned conductor. Compared to a more recent recording by Monserrat Caballé (Vic. LSC 6180), it has more fire. (We must remember Toscanini's penchant for fast tempi.) Albanese and Toscanini were able to create the heroine caught in a great struggle of conflicting passions much more tell-ingly than Miss Caballé. A contributing factor no doubt was that the Toscanini recording was made before an audience in a radio studio and was broadcast nationwide, instantaneously. The Caballé recording was made in a recording studio in Rome.

Let us examine some of the matters of interpretation of this aria. In the opening recitative (Section I) some singers hold the high B♭ in measure 14 (Caballé did; Albanese did not). In measure 21 of this recitative, Albanese sang the little ornament fast (it is marked "Allegro"); Caballé did not.

In the Andantino, there are certain traditional alterations. Although there is a phrasing mark to connect "–ma" in measure 8 to "solinga" in measure 9, most singers breathe between the measures. Almost all inter-preters hold the high A♭ (mm. 10 and 18) softly, much longer than written (both Albanese and Caballé did). Most singers add an anticipation note (F) at the end of the E in measure 28, with a portamento from E to F, and then take a breath before continuing with measure 29. When the second verse of the Andantino is performed, the above comments again apply.

The cadenza* at the end of the Andantino (m. 91), with its many

* Compare the remarks on p. 17.

chromatic inflections, presents intonation problems. For this reason a different cadenza is often sung here. Albanese used this one:

The one used by Caballé more closely resembles Verdi's original, but it lacks the chromatic alterations:

The Allegro (Section II) that follows is almost always sung as written. Some singers put a tenuto on the high C in measure 16 (Albanese did not; Caballé did). How to sing "gioir" in measures 17–18 is open to different interpretations. Most often the first will be sung loud, and the second, like an echo, rather soft. Since the first is marked "dolce," it seems logical that it also be sung softly, and that its repetition, marked "a piacere," can be louder. Almost all singers will object to an *ee* vowel on a high D♭; thus the syllable "–ir" is sung only on the first E♭ in measure 19, the remainder of the phrase is then sung on "ah."

In Section IV, marked "Allegro brillante," many singers omit the trills in measures 10, 14, and 24. Little is lost, for the trills occur in the orchestra as well. Again, because of the difficulty in singing *ee* vowels on high notes, measures 20–22 are altered slightly, with a portamento from the high C to the octave below:

At the end of measure 22, "con effetto questo ripiglio" (this repetition with effect) urges the singer to repeat the music of "Sempre libera" with more drive and enthusiasm; thus a slight ritard is possible in measure 26. In measure 32, "–lar" is usually sung only on the first E♭, and the remainder of the phrase is sung on "ah" until "il pen–" at the end of measure 35.

During Alfredo's offstage singing in the Andantino, Violetta's exclamation, "Oh!" in measure 39 can be parlando, and "oh amore" in measure 43 can be sung breathily, to indicate her surprise and pleasure at hearing his voice. The "fol–" at the end of measure 50, which is Violetta's latest renunciation of her feelings for Alfredo, must be sung later than indicated; it can safely be made a sixteenth note. For a third time, the problem of an *ee* vowel on high notes appears; thus an adjustment of words is made in measures 51–54. One possibility is as follows:

The problem with "gioir" in measure 56 is handled as before, with "–ir" only on the first E♭ and the remainder of the phrase on "ah."

In the final 6/8 section, measures 70–72 are handled as before, as is measure 82. Many singers will find it necessary to slow down the tempo a trifle beginning with measure 86, though apparently Toscanini felt it preferable to keep the tempo moving ahead, even at the expense of some intonation on the part of Miss Albanese!

One often hears some omissions in the vocal line near the end of the aria. The authors firmly believe that it is highly effective as Verdi wrote it, and that nothing needs to be omitted from measures 102–110. One small concession is allowed: the last note can be sung an octave higher.

The Text

Literal Translation

Recitative

1. It's strange . . . in heart carved I-have those words!
2. Would-be for me misfortune a serious love? What resolve-you, O disturbed spirit my?
3. No-man yet you-aroused . . . O joy that-I not knew, to-be loved loving!
4. And to-spurn-it can-I for the-barren follies of-the life my?

Aria

5. Ah, perhaps-is he that the-spirit alone in-the tumults
6. enjoyed often to-paint with its colors mysterious . . .
7. He, who, modest and vigilant, to-the-ill thresholds ascended,
8. and new fever kindled, waking-me to-the love.
9. To that-love, that-love which-is pulse of-the-universe, of-the-universe entire,
10. mysterious, haughty, cross and delight to-the heart.
11. To me, girl, an ingenuous and trembling desire,
12. this-depicted sweetest Lord of-the-future,
13. when in-the skies the ray of his beauty I-saw,
14. and wholly myself I-fed on that divine mistake.
15. I-felt that love is pulse of-the-universe entire,
16. mysterious, haughty, cross and delight to-the heart.

Recitative

17. Follies! . . . Delirium vain is this!
18. Poor woman, alone, abandoned in this populous desert that they-call Paris?
19. What I-hope now more? What to-do must-I? Enjoy!
20. Of pleasure in-the whirlpools to-perish! Enjoy!

Aria

21. Always free must-I act-foolishly from joy to joy,
22. I-wish that may-glide the life my along the paths of-the pleasure.
23. Is-born the day, or the day dies, always merry in-the parties,
24. to delights always new must fly the my thought.

Idiomatic Translation

Recitative

1. It's strange . . . I have those words carved in my heart!
2. Would a serious love be a misfortune for me? What are you resolving, O my anguished spirit?
3. No man ever aroused you before . . . O joy that I did not know, to love and to be loved!
4. And can I spurn it for the barren follies of my present life?

Aria

5. Ah, perhaps it is he whom my spirit, alone amid tumults,
6. often enjoyed painting with its mysterious colors . . .
7. He, who, modest and constant, came to my sickroom door,
8. and kindled a new fever, waking me to love.
9. To that love, which is the pulse of the entire universe,
10. mysterious, aloof, the cross and delight of one's heart.
11. When I was a girl, an innocent and trembling desire
12. depicted him, the tenderest lord of my future,
13. when I saw in the skies the glow of his beauty,
14. and I fed myself wholly on that divine fancy.
15. I felt that love is the pulse of the entire universe,
16. mysterious, aloof, the cross and delight of one's heart.

Recitative

17. Folly? This is a hopeless dream!
18. A poor woman, alone, abandoned in this crowded desert they call Paris,
19. what more can I hope for now? What must I do? Enjoy myself!
20. Perish in the whirlpools of pleasure! Enjoy myself!

Aria

21. Always free I must flit giddily from joy to joy,
22. I want my life to glide along the paths of pleasure.
23. Whether the day is dawning or dying, always merry at parties,
24. my thoughts must always fly to new delights!

The Scenic Picture

The U center door leads to the ballroom where the guests were dancing earlier and from where they entered to bid farewell to their hostess. There are also two side doors, DR and DL. The one on the R was used by the servants who brought in the trays with drinks and refreshments; Alfredo departed through the L door, and it is consequently this DL direction which is now associated with him and with his glowing devotion to Violetta. It is also from the DL that his voice will be heard in the middle section of the final Cabaletta. Much of Violetta's rejection of Alfredo's plea and her intention to continue her life of pleasure will be identified with the opposite, R and DR, directions. There are two tables and two small settees. One table stands in the UR corner of the terrace, the other in the middle of its left half. One settee is placed UR of the left table and the other in the middle of the right portion of the terrace. There are half-filled wine bottles and clean wine glasses on both tables. The diamond bracelet which Violetta removes from her wrist during Alfredo's offstage serenade is a gift of Baron Douphol, her lover of the moment. It symbolizes her status as a "kept woman," and shows that yielding to Alfredo's genuine love will involve a financial sacrifice on her part, a dramatic motif that plays an important role in each of the subsequent acts of the opera.

The Stage Actions Explained

In this, as in most of Verdi's arias, the intensity of the expression is generated by a violent conflict of emotions. Violetta, who in the beginning of the opera seems reconciled to her role as a plaything of the rich, suddenly finds herself confronted with the possibility of a serious attachment. "Ah, fors' è lui?" (Perhaps it is he?) she wonders in the Andantino. Perhaps Alfredo Germont is the man whom she had pictured in her dreams of romantic happiness? Although this idea fascinates her, she is aware that for a woman in her position true love is nothing but "folly," and "a hopeless dream." In the Exposition of the "Sempre libera" she announces her intention of resuming her life of superficial pleasures, and to continue to "flit giddily from joy to joy!"

In the Middle Section, the offstage voice of Alfredo, singing the praises of the "mysterious emotion" that is a "cross and delight to the heart," again makes her vacillate. Although greatly moved by his appeal, she rejects once more the lure of serious love and, in the Recapitulation of the Allegro Brillante, restates her determination to lead a "life of Joy!"

It is only in the Coda, when Alfredo's entreaty is heard with the added urgency of the faster tempo, that Violetta finds herself unable to resist his passionate call of love. Although her words at this moment — "dee volar il mio pensier" (my thoughts must fly) — are still ostensibly in reference to the earlier "diletti nuovi" (new delights) it is possible to interpret them as a joyous "giving in" to the intensity of Alfredo's passionate plea.

The tenor's entrance at this point is an action not indicated in the score and not envisioned by the composer.* It has two great advantages however: it not only provides a most effective "curtain" for the first act but also serves as a logical transition to the idyllic happiness of the lovers which Alfredo describes so eloquently in the beginning of the next scene.

The opening scene of the second act is set in the autumn. Alfredo enters dressed in a hunting outfit and states that three months have passed since Violetta has abandoned her former mode of life. It seems reasonable, therefore, to assume that the first act takes place in June or July, and this makes it possible to set it on the terrace of Violetta's Parisian home. This rather unconventional procedure permits us to imagine a "stand-up" party with food and drinks served on trays and thus avoid the profusion of tables and chairs that always look so unsightly in the later portions of the first act. It also established more securely the location of Alfredo's offstage serenade which, according to the score, comes from "under the balcony." The actions recommended for Violetta in this aria will, however, function just as well if the scenic picture follows the instructions in the score and represents a *salotto,* a small salon or living room in Violetta's apartments.

Recitative (Section I) — 22 Measures

Violetta's behavior during these measures illustrates her indecision. Can she dare to yield to Alfredo and the dream of serious love? Or should she spurn it for the "barren follies" of her present existence? As the first orchestral interlude begins, she starts going toward the DL door through which Alfredo left earlier, but she changes her mind almost immediately and moves R, away from Alfredo, continuing to go in this direction during the following instrumental passages. The vocal embellishment on the word "gioia" in the fourteenth measure induces her to face again toward DL, while the thought of her "barren follies" makes her glance at the wine bottles UR and the bracelet on her wrist. At the very beginning of the Recitative, Violetta stands near the center entrance and faces upstage looking after the departing guests.

Measures

1. She turns Cclw and gazes into the distance toward DR.
2. With the second "è strano," she continues to turn Cclw and looks DL toward the door through which Alfredo left earlier.
4. With "accenti," she goes DL toward the L bench, but stops suddenly and turns Clw.
5. She takes a step or two to the R.
7. With "sventura," she looks over her L shoulder.
8. After "amore," she looks R and takes a few more steps in that direction.
14. With "gioia," she turns LSB and backs slightly to UR.

---

*At the end of what is essentially a "solo" scene, no prima donna of the nineteenth century would have tolerated a sharing of the applause with another singer!

16. With "amando," she goes slightly DL to CC.
19. With "Follie," she turns Clw and looks over her R shoulder at the wine bottles on the UR table.
21. With "mio," she looks at the diamond bracelet on her L wrist and touches it with her R hand.

Andantino (Section II) — 92 Measures

Although the musical content of the two stanzas is identical, the ideas expressed in their opening sections are quite different. Whereas during the twenty-four measures beginning with "Ah fors' è lui," Violetta sings only of Alfredo, the corresponding section of the second stanza, "A me fanciulla," etc., is devoted to her childhood dreams and hopes. The difference between these two verses must be brought out not only by the change in stage position and eye focus, but also by a more childlike vocal color in the second stanza and by the changed emphasis on the key words: "trepido desire," as compared with "solinga ne tumulti," and "signor del avvenire," as opposed to "colori occulti." Unless the singer can do justice to these subtle nuances, she may feel safer in skipping the second stanza and proceeding directly from the end of the first verse to the Coda, that is from the forty-fourth to the eighty-eighth measure of the Andantino.

Andantino Stanza 1 (mm. 1–44)

Measures

1. Violetta goes slowly to the L bench and sits down facing DL.
11. She turns Clw and repeats the words of the preceding two measures while looking into the distance DR.
19. She turns Cclw and repeats the words of the preceding two measures, gazing at the L door.
23. She rises from the bench.
25. She goes L, Xing above the table, to UL of it.
27. She looks heavenward over her R shoulder.
28. At the end of this measure, she turns RSB.
29. She backs slightly to UL.
35. With the repetition of "dell' universo," she goes DR, Xing the table to DR of it.
39. With the repetition of "misterioso," she looks heavenward over her L shoulder.
41. She turns LSB and backs UR to CC.

Andantino Stanza 2* (mm. 45–94)

45. Violetta turns Clw, goes slowly to the R bench, and sits down facing DR.
55. She turns Cclw and repeats the words of the preceding two measures looking into the distance DL.

* If this Stanza is omitted, the actions must be resumed as of measure 88.

61. Recalling Alfredo to mind, she looks at the L door.
63. She turns Clw and repeats the words of the preceding two measures gazing into the distance DR.
65. She looks heavenward.
67. She rises from the bench.
69. She goes R to DR of the bench.
72. She turns her head Clw, to look at the L door.
73. She turns LSB and backs slightly to UR.
79. With the repetition of "dell' universo," she goes L, Xing above the R bench to UL of it.
83. With the repetition of "misterioso," she turns Clw and looks into the distance toward DR.
85. She turns LSB and backs slightly to UR.
88. With "croce e delizia," she goes L.

Coda

89. As she moves toward the L bench, she looks DL as if evoking Alfredo's image in the distance.
91. She backs slightly and, while singing the embellishment, turns slowly Clw. Then, with "delizia," she turns Cclw and gazes at the L door, remaining in this pose as if hypnotized, until the following Allegro.

Recitative (Allegro) (Section II) — 20 Measures

1. Violetta shakes herself as if awakening from a dream and, after the first "Follie!" turns Clw.
2. She goes DR and continues, Xing the R bench, to DR of it.
5. With "povera donna," she stops and gazes into the distance DR, as if seeing the streets and houses of Paris.
11. After "Parigi," she backs to UR of the bench and turns Cclw.
12. With "che far," she goes L, Xing above the bench, to UL of it.
14. She turns RSB and backs to UL.
16. With the vocal embellishment, she turns Cclw to face DL.
19. With the vocal embellishment, she turns Clw.
20. She continues to turn Clw until she looks at the wine bottles on the UR table.

Allegro brillante (Exposition) (Section IV) — 116 Measures

1. Violetta goes UR to the table, picks up a bottle, and pours some wine into a glass.
4. She puts down the bottle, picks up the glass containing the wine, turns Cclw, and goes DL, Xing above the bench, to CC.
8. Before attacking her lines, she lifts the glass high, as if pronouncing a toast.
22. After ending the high C, she takes — or rather pretends to take — a sip from the glass. She then starts to move DL toward the bench. The first step she takes coincides with an extra downbeat for this

measure, which makes it easier for the conductor (or accompanist) to synchronize precisely the last two notes of this measure.

26. She sits down on the bench.
27. She puts the glass on the table.
28. She turns Clw to face DR.
30. She rises.
32. She goes slowly DR and stops at CC.

Middle section (Andantino)

36. Alfredo's voice comes as a great shock, so that for a few measures Violetta remains motionless, listening intently.
39. She turns LSB and stretches her L arm toward DL.
41. She goes L, Xing the table, and stops at its DL corner.
44. She notices the bracelet, slips it off her L wrist and — continuing to gaze DL — places it without looking on the table behind her.
48. She takes another step or two toward DL.

Recitative (Allegro)

51. With "Follie!" she turns Clw and goes UL to the UL corner of the table.
52. She turns Cclw, spraying the long A flat.
54. During the fermata, she moves closer to the table and picks up the glass with her L hand.
55. She passes the glass into her R hand.
56. With the high D♭, she raises the glass.

Recapitulation (Tempo I)

58. During the fermata, Violetta drinks, then places the empty glass on the table. Passing between the table and the bench, she takes a few steps toward DR.
72. The synchronization between the voice and the accompaniment is handled in the same manner as in measure 22 of the Exposition.
76. At some point between here and the Coda — it does not matter exactly where — she moves DR, so that by the time Alfredo sings, she is standing DR of the R bench.

Coda

86. Alfredo appears in the DL entrance and standing there sings the first three measures. He sings them with great emotional intensity, but not too loudly.
87. Violetta executes this scale not yet realizing that Alfredo is on stage.
89. As he finishes "universo," Alfredo goes R to the center. Violetta turns LSB, and BU to UR of the bench.
90. Her first "Ah!" must have the quality of joyous surprise at seeing Alfredo.
94. He stretches both arms toward Violetta.

95. She goes toward him, Xing above the bench.
96. She stops as if still uncertain whether she should accept his love.
97. She goes to Alfredo.
98. She puts her hands into his. He kneels DL of her and kisses her hands with loving rapture.
111. She backs slightly pulling him up. They gaze at each other.
114. As the curtain begins to descend, she falls into his arms.

Die Zauberflote takes place in Egypt, therefore Pamina wears a stylized Egyptian costume to which is added the dagger her mother gave her.

"Ach, ich fühl's"
from *Die Zauberflöte,* Act II
by Wolfgang Amadeus Mozart

The Drama

The noble and wise Sarastro has abducted Pamina and keeps her in his realm to protect her from the malicious influence of her wicked mother, the Queen of the Night. Prince Tamino, who is sent by the Queen to rescue her daughter from the supposedly evil intentions of Sarastro, soon discovers the true state of affairs. He becomes eager to join the brotherhood of Sarastro's knights and is completely willing to undergo the necessary tests of manly steadfastness and courage.

The birdcatcher, Papageno who accompanies Tamino on his mission, is not in the least interested in disciplining himself for the sake of some nebulous spiritual reward. He yearns only for food, drink, and sleep, and dreams of soon sharing all these delights with a pretty, young wife.

The first test that Tamino and Papageno are asked to undergo is that of silence. Subjected to questioning by the three ladies of the Queen, Tamino remains deaf to their wiles, and somehow manages to prevent Papageno from too serious a breach of the imposed silence. The next test of fortitude — with which we are mostly concerned here — puts an infinitely greater strain on Tamino, for it involves Pamina, the girl with whom he has fallen in love and to whom he has sworn eternal faith.

Pamina, in the meantime, has undergone a shattering experience. Her mother appeared at her side and forced a dagger into her hand. "Since the young man whom I sent to rescue you," said the Queen, "has gone over to our enemies, you my daughter, must take things into your own hands and, with this dagger, kill the wicked Sarastro. Unless you perform this necessary deed," the Queen added before departing, "I shall invoke a dreadful curse upon you, and no longer call you my daughter!" The horrified Pamina finds herself utterly unable to obey her mother's command. Fortunately, Sarastro, who is aware of Pamina's turmoil and agony, reassures her that he harbors no desire for revenge and that in the realm of the priestly knights there is no room for any feelings except those of compassion and brotherly love.

It is necessary here to say a few words about the dagger given to Pamina by her mother. It happens to be part of a discrepancy that mars the second act of this opera and that, because it affects Pamina's actions both during and following her aria, is pertinent to our discussion.

In the complete sequence of events as they are presented in the opera, the wicked Monostatos, who has overheard everything the Queen said to her daughter, snatches the dagger from Pamina and, when she repels

his amorous advances, lifts his arm threatening to kill her. Sarastro's op-
portune arrival stops Monostatos, who soon leaves the stage, remarking
in an aside that since he cannot win Pamina's love he might as well join
hands with Sarastro's enemies.

There is no stage direction in the libretto or in the score that indicates
just what happens to the dagger at this point, and there is no further mention of it until much later in Pamina's "Suicide" scene when she carries
the dagger with her, mentioning specifically that it was given to her by
her mother. It is clear, therefore, that Pamina must somehow regain
possession of the dagger, and the simplest way to arrange this is to have
Sarastro wrest it from Monostatos and give it back to the girl, either while
he sings his solo, or earlier, during his spoken lines when he denies all
thoughts of vengeance. Having regained the dagger — and needing it
later — Pamina brings it with her when she hurries to rejoin her lover,
and thus is able to refer to it in the aria. The discrepancy which we mentioned earlier becomes apparent during the events that follow Pamina's
aria. It was Ernst Lert* who first pointed out that Pamina's next appearance in the opera should not be in the Trio with Tamino and Sarastro,
but in the scene with the three Spirits where she behaves as if she were
half demented, and makes it evident that her decision to commit suicide
is prompted by sheer despair. Tamino has forsaken her and will not speak
to her — so she tells the Spirits — and therefore she might as well die.
All this makes excellent sense if it alludes to the scene of Pamina's aria
during which Tamino was not allowed to say a single word. But it is completely illogical if it comes after the Trio when Tamino does speak to
Pamina and when Sarastro repeatedly assures her that she is certain to be
reunited with her lover. We are in full agreement with Dr. Lert's suggestion that the best way to set things right is to reshuffle the sequence of
events, to have Pamina's aria followed by Papageno's F-major song, "Ein
Mädchen oder Weibchen" (No. 20), and to proceed directly from there
to the opening section of the Finale, "Bald prangt, den Morgen zu Ver-
künder," (No. 21), the scene with the three Spirits, Pamina, the dagger,
and the attempted suicide. There are several possible ways in which the
remaining scenes of this act can then be rearranged, but since this does
not affect Pamina's actions, a discussion of this additional problem would
lead us too far afield.

After Sarastro's aria addressed to Pamina is finished, there is a change
of scene and when the curtain rises again we are in a "Hallway with a
stone bench on each side of the stage." Since in the action of Pamina's
aria only the L bench is used, we can for our purposes dispense with the
other.

In the beginning of this scene, Tamino and Papageno are addressed by
the three Spirits, who bring them food and wine and restore to them the

* See Ernst Lert, *Mozart auf dem Theater* (Berlin: Schuster & Loeffler, 1921),
p. 405.

"magic" flutes and bells that were earlier taken away from them by the priests. Papageno takes the basket with the wine bottle and the food to the bench on the L, and begins to eat and drink quite happily, while Tamino tries a few strains on his flute.* It is this music that attracts Pamina and leads her to her beloved Prince. She is naturally very anxious to tell him of her recent, unsettling experiences.

Papageno's presence during part of the spoken section that precedes the aria is essential for the enactment of this scene, but he must not be permitted to disturb the deeply pathetic content of the rest of this piece by his clownish antics. After his part in the action is completed, he must be allowed to go upstage and, while remaining visible, becomes completely passive and "faceless."

The Music

This aria of forty-one measures consists of four separate sections preceded by an introduction and followed by a Coda. While the introduction is barely long enough to establish the key of G minor, the Coda features an expressive device of unusual musical and dramatic interest. The four sections of the main body of the aria are built around the four complete sentences of the text. To accommodate the expansion of the musical phrases, each sentence is extended by a more or less elaborate repetition of its words. Since in the acting-out of this aria each of these ten verbal extensions will be exteriorized and emphasized by some form of stage movement, the singer will find it useful to examine the text in a form that clarifies this particular feature of its construction.

1. Ach, ich fühl's, es ist verschwunden, ewig hin mein Ganzes Glück,
   ewig hin der Liebe Glück! (mm. 1–7)
2. Nimmer kommt ihr Wonnestunden, meinem Herzen mehr zurück,
   meinem Herzen,
   meinem Herzen mehr zurück! (mm. 8–16)
3. Sieh, Tamino, diese Tränen fliessen, Trauter, dir allein,
   dir allein! (mm. 17–22)
4. Fühlst du nicht der Liebe Sehnen,
   der Liebe Sehnen, (mm. 22–38)

* A few snatches from Tamino's first act—aria:

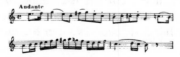

* A few snatches from Tamino's first act—aria:
are usually heard here, but it is possible to anticipate the opening measures of the flute passages played in the later "Fire and Water" trials:

So wird Ruhe,
So wird Ruh' im Tode sein;
Fühlst du nicht der Liebe Sehnen,
Fühlst du nicht der Liebe Sehnen,
So wird Ruhe,
So wird Ruh' im Tode sein,
                im Tode sein,
                im Tode sein!

The instrumental Coda (mm. 38–41) features a "change of diaeresis,"* a deviation from an established rhythmic pattern that Mozart reserves in his operas only for very severe emotional upheavals. It is a disruption of normal accentuation in which, for a time, a basic grouping of three units is suddenly changed into a binary grouping or, on the contrary, a triple rhythm is superimposed on a duple or quadruple one.† In 6/8 the distribution is changed so that instead of the normal and expected we are suddenly faced with a string of This is exactly what happens in this Coda which, although it is written as a continuity of four measures in 6/8, actually sounds and functions as if it were notated as a six-measure phrase with a changed meter signature.

The feeling of emotional turmoil induced by this rhythmic change is further enhanced by the crescendo and the forte, while the hopelessness of Pamina's appeal is highlighted by the sudden piano, the poignancy of the Neapolitan sixth, and the resigned return to the triple rhythm.

*This very useful term was introduced by C. F. Abdy Williams in *The Rhythm of Modern Music* (London: Macmillan & Co., 1909).

† The insertion of several strongly accented 3/4 phrases into an allegro in 4/4 lends a particularly frantic character to Electra's jealous frustration in the first act of Mozart's *Idomeneo*.

An interesting observation concerning the right tempo for this aria is found in George N. von Nissen's biography of Mozart. Nissen married Mozart's widow Constanze and had the invaluable advantage of his wife's recollections of her former husband.

In the footnote on page 123 of the Appendix* to the original edition of 1828, we read: "Pamina's aria: 'Ach ich fühl's es ist verschwunden, etc.' is often made boring to the audience by performers who take it in the slowest possible *Andante*, almost as an *Adagio*. This aria must move at a speed of 6½ Rhenish inches. That was also the tempo at which Mozart himself conducted it."

This statement points in the right direction, although — with all due respect to Nissen and to Constanze — it should be taken with a grain of salt. Personal recollections of performance details after the passage of many years — particularly in the matter of tempo — are notoriously untrustworthy. A speed of six-and-a-half Rhenish inches converted into the more familiar metronome markings† is equal to ♪ = 144 which is *very much* faster than anyone today would consider possible. In the recording conducted by Karl Boehm and sung by Hilde Gueden this aria is taken at approximately ♪ = 50. But of course it is not a question of whether any tempo seems "boring" but whether, in the given dramatic situation, it is in keeping with the thoughts and feelings of the opera's character. In the controversial Salzburg production of *The Magic Flute* in 1937, Toscanini's tempo for this aria seemed almost scandalously fast to his colleagues. Asked to justify it, the conductor pointed out that Pamina was in despair over the behavior of her beloved Tamino whose unwillingness to answer her, or even to look at her, seemed to prove his indifference. "A young girl who, in this situation, thinks of committing suicide," so Toscanini is reputed to have said,** "cannot just sing *cantabile* — she must sing *agitato!*"

Between Boehm's recorded ♪ = 50 and the ♪ = 144 recommended by Nissen and Constanze Mozart, there is room for a multitude of possibilities. Artists endowed with mature, opulent voices and used to performing in large opera houses accompanied by sonorous orchestras will obviously take this Andante considerably slower than young, light-voiced sopranos singing in small halls and accompanied only by a piano. It may be pertinent to recall that Anna Gottlieb, for whose voice and personality Mozart fashioned this role, was only seventeen years old at the time he conducted *The Magic Flute* in a theater seating only one thousand spectators.

Personally, I (B.G.) like this aria performed faster than it is usually

* This Appendix was published after Nissen's death, so that the footnote is probably not his, but Constanze's.

† See Rosamond Harding *Origins of Musical Time and Expression* (London: Oxford University Press, 1938), p. 26.

** This was related to me by Dr. Herbert Graf who was the stage director of this production. (B.G.)

taken, though of course much slower than the "impossible" $\flat = 144$. In my opinion, $\flat = 84$ seems just about right for a young Pamina who is truly heartbroken over Tamino's sudden and, to her, inexplicable coldness.

The Vocal Aspects

Since this is the only aria in this collection which is preceded by a spoken dialogue, it is necessary to make a few remarks concerning its proper execution. Singers are not usually skillful at interpreting spoken lines. The reason is obvious. Whereas the composer provides the singer with quite exact instructions for "saying" the words (speed, intensity, relative length and stress of syllables and words, pitch, even color), none is provided for the spoken dialogue. We can say that an actor in the spoken drama "composes the music" for his text, for it is he, with the aid of the director, who decides how loud, how fast, and with what color, pitch, and intensity each word and syllable will be spoken. But singers have been trained to depend on the composer for such information. They are concerned only with the execution of the composer's instructions, and therefore are not adept at "composing their own music." Thus a certain amount of special practice is necessary to perform spoken dialogue well. The singer must not be afraid to practice his text, experimenting with various interpretations, putting stress on different words and syllables, and employing different speeds, different colors, and different intensities, in order to find the desired interpretation. He must also learn to project his speaking voice in the same manner that he projects his singing voice. He must learn not to drop the ends of sentences, which is something he does naturally in normal conversation. This may make him feel a bit foolish — he fears he is overdoing it. But he should remember that he does not feel foolish when he is "overdoing it" in singing; he is only making sure that he will be audible and understandable above the orchestra and that he is expressing his thoughts and emotions to the proper degree. Because he does not have to raise the level of his speaking voice over an accompaniment, he tends to underproject. Feeling uncomfortable because he must "compose the music" for his text, he speaks too rapidly and too softly. We have found it necessary to give singers the exact interpretation of spoken lines, particularly in matters of stress and intensity, and to ask them to imitate the model given. Most dramatic actors would resent being spoonfed in this fashion, but most singers welcome such assistance with gratitude.

Mozart was usually very careful to set his text in such a way that unimportant words were seldom set to long, high, or stressed notes. But measure 2 of the aria is an exception. Here the singer must be careful to sing "ist" very gently and carefully because of the octave skip. The less attentive singer will simply sing the note louder because it is an octave higher than the preceding one. Yet the word "ist" is the least important word in the phrase.

Care must be taken to sing the four thirty-second notes at the end of measure 3 without haste or uneveness. In measure 4 the written-out appoggiatura need not be hurried. The G comes on the beat, and both G and F♯ are sixteenth notes. In measure 6, some singers may wish to modify the vowel sound *ee* for the high B♭. (See discussion of "vowel modification" on page 34.)

When the aria is sung at the recommended speed of ♪ = 84, most singers should be able to sing from the middle of measure 13 through the end of the phrase in measure 16 in one breath. There is an unfortunate tendency, when the aria is sung too slowly, to take a catch breath at the end of measure 14 and then to sing the first four sixteenth notes in in measure 15 too detached. Composers are prone to use the marking ⌢ . . . ⌣ to mean singing the notes distinctly, non legato, but they certainly do not mean an ordinary staccato. (See discussion of vocal aspects of "Oh, patria mia" on page 33.) In this case it is wiser not to detach the notes at all but simply to sing them very distinctly.

The written-out appoggiatura in measure 21 consists of two sixteenth notes, with the B♭ coming on the beat. The situation is identical in measure 22. The diminished-seventh skip on "Seh–" in measure 24 should be sung legato, with a small relaxation of tempo if necessary, to give the proper connotation to "longing."

As in measure 6, the high B♭ on the *ee* vowel in measure 29 may require some modification. Sometimes singers are careless about the C♯'s and C♮'s in measure 31; this measure needs careful study so that the proper pitches are sung. It is preferable to sing "so wird Ruh im Tode sein" the first time (middle of m. 31 through first quarter of m. 33) in one breath. When the same words are repeated the singer may feel the need to breathe before attacking the low C♯ at the end of measure 34. It should not be necessary to modify the *oo* vowel on the high G in measure 34 because it is sung softly.

It does not seem necessary for the singer to employ a true chest tone anywhere in this aria, though there may be a tendency to do so on the low C♯ and D in measures 34–35. Measure 37 can obviously be sung a piacere with a relatively short fermata on the E♭; the four descending thirty-second notes need not be hurried and should be sung legatissimo.

There are no dynamic makings in the vocal line of this aria. Generally, in such a case, it is wise to consult the accompaniment for dynamics. In this aria, the dynamic level is almost constantly piano, with a few exceptions during the interludes when the voice is silent. In measure 27, however, there is one forte outburst in the vocal line, and then the remainder of the aria is again piano or softer.

The Text

Literal Translation

1. Ah, I feel-it, it is disappeared, forever gone the love happiness!

2. Never come you, joy-hours, to my heart more back.
3. Look, Tamino, these tears flow, beloved, to-you alone.
4. Feel you not the love longing, so will rest in-the death be.

Idiomatic Translation
1. Ah, I feel it — love's happiness has disappeared, forever gone!
2. Never will you come back, hours of bliss to my heart.
3. Look, Tamino, my tears flow for you alone, my beloved.
4. If you do not feel love's longing, then rest for me will come only in death.

The Scenic Picture

The setting shows a large rocky opening in the subterranean caves of Sarastro's realm. Various stone structures are visible in the background. A bench is standing downstage, L of CC.

The Stage Actions Explained

It seemed inappropriate to include the German text when describing the actions of the spoken section that precedes the aria. The English version given here is a quite exact translation of the original text. We know from experience that very few singers can speak lines in a foreign language with ease and fluency. We suggest that they do not attempt to do so in the dialogue scene that precedes this aria. We have given a literal translation of the dialogue of this scene to acquaint the singer with the meaning of the words and the sense of the situation. We suggest that it may be used as an acting version in English even if the aria itself is sung in German. It is *not* a definitive translation however, but only a guide to the original.

Spoken Lines

Papageno, occupied with food, is seated on the L bench. Tamino, playing his flute, is walking about in the DR area of the stage. Pamina enters from UL and goes DR to UL of Tamino. He stops playing and turns UL to face Pamina.

PAMINA (*addressing Tamino joyfully*)
You are here! (*looking to heaven*) Kind heaven, I thank you for having led me to this place. (to *Tamino*) I heard your flute and sped toward the music like an arrow. (*pause*) Why do you look so sad? (*Tamino turns Clw and stares DR.*) Won't you say a single word to your Pamina?

TAMINO (*sighs*)
Ah! (*motions with his L hand, asking Pamina to leave*)

PAMINA (*backs slightly to UL*)
What? You want me to go away?

TAMINO

(*repeats his last actions more emphatically*)

PAMINA

Am I to leave without knowing why? Tamino! Dearest! Have I
offended you? Do not treat me in such a way. I need your
affection! (*She takes out the dagger which she carries in the belt
of her dress and tries to show it to Tamino. He does not see it.*)
I need your advice and help. . . . How can you reject my love?
Don't you love me anymore?

TAMINO (*sighs*)

PAMINA

(*still holding the dagger in her hand, turns Cclw and goes L, to UR
of Papageno*) Papageno! Please tell me what happened to our
friend!

PAPAGENO

(*turns Clw toward Pamina, makes humming noises through a mouth-
ful of food, motions her to go away, and then returns to his dinner*)

PAMINA

What's this? You won't talk to me either? Won't you at least explain
the reasons for your silence?

PAPAGENO

Sh! (*motions her to leave, then gets up, picks up the basket with the
wine bottle and the food, goes L past the bench, and then U, where
he finds a hiding place above a rock or some other piece of scenery.
During Pamina's conversation with Papageno, Tamino turned Cclw
and went slightly L to listen. When Pamina asked for an explanation of their behavior, he took another step L, half-hoping, half-
afraid that Papageno would tell Pamina about their vow of silence.
When Papageno says: "Sh!" Tamino turns Clw and goes very slowly R, to a position slightly U of where he was standing when first
addressed by Pamina.*)

PAMINA

(*goes L, to above the bench, and puts the dagger on the R corner
of the bench. Then, following Papageno with her eyes, she turns
Cclw and continues to turn until she faces R. Here, she becomes
aware that Tamino is also walking away from her. She looks over
her L shoulder toward heaven, DR.*) This treatment is worse
than . . . (*she glances at the dagger*) worse than death! (*After a
short pause, she runs UR to UL of Tamino.*) Dearest, darling
Tamino! (*Tamino remains silent and motionless.*) (*Pamina turns
slowly Cclw and goes slightly DL. Orchestra begins to play.*)

Aria

(Pamina sings the opening four measures gazing into the distance, DL.)

Measures

5. With the repetition of "ewig," she turns RSB, backing very slightly,
   and finishing the sentence toward DR.

6. Pamina's high B♭ affects Tamino so strongly that he trembles, turns slightly Cclw, and looks at her over his L shoulder, almost ready to say something.

7. Noticing his reaction, Pamina goes R to UL of Tamino and touches his L arm. Afraid that his resistance is weakening, Tamino goes DL to CC, Xing Pamina. She keeps looking at him and turns LSB.

9. On "Wonnestunden," she gazes heavenward as if reliving those hours of bliss when she was certain of Tamino's love.

12. With the repetition of "meinem," she turns Clw.

13. With the repetition of "Herzen," she puts the palm of her R hand on her L bosom. To emphasize the second repetition of "meinem," she walks slightly DR.

14. With the second repetition of "Herzen," she puts the palm of her L hand on the back of her R hand.

16. She turns Cclw and, with the flute and oboe scale, goes UL to UR of Tamino.

18. With the second flute and oboe scale, Tamino turns slightly Clw and looks at Pamina over his R shoulder.

19. She points to the tears on her cheeks.

20. With "Trauter," he turns slightly Cclw to gaze DL.

21. Tamino goes DL to UR of the bench. To emphasize the repetition of "dir," she backs slightly to UR and stretches both arms toward him.

23. With the repetition of "der Liebe," she turns Clw and gazes DR.

25. With the repetition of "so wird," she walks sadly R.

26. As she sings "Tode," Tamino notices the dagger which he has not seen before. The idea that Pamina might use it on herself passes through his mind and induces him to turn Cclw, so that he stands with his back to the audience.

27. With "fühlst du nicht," Pamina turns LSB and backs UR while looking at Tamino.

28. With the repetition of "fühlst du nicht," she goes L to UR of Tamino.

29. Pamina's high B♭ affects Tamino so strongly that he looks at her over his L shoulder and then turns Clw and walks DL, Xing the bench to L of it.

31. With the repetition of "so wird Ruh," Pamina looks at the dagger and goes DL to above the R corner of the bench.

32. On "Tode," Tamino lowers his head and covers his forehead with his clenched fists.

33. Pamina picks up the dagger.

34. She looks heavenward and turns slowly Clw.

35. She looks at the dagger in her R hand. Tamino turns Cclw and, walking slowly, takes two or three steps toward U.

36. Continuing to look at the dagger, Pamina walks R beyond CC.

37. On the last "Tode," she looks once more at the dagger, and then

turns her gaze to heaven. Tamino turns Cclw and goes R to above R corner of the bench as if ready to speak to Pamina.

*   *   *

The unusual "change of diaeresis" which is the special musical feature of the instrumental Coda, must receive an appropriate dramatic exteriorization. This is facilitated by a subtext that is based on a sixfold repetition of "Tamino," and thus serves as an eloquent expression of Pamina's last, wordless appeal to her lover. On the first "Tamino," she turns Cclw to look at him; during the second, they gaze at each other; with the crescendo of the third "Tamino," she goes UL to his R. On the fifth, she touches him with her L hand, but he turns Clw and goes slightly UL, turning his back on her. With the sudden piano in the fortieth measure, she looks at the dagger as if to say: "Well then! Only death is left for me!" and then goes L, Xing Tamino, and exits into the L wing.

Background Texts

Aida — There is no authentic background text to Verdi's *Aida*, but readers may be interested in studying a freely imagined background story, "Radames' letter to his uncle" by Boris Goldovsky in *Bringing Opera to Life* (New York: Appleton-Century, 1968), p. 399.

Il Barbiere di Siviglia — Pierre Caron de Beaumarchais, "The Barber of Seville," in *The Genius of the French Theatre*, trans. Albert Bermel (New York: New American Library), paper.

La Bohème — There are several English versions, all of them out of print. *Vie de Bohème*, trans. Norman Cameron (London, 1949). *Also*, the Folio Society (London, 1960). *Also*, Société des Beaux-Arts (New York).

Carmen — Prosper Merimée, *Carmen*, trans. John Wood (Baltimore: Penguin Books, Inc., 1965), paper. *Also*, The Modern Library (with *Sapho* and *Manon Lescaut*), (New York: Random House).

Cavalleria Rusticana — Giovanni Verga, "Cavalleria Rusticana" (play) English version by Eric Bentley in *The Modern Theatre* (New York: Doubleday, 1955), paper (Anchor Book).

Don Giovanni — Tirso de Molina, "The Trickster of Seville," in *The Classic Theatre*, Vol. III, trans. Roy Campbell (New York: Doubleday, 1961), paper (Anchor Book). *Also, The Theatre of Don Juan* (Univ. of Nebraska Press, 1963).

Faust — Goethe, *Faust*, Part I, trans. Bayard Taylor (New York: Collier Books, 1962), paper.

La Forza del Destino — Duque de Rivas, "Don Alvaro o la Fuerza del Sino" (Spanish), in *Tres Dramas Romànticos* (New York: Doubleday, 1962), paper.

La Gioconda — Victor Hugo, "Angelo, Tyrant of Padua," in *The Works of Victor Hugo*, trans. Burnham Ives (Boston: Little Brown, 1909).

Manon — Antoine Francois Prévost, *Manon Lescaut*, trans. D. C. Moylan (New York: Doubleday, 1960), paper. *Also*, The Modern Library (with *Sapho* and *Carmen*), (New York: Random House).

Madama Butterfly — David Belasco, "Madame Butterfly," in *Six Plays by David Belasco* (Boston: Little Brown, 1928).

Le Nozze di Figaro — Pierre Caron de Beaumarchais, "Figaro's Marriage," in *The Classic Theatre*, Vol. IV, English version by Jacques Barzun (New York: Doubleday, 1961), paper (Anchor Book).

Don Pasquale — Ben Jonson, *Epicoene, or The Silent Woman* (Univ. of Nebraska Press, 1966), paper.

Rigoletto — Victor Hugo, "The King Amuses Himself," trans. F. L. Slous (New York: Washington Square, 1964), paper.

Romeo et Juliette — Shakespeare, *Romeo and Juliet*.

Tannhäuser — E. T. A. Hoffman, "Der Kampf der Sänger" (German), in *Die Serapionsbrüder*, Vol. II (Salzburg: Das Berglandbuch).

Tosca — Victorien Sardou, "La Tosca" (French), in *Theatre Complet*, Vol. I (Paris: Albin Michel, 1934).

La Traviata — Alexandre Dumas (fils), *Camille* (play), English version by E. Reynolds and N. Playfair (New York: Hill & Wang, 1957), paper. *Also Camille* (novel), Modern Library (New York: Random House).

Die Zauberflöte — August Jacob Liebeskind, "Lulu oder die Zauberflöte" (German), in *Dschinnistan*, Vol. III, Wieland's Collection of Fairy Tales (Winterthur, 1810).

Louise, Pagliacci, and *The Old Maid and the Thief* are based on original stories by their composers, and no background texts are available.